Setting the Theme

For Such A Time As This
Daily Moments With God

SETTING
the
THEME

For Such A Time As This
Daily Moments With God

BONNIE J MARTIN

Except for scripture quotations, and unless otherwise indicated, this book reflects the author's personal experiences and in no way replaces the work of God in the life of a believer. The intentions of the author are for encouragement and inspirational purposes for the reader.

Cover design by Bonnie J Martin
Book design by Bonnie J Martin
Published by Bonnie J Martin

www.bonniejmartin.com

ISBN 979-8-9940554-0-3

For my family.
When God places something on your heart and mind, do it.
He will be faithful to help you finish.

Contents

Prologue

The intentions of my heart are written on these pages. Snippets for each day of the year to draw you and me closer to our Creator. Space for you to contemplate your relationship with Him. Space to give Him praise and thanksgiving. It is for Him. It is for you. It is for me.

I pray that as you move through the pages you will develop a habit of sitting quietly, uninterrupted for just a moment of reflection and meditation. Your relationship with God is the most important relationship you will ever have. It is worthy of this time of devotion.

Let me back up before I move forward. Allow me to introduce you to the Creator. He is the One that thought the world needed you. He formed you in your mother's womb and knows the number of hairs on your head. He designed your fingerprint. He knows everything there is to know about you.

But there's a problem. Sin. It keeps us from drawing near to Him. It causes separation and division. But your perfect Creator has a solution for that separation. Jesus. God made the only way across the chasm of sin so that we can draw near to Him.

Jesus took all the sin that has ever and will ever exist and called us righteous. He took the punishment we all deserve for the sin He didn't commit and placed us in right relationship with God. But only if we accept His gift of forgiveness. Will you accept it? Will you accept Him?

If so, keep reading. If you haven't decided yet, keep reading. I pray you will find Him in these pages and live the purpose He created just for you.

Grab a journal and make notes as you go. Or use the extra space in the margins. I pray you will have a year full of fellowship with God.

"FOR IF YOU REMAIN SILENT AT THIS TIME, RELIEF AND DELIVERANCE WILL ARISE FOR THE JEWS FROM ANOTHER PLACE AND YOU AND YOUR FATHER'S HOUSE WILL PERISH. AND WHO KNOWS WHETHER YOU HAVE NOT ATTAINED ROYALTY FOR SUCH A TIME AS THIS?"

ESTHER 4:14

Introduction

"For if you remain silent at this time, relief and deliverance will arise for the Jews from another place and you and your father's house will perish. And who knows whether you have not attained royalty for such a time as this?"
Esther 4:14

Sitting in a palace, Esther was in the most unlikely place. She was a simple young woman that happened to find favor with the king. She had become a queen. But her people were on the brink of disaster. She could sit back and do nothing, or she could approach the king on behalf of her people and do something about it. Scared. Unsure of herself. She had a 50/50 shot at reaching the ears of the king. One word from the king would decide her and her people's fate. Rejection by the king would bring doom. Acceptance by the king gave us the story we share today.

She was in a place at just the right time for such a time as this. You are in this place for such a time as this. Esther was prepared for the role she found herself in. God has and will prepare you for the role He has for you. Your divine assignment is uniquely yours. Each assignment is different. Each talent is different. The giftings God pours out vary like our personalities. Unique. Blessed. Appointed to do excellent work for His kingdom.

Each day of this year, you will be presented with questions and opportunities. Journaling is only one way to express your answers and responses. Yours may be something completely different. Make each Call to Action unique to what God is calling you to. Make this your personal space with Him. Ask Him to meet you there. He will be there faithfully.

Holy Father, as we begin a new year, I ask that You speak life into us. Allow us to be purposeful in planning out the life You desire. Let our intentions match Your will for our lives. Prepare us even now for such a time as this. In Jesus' name. Amen.

COMMIT YOUR WORKS TO
THE LORD
AND YOUR PLANS WILL BE
ESTABLISHED.
PROVERBS 16:3

January

Commit your works to the LORD
And your plans will be established.
Proverbs 16:3

A new year of promises ahead! How exciting to think of all the possibilities in front of you! Maybe this is the year you will finish that project in your house you have wanted to do for so long. Maybe you have wanted to learn how to make sourdough bread and this is the year you will do just that. Maybe you will run a marathon. Maybe you will read the Bible. Do it!

As you begin the journey of a new year, reflect on the plans you will follow Him into. Our plans will only be successful if they are committed to His honor and glory. He will establish a sure footing for you as you draw close to Him in your divine assignment.

Winter is the perfect time to set the stage. A blank canvas sits in front of you. What shapes can you see forming on the white backdrop? Will the year be painted with vivid colors or muted tones? Perhaps some of each?

If the page already has the beginning of something for you, what actions will you take to influence the outcome? What will your script be in this fresh beginning? How will you change the narrative this year? Have you made any resolutions? Will you keep them?

You get to decide if you will follow through or not. I am here to help you. Creating a daily habit of meditation will help you focus your attention on what God wants to do in and through you. Draw near to Him through the pages of this book.

January 1

Therefore if anyone is in Christ, he is a new creature; the old things passed away; behold, new things have come.
2 Corinthians 5:17

Christ became man for just a little while and moved on, leaving behind a trail of hope leading us to Himself. Leaving behind examples of transformation for good. Him resurrected gives us the example of new life with Him. Him raising us from the past into new things to come.

Leaving the past behind. Whatever last year held, there is a new year in front us. Fresh opportunities are waiting. Can you see them up ahead?

A fresh start. Today. Waiting on us to move into His calling of hope. He made us new so that we can live in this hope. For us, an exciting prospect for what is ahead. Are you excited to see what He will do with your faithfulness? I am. I am excited to see Him work through you.

Let's Pray

Holy Father, thank You for Your example through the life, death, and resurrection of Your Son. It is only through Him that we can come to Your throne of grace and mercy. Thank You for creating in me a new creature. I commit to serving You in this new year. In Jesus' name. Amen.

Call to Action

Will you commit to service for Him this year? What ideas do you have? How will you serve Him with the talents He gave you? Write it out.

January 2

'For I know the plans that I have for you,' declares the LORD, 'plans for welfare and not for calamity to give you a future and a hope.'
Jeremiah 29:11

God makes the plans. He orchestrates the seasons of the earth and your life. He has numbered the hairs on your head and the days of your life. He has only good in mind for you.

He knows what this year will bring so you don't have to worry about it, but you do need to seek Him in making plans. Continual communication with Your Creator and reading His Word connects You with Him.

Engaging in a like-minded group of believers who encourage and edify one another strengthens your walk. Helping others from the overflow He has given you brings joy. Seeking His face in everything you do ensures your plans align with His.

Let's Pray

Holy Father, I trust You with this new year. Transform and renew my mind so that the plans I make will be directly in line with what You have for me. In Jesus' name. Amen.

Call to Action

Are you entering a new season? Are you anticipating good things to come in this new year? Have you prayed about your plans? Do they agree with God's plans for you? Write it out.

January 3

But the noble man devises noble plans;
And by noble plans he stands.
Isaiah 32:8

Plans made with God will be established. The security of walking with Him does not negate struggles but it does provide assurance that He is in control. His provision is constant and complete.

Your obedience in following Him and seeking Him brings contentment. True contentment. Like filling your lungs with clean, fresh, crisp air and exhaling in full confidence that another breath is right there waiting for you. No doubting of the provision He gives.

Walk in His security for the plans He gives you. Be confident that each step you take is already known by Him. He had it planned before you were born.

Let's Pray

Holy Father, we lay our plans at Your feet in full submission to Your plans for us. We trust Your plans. In Jesus' name. Amen.

Call to Action

Making plans requires intentionality. You wouldn't start building a house without a blueprint. Your life is no different. God owns the rights to the blueprint of your life. He drew it. What are His plans for you? Write it out.

January 4

Prepare plans by consultation,
And make war by wise guidance.
Proverbs 20:18

Working with a team of trusted advisors who seek God for their own plans ensures adequate resources for your own plans. Tackling any problem becomes much easier when others are consulted. Teamwork may sound daunting but when each one brings to the table the thoughts and characteristics ordained by God, tasks become less daunting.

Carefully selecting your team from those you trust with the right skill set for the task at hand makes quick work of something you may struggle with alone. Each person is gifted with abilities that bring different problem-solving skills. Monumental tasks shrink.

All hands-on-deck assures completion. Tools and resources gathered. Instructions written. God consulted. Execution is about to commence.

Let's Pray

Holy Father, prepare us for the execution of Your plans for our lives. Connect us with others that can help us, and we can in turn help as well. In Jesus' name. Amen.

Call to Action

List the people in your inner circle. Who will help you with your plans? Write it out.

January 5

Without consultation, plans are frustrated,
But with many counselors they succeed.
Proverbs 15:22

Did you list your team of trusted advisors yesterday? Do they know they are your trusted counselors? Maintain regular communication with the people you trust. Let them know how important they are to your plans for walking with God.

Are you a trusted counselor to someone? Your actions in helping someone else convince them of your willingness to be there for them. Sharing the load of plans or burdens distributes weight more evenly, allowing everyone involved to participate more easily; encouraging one another.

Isolation limits effectiveness. Finding the right people for the plans at hand brings insight and fellowship. Honoring God with Your plans as you all work toward a common goal.

Let's Pray

Holy Father, bring people alongside us in our work for You. Direct each one to use the talents and resources You provide to further Your kingdom. In Jesus' name. Amen.

Call to Action

What does each one bring to the table? Creativity? Administration? Leadership? Vision? Each one has gifts given by God. Can you identify the gift in each member of your team? What about yours? What is the gift God has given you? Write it out.

January 6

The mind of man plans his way,
But the LORD directs his steps.
Proverbs 16:9

In His Sovereignty, He directs our steps even when we have meticulously planned our way. He already knows our successes. He already knows our failures. Each one used for His glory.

Expect the unexpected. It will come. Your plans will feel like they are falling apart. After days or weeks or months or years of planning, something will present a unique challenge.

Your circumstances may change. But God is still directing your steps.

The group of trusted counselors may fall apart. But God is still directing your steps.

The plan may have to be reconfigured entirely. But God is still directing your steps.

Let's Pray

Holy Father, help us to trust in Your Sovereignty. When things get hard remind us You have everything in Your Mighty Hands. In Jesus' name. Amen.

Call to Action

Have you experienced an upset in plans in the past? What helped you get through that time in your life? How did it allow growth in your relationship with God? Write it out.

January 7

Many plans are in a man's heart,

But the counsel of the LORD will stand.
Proverbs 19:21

Everyone is attempting to convince us to do things their way. Their way is the best way to do it. No matter if there are twenty others telling you the same thing, their way is the best. They draw you in with clever presentations making you want to be just like them. Making you want to imitate them. Do you really want to do whatever it is they are doing or is it just the latest and greatest trend, and you want on the bandwagon? It can be overwhelming.

The world will do it's best to pull you away from the counsel of the only One that truly has the best way to do anything. His counsel presents you with the best opportunity. The world will only disappoint after considering His options.

Guard your heart from all the latest trends. Put your trust in God. His counsel will never fail.

Let's Pray

Holy Father, thank You for the best counsel. Protect our hearts from being tempted by all the latest trends. We seek Your guidance in our plans. In Jesus' name. Amen.

Call to Action

Are there trends that have captured your attention? Are they wasting precious resources? Do you need to move past them? Write it out.

January 8

The counsel of the LORD stands forever,
The plans of His heart from generation to generation.
Psalm 33:11

God's plans have been perfect from the beginning of time. The counsel He gives paves the way for peace. Taking matters into our own hands and veering off the path He lays out brings calamity. Remember the Garden of Eden?

When we continue to ignore His counsel, we become confused and distracted. Our actions become evidence of our disobedience. Discontentment and disconnection result from our disobedience.

But standing firm in His counsel provides assurance of contentment. The desire of His heart is fellowship with you and generations to come. Intentionally walking with Him provides peace.

Let's Pray

Holy Father, thank You for Your perfect plan. In Your wisdom You order our days. Allow us to be an example for future generations of abiding with You. In Jesus' name. Amen.

Call to Action

Have you attempted a project without His counsel? How did that work for you? What would you do differently now? Write it out.

January 9

The plans of the diligent lead surely to advantage,
But everyone who is hasty comes surely to poverty.
Proverbs 21:5

God provides so much proof of His surety in our obedience. But He isn't in a hurry. Our decisions and plans can be thwarted by quickly acting without His wise counsel.

Diligently seeking Him with the plans you make will give you an advantage. When you seek Him, earnestly, continually, you come to know Him better. Spending time in His Word and in prayer are only two ways to get to know Him. Spending time with other believers and living on mission with rejoicing and praise focuses your mind and heart on those things that are honoring and pleasing to Him.

Set the intentions of your mind and heart on Him. Move forward in His time, as He leads. Stay in constant contact with Him and help those around you do the same.

Let's Pray

Holy Father, draw us closer to You. Teach us, Holy Spirit, those things that You would have us understand. Give us discernment and wisdom in seeking You. In Jesus' name. Amen.

Call to Action

Does your timeline agree with God's? What adjustments do you need to make? Write it out.

January 10

The plans of the heart belong to man,
But the answer of the tongue is from the LORD.
Proverbs 16:1

I felt the attack coming hard. It had pelted away at my mind and heart all day. The onslaught of fiery arrows besieged me from all directions. But a still small voice called me. It warned me.

My heart can deceive me sometimes. The environment around me can attempt to persuade it to want what is contrary to what is good for it. Constant bombardment of worldly desires will surely leave me empty and disappointed.

But God provides the path to life. He is steadfast and sure in His Word. He gives us all we need to navigate thoughts; discerning those that destroy fellowship with Him. His Holy Spirit leads us away from destruction. We must be attentive to Him and then purposefully follow. Taking our thoughts captive will allow us to steer and guard our hearts to Him.

Let's Pray

Holy Father, thank You for Your Holy Spirit. Thank You for providing that still small voice in a world of loud chaos. Guard my heart and mind. In Jesus' name. Amen.

Call to Action

The world calls them triggers. But the world claims they win every time. They won't. God does. What do you need to give to God and tell the world it lost? Write it out.

January 11

O LORD, You are my God;
I will exalt You, I will give thanks to Your name;
For You have worked wonders,
Plans formed long ago, with perfect faithfulness.
Isaiah 25:1

Do you know He is faithful to you? He is. Long before you existed, He had plans for you. Wonderful plans of peace and hope. Wonderful plans for you to diligently seek Him and find Him in small and big moments of life.

He has been with you throughout your life. Waiting for you to notice. Today is the day for you to think back on your life and discover those times He has protected, provided, healed, satisfied, comforted, sustained, strengthened and whatever it is He has done for you.

Now thank Him for each time you recognized.

Let's Pray

Holy Father, I praise Your Holy name for these times You have shown up. Please forgive me for not recognizing Your presence in the moment. Help me to continually recognize Your presence. In Jesus' name. Amen.

Call to Action

Make a list of times God has shown up. Ask Him to allow you to see those moments. How did He help? What mess did He turn into a message in your life? Write it out.

January 12

Woe to those who deeply hide their plans from the LORD,
And whose deeds are done in a dark place,
And they say, "Who sees us?" or "Who knows us?"
Isaiah 29:15

Evil lurks in dark places. Waiting to devour unsuspecting victims. Wanting to steal what doesn't belong to him. Using his tried and proven methods to take you down. He wants to take from you the promises God has proclaimed for you since before the beginning of time.

Staying in dark places invites evil to take up residency. The cycle continues if your residency is planted in those dark places. Moving to the light will reveal the promises God has given you.

How do you do that though when you have lived in darkness for so long? Ask God to lead you. Pick up a Bible and start reading. Lay down anything that keeps you from fellowship with God. Get connected with a group of believers. That is where you start.

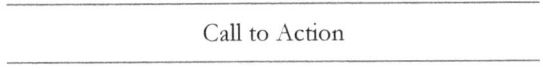

Let's Pray

Holy Father, it is only through the blood of Jesus that we move into Your Light and leave the darkness. In Jesus' name. Amen.

Call to Action

What is your action plan? You need to put it in a place that you will see it often. Write it out.

January 13

"For we will surely die and are like water spilled on the ground which cannot be gathered up again. Yet God does not take away life, but plans ways so that the banished one will not be cast out from him."
2 Samuel 14:14

Tomorrow will not return to allow you to live it again. You have right now. Today is the day to live. Whatever you have poured out already is done. You cannot pick it up.

God allows a fresh filling for you. Every breath gives you another moment to seek Him. His offering is continually in front of you. His redemption is renewing you persistently.

Only refusing Him will keep you separated from Him. His plan is for you to have life with Him. He won't take that offering away. It is up to you to receive it.

Let's Pray

Holy Father, Your life-giving plan redeems all the poor choices I have made. You provide me a way to return to You over and over. Thank You for the breath in my lungs that remind me of your constant renewing. In Jesus' name. Amen.

Call to Action

Have you poured out and found yourself unable to reclaim whatever it was you poured out? Do you really want to pick it up? Or instead, do you want a fresh filling? Tell God your desires and ask Him to fill you with fresh abundance. Write it out.

January 14

"For God has put it in their hearts to execute His purpose by having a common purpose, and by giving their kingdom to the beast, until the words of God will be fulfilled."
Revelation 17:17

God's purposes will not fail. His execution is orchestrated skillfully. Nothing is wasted. Even when I think all is lost and that the thousandth mistake will be the one that seals my fate, He steps in and reminds me that He is my Savior. He assures me all is not lost and that He is near.

He is sovereign and all will bow to Him. His plan is greater than anything we can imagine. We will continue in our quest to know Him by walking out His purpose for us. He holds great mysteries that will be revealed in His time, not ours.

Trusting His fulfillment is our responsibility. We must stand firm in the faith of the One who will see all things to completion. All things done for His glory and honor.

Let's Pray

Holy Father, You alone are worthy of all praise. I trust Your plan and purpose for my life. Help me in my plans so that I am walking in fellowship with You. In Jesus' name. Amen.

Call to Action

Do you know the purpose and plan God has for your life? Do your plans for this year include walking out His purpose for you? Write it out.

January 15

For God has not called us for the purpose of impurity, but in sanctification.
1 Thessalonians 4:7

Clean hands. Pure heart. Genuine intention. Sincere actions. Working together in purity.

The process of sanctification is continual. Our desires may shift and change causing us to take our eyes off God for periods of time. The returning to Him, learning from our mistakes, finding Him still there, waiting for our return, sanctifies us.

He cleanses us as we walk through life. Circumstances and situations will attempt to pull us away from Him. Through the perfect sacrifice of the blood of Jesus, He purifies us so that we can live in harmony with Him.

Let's Pray

Holy Father, take my messes and turn them into Your glory. My life belongs to You and is only complete when I walk in submission to Your will for my life. I lay my plans at Your feet. In Jesus' name. Amen.

Call to Action

Have you experienced sanctification in a specific area of your life? Did something hold you in bondage until you realized the sanctifying blood of Jesus? Are you walking through something right now that is bringing about sanctification? Write it out.

January 16

"I know that You can do all things,
And that no purpose of Yours can be thwarted."
Job 42:2

Each day we rise to a new opportunity to serve God. Even if the plans you made seem unreachable, if you made them with God, He will see them through to completion. Today is a new day for you to adjust your plan so that it will be in line with His.

It is a great and wonderful thing to search for Him and find Him in your plans. He is evident when you earnestly seek Him. He can do all things.

Trust Him with your plans. Ask Him to take your plans. Ask Him what His plans are for you. Then evaluate your plans to see if they include Him. If not, start fresh. If they include Him, know that they will succeed.

Let's Pray

Holy Father, Your plans, and purpose for me are greater than anything I can imagine. Guide me in fulfilling what You have placed in front of me. In Jesus' name. Amen.

Call to Action

Now that you have fully evaluated your plans considering what God has for you, take some time to thank Him. Give Him praise for His work in your life. Write it out.

January 17

Now accept the one who is weak in faith, but not for the purpose of passing judgment on his opinions.
Romans 14:1

In our sin, Jesus offered the way for us to be righteous and accepted by God. The blood of Jesus covered all sin and does not discriminate. Perfect Jesus accepts all regardless of their past. Each one only must draw near Him and believe.

In drawing near, we learn His characteristics and those characteristics begin to become part of our characteristics. The more we know Him the more we imitate Him. This allows us to treat others in His nondiscriminatory love.

He gives us discernment to righteously view others, not to judge, but to show them the way to Christ. He desires us to be examples to glorify Him. Our lives become a reflection of the love He has for us and allows us to be kingdom builders.

Let's Pray

Holy Father, You gave me a precious gift and responsibility to lead others to You. Keep me from becoming an obstacle but instead an encourager in the faith. In Jesus' name. Amen.

Call to Action

Do you recognize your responsibility in the kingdom? Write it out.

January 18

Now He who prepared us for this very purpose is God, who gave to us the Spirit as a pledge.
2 Corinthians 5:5

Gracious God gave us His Spirit. He gave us His constant presence to guide us. He comforts us. He intercedes for us. He gives us the assurance of eternal life.

Almighty God, in His sovereignty, enters us in His Spirit when we accept His gift of forgiveness and believe in Him. He takes up residency in us. Did you know God dwells within you if you are His child?

He prepared you for now. For this very moment in time, He formed and fashioned you to carry out a purpose no other person could carry out. He gave you the pledge of His Spirit to accomplish His purpose through you.

Let's Pray

Holy Father, I praise You for Your presence in my life. Thank You for Your Spirit dwelling in me. I surrender to Your purpose for my life. In Jesus' name. Amen.

Call to Action

Does the knowledge of God's Spirit dwelling in you change your view of the plans you have made? Does it cause you to desire different outcomes for your life? Will you make any changes because of this knowledge? Write it out.

January 19

The end of all things is near; therefore, be of sound judgment and sober spirit for the purpose of prayer.
1 Peter 4:7

Prayer is a constant conversation with God. Two-way communication with the One that formed you in your mother's womb. It is a perpetual discussion with Almighty God.

The temporary status of the world may pull you away from this communication. Obstacles will attempt to keep you from acknowledging His communication with you. Your relationship with Him is the most important relationship you have. Therefore, communication with Him is the most important communication you have.

Prayer allows you direct access to your Holy Father. Oh, how He loves to communicate with you! He is right there with you now. Talk with Him. But remember it is two-way communication. Don't be the one doing all the talking. Be still and listen.

Let's Pray

Holy Father, to fully realize the gift of communication with You is overwhelming to consider. Through Jesus, You allow us into the holy of holies, into Your presence. In Jesus' name. Amen.

Call to Action

Do you journal your prayers? It allows me to focus on Him. Try it. Write it out.

January 20

But He said to them, "I must preach the kingdom of God to the other cities also, for I was sent for this purpose."
Luke 4:43

The message of the gospel is not isolated to a specific people group or location. You may look around you and think there are areas of your city, county, state, or nation that will never have the gospel message. It is to be shared to the uttermost parts of the earth.

Jesus even traveled to other areas to share the message of salvation and hope. He spread the message through healing those with a faith that overcame their circumstances. He spread the message by preaching to large groups.

Part of your purpose is to share Him with others. It is your message to share. In the unique way God created for you. It doesn't have to imitate anyone else. Seek Him and be prepared to share His message of salvation whenever the opportunity arises.

Let's Pray

Holy Father, thank You for the example of sharing Your kingdom through those You gave us in Your word. Thank You for the privilege of being messengers for You. In Jesus' name. Amen.

Call to Action

Is sharing the message of Christ included in your plans this year? Write it out.

January 21

I have sent him to you for this very purpose, so that you may know about us, and that he may comfort your hearts.
Ephesians 6:22

You have a mission field whether you realize it or not. Not all missionaries travel far distances to carry the good news of Jesus Christ and the salvation He offers. Your mission may be to tell your children the good news. It may be raising them to carry the message a little further.

A mission field is not always some place away from your circle of influence. Home, work, restaurants, stores, medical offices, or wherever you go is a mission field. You just need to look for opportunities. They surround you every day.

The message you share may be a simple smile. It may be holding a door for someone. It doesn't have to be complicated, but it does need to be genuine and sincere.

Let's Pray

Holy Father, thank You for the opportunities to share Your love with others. Help me to discern those divine moments and guide me in action and words as needed. In Jesus' name. Amen.

Call to Action

Have you shared Jesus with a stranger? How did it feel? What would you do differently? Write it out.

January 22

But have nothing to do with worldly fables fit only for old women. On the other hand, discipline yourself for the purpose of godliness;
1 Timothy 4:7

After lunch each weekday, my grandparents would sit in their recliners with the television on and watch what they called their "stories." It gave them a temporary reprieve from the lack of anything else to do and rest for their aging bodies. Always plagued with scandal and romance, these shows provided entertainment only. Not much eternal value found in these "stories."

I am guilty of doing the same thing. Filling my time with meaningless entertainment instead of being disciplined with my time and purpose of kingdom building. We have been conditioned to believe we need constant entertainment.

What value is the entertainment you are consuming bringing to your life? Is it pleasing to God? Devote yourself to kingdom building so you don't need mindless entertainment.

Let's Pray

Holy Father, thank You for providing kingdom work. Find our efforts acceptable. Keep us from mindless activities that draw us away from You. In Jesus' name. Amen.

Call to Action

Is there something you need to give up that is drawing you away from God? Write it out.

January 23

And we know that God causes all things to work together for good to those who love God, to those who are called according to His purpose.
Romans 8:28

God doesn't abandon His plans for you. He works them out even if your plans seem to fall apart. His plans are perfect. Sometimes we can get in our own way of staying on the path He has laid out for us. He directs our steps when we are diligent in seeking Him.

Have the plans you made crumbled in these first few weeks of the new year? Today is a new day. You have the opportunity to start fresh. What will you do with that opportunity?

God will work things out and you will be blessed if you love Him. It may not look exactly like you expected or what the world defines as success. But the work of God far surpasses anything that we can imagine. Trust His hand with your plans.

Let's Pray

Holy Father, You are worthy of all praise for the work you complete in my life. I owe everything to You. You are faithful even when I am not. Thank You, Holy Father. In Jesus' name. Amen.

Call to Action

How have you seen the hand of God work something seemingly impossible out in your life? Did you thank Him for it? Now is your chance. Write it out.

January 24

Therefore, since we have so great a cloud of witnesses surrounding us, let us also lay aside every encumbrance and the sin which so easily entangles us, and let us run with endurance the race that is set before us, fixing our eyes on Jesus, the author and perfecter of faith, who for the joy set before Him endured the cross, despising the shame, and has sat down at the right hand of the throne of God.
Hebrews 12:1-2

Staying in the lane God has set out for me has proven difficult at times. So many interests pull at me to divert my attention away from the current task set in front of me, a task assigned by God. God assignments are priorities. All the other stuff is just the enemy getting in the way.

Jesus joyfully approached the wrath I deserve so that I could joyfully accept the assignments from God. He gave me the path; it is mine to walk. I have a vast number of people watching me run the race.

My devotion to God turns into devotion to the task set in front of me. His glory will be revealed. It is up to me to run my race so I can reflect His glory. I want to run well.

Let's Pray

Holy Father, thank You for allowing me to take part in furthering Your kingdom. Keep my feet going in the direction You have for me. Keep my focus on You. In Jesus' name. Amen.

Call to Action

What race is set before you? Write it out.

January 25

I have fought the good fight, I have finished the race, I have kept the faith.
2 Timothy 4:7

In the eighth grade, I had to write my first research paper. I still remember my topic: Marsupials. I chose that topic because one of my favorite people loved koalas. I worked hard on that paper without the use of the internet. My resources came from books in the library of my school.

I will never forget the satisfaction that came when my grade was awarded: A. The teacher, Mrs. Johnson, thought the work I put into that paper deserved a high mark of achievement. I went on that year to receive the English award for my grade.

It did my insecure heart good to accomplish something seemingly insignificant. I put the work and time in with my best effort. It was a race I finished well.

Let's Pray

Holy Father, at the time it didn't seem like much but looking back, You were faithful to me even in completing a simple school assignment. I can recall so many other times where Your faithfulness was evident. May I be found faithful to You. In Jesus' name. Amen.

Call to Action

What races have you finished well? Even as a child, our races can be contributed back to God's faithfulness toward us. Will you give Him praise for His faithfulness? Write it out.

January 26

Do you not know that those who run in a race all run, but only one receives the prize? Run in such a way that you may win.
1 Corinthians 9:24

Look around you. Go ahead, look around. If you are alone, then look with your mind. Who are the people running beside you? Are you all running for a common goal? What is your goal? Have you named it? What prize are you aiming to receive? So many questions!

Your race is not necessarily a physical race. Your race may have the goal to share the good news of Jesus to as many people as possible. It may be to raise your children to love God with all their hearts, minds, souls, and strength. It may be to care for your aging parents.

Whatever your race looks like, run it so that at the end, you can face God and hear "Well done!"

Let's Pray

Holy Father, thank You for the equipping needed to run the race set before me. I am confident in Your blessings on my life to accomplish what You have called me to do. Without You I am unable to run this race. Help me to finish well. In Jesus' name. Amen.

Call to Action

Will you ask God to help you in your race? Ask Him if you are in the right lane. Sometimes we skip lanes and need to move back into our own. Write it out.

January 27

I press on toward the goal for the prize of the upward call of God in Christ Jesus.
Philippians 3:14

Press on. Keep going. Move forward. You won't see where you are going with your head down. It may be scary to trust the ground under your feet. It may feel like you are taking the wrong steps if you can't see your feet. Look up!

For most of my life, I have walked with my head down. I look at the ground to keep from falling, like I did after school one afternoon walking to the bus with a heavy load of books in my arms. But it got me in trouble once. Head down, I walked into the trunk of a bent tree. I fell.

When I raise my head, I can see the horizon. My perspective shifts upward to give me a larger view. I can drop my eyes on occasion to check the ground, but I can see so much more if I keep my head up. Scan the horizon for the possibilities in front of you.

Let's Pray

Holy Father, You open the whole world up to us. With you, our reach is limitless. Thank You for walking with us through every step of life. In Jesus' name. Amen.

Call to Action

What posture keeps you from moving in the direction God guides? Write it out.

January 28

Are you so foolish? Having begun by the Spirit, are you now being perfected by the flesh?
Galatians 3:3

Relying on the gift of His Holy Spirit means you are never facing the future alone. No matter what your circumstances may be, He is your constant companion. He will never leave you.

Our flesh will fail us. We age and our strength lessens. Our mental abilities may diminish. God never fails. God's strength is the same yesterday, today and tomorrow. God knows everything and He won't forget it.

Holy Spirit resides in those who have placed their trust in Jesus Christ. If you have done so, you are sealed by the salvation promised by the blood of Jesus. Be still and know His presence.

Let's Pray

Holy Father, forgive me for taking my eyes off You. Return me to the place of knowing You are always with me. Thank You for Your Holy Spirit. In Jesus' name. Amen.

Call to Action

Have you lost focus of His presence with you? Can you name what caused your focus to waver? Identify the obstacles and take action to remove them from your life. Take some time to pray and ask God to reveal Himself to you. Write it out.

January 29

But now finish doing it also, so that just as there was the readiness to desire it, so there may be also the completion of it by your ability.
2 Corinthians 8:11

You have looked forward to working on this project for so long. Your energy is high, and you feel like you could finish it all in one day. You can see the finished work in your mind. Your hands are moving as fast as they can. The day ends. You are not finished.

Ending the day defeated, you wonder if you should give up. Things didn't go as planned. You didn't have all the materials you needed. One area took longer than you expected. The partially finished project is a sad comparison to what you envisioned.

The next morning, what will you do? Will you rise in eager anticipation of working well to finish what you started? Will you complete the project and make it live up to your effort? Or will you stay discouraged and allow the project to stay unfinished? It is your choice.

Let's Pray

Holy Father, you call us to finish what You have us begin. You provide all the necessities for us to finish the work You place in front of us. Help us to finish well. In Jesus' name. Amen.

Call to Action

What project do you need to finish well? Write it out.

January 30

But I do not consider my life of any account as dear to myself, so that I may finish my course and the ministry which I received from the Lord Jesus, to testify solemnly of the gospel of the grace of God.
Acts 20:24

"Amazing Grace" rolls off the tongue in choirs all over the world. Just saying the name brings the melody to mind. The words a reminder of the wretchedness of a life without Christ and the redemption found in His grace.

In my meritless condition, He calls me worthy to share His good news of grace. Deserving of the death He faced, instead I am given salvation from wrath. Why would I not testify to this eternal gift of life?

So, allow me to share His good news with you. God provided the once and done sacrifice for all sin. Nothing is excluded under this sacrifice except the outright rejection of this precious gift. Will you accept His gift of eternal life?

Let's Pray

Holy Father, I confess that I am a sinner. I recognize the sacrifice of Jesus as the only way for my redemption. My life belongs to You. You are Lord of my life. In Jesus' name. Amen.

Call to Action

Will you confess your need for Him? Write it out.

January 31

Not that I have already obtained it or have already become perfect, but I press on so that I may lay hold of that for which also I was laid hold of by Christ Jesus.
Philippians 3:12

Have you confessed your need for Jesus Christ? Has He captivated your heart and mind for His purpose? If your answer is yes to both questions, you are called to press on for His glory.

Your life is no longer your own. You have decided to lay aside everything that keeps you from His purpose and devote yourself to the work He has for you. You are on a mission.

This divine work may come with the loss of some friends. You will have to give up old habits. You may even need to change the language you speak.

The rewards far outweigh anything you must give up. You will face challenges along the way, but you are surrounded by an army of protection. Take hold of your purpose.

Let's Pray

Holy Father, I commit the work of my hands to Your purpose. Nothing is worth doing without You. May my effort be acceptable to You. In Jesus' name. Amen.

Call to Action

Are you ready to make a commitment to Him? Once you put it in writing, sign, and date it. Tell Him. Write it out.

BUT NOW FAITH, HOPE, LOVE,
ABIDE THESE THREE; BUT THE
GREATEST OF THESE IS LOVE.
1 CORINTHIANS 13:13

February

But now faith, hope, love, abide these three; but the greatest of these is love.
1 Corinthians 13:13

The world confuses the object of love. Love is to be directed at the spirit, not flesh, not pride, not what can be seen and touched. Idolatry replaces love all too frequently. Love comes from the deep longings in a person's soul. Therefore, love is an eternal condition.

We throw the word around when we refer to food or clothing or cars or houses. We claim to love someone when in just a few days or months or years we dismiss them from our lives wanting nothing more to do with them. This is not love. These are fleshly desires.

The object of our love should first be God. Without the proper placement of our first and most important love, all others will disappoint. Misplaced devotion misdirects the intentional love God planted within us. Misplaced love confuses our emotions.

Take February to review what God tells us about love and the connection of the heart. Emotional reactions are not always tied to love or the lack thereof. Emotions can mislead us. Reactions to environmental or physiological circumstances may also mislead us.

Know what God says about love. Know what God says about the heart. He gave us His word so that we can know Him and grow in our faith, understanding, and wisdom. It is our responsibility to study Him. When we do, He meets us there and through His Holy Spirit, He teaches us.

Seek His heart and love.

February 1

Beloved, let us love one another, for love is from God; and everyone who loves is born of God and knows God.
1 John 4:7

Do you find it difficult to love everyone? Words spoken can hurt. Actions taken can offend. You get cut off in traffic when you are already running late. The enemy loves to present opportunities to you for revenge and hatred. But that is not what God has called us to do.

God's love calls us to love one another. God poured out for us His perfect love. Our love becomes an example for others, even in moments where it is most difficult, of God's love for us. It becomes proof that we belong to Him.

You will have opportunities today to seek His help in loving others. In the moment where you are most tempted to strike out against someone, remember the grace given to You through the blood of Jesus and offer the same grace of love to someone. Reflect the example of Jesus.

Let's Pray

Holy Father, instead of striking back, teach me to offer grace. In undeserved moments, let me show love to those that may cause me harm. Thank You for Your love. In Jesus' name. Amen.

Call to Action

Think back on one moment you showed love in a difficult circumstance. Write it out.

February 2

Your word I have treasured in my heart,
That I may not sin against You.
Psalm 119:11

Falling in love with God's word draws us near to Him. We see the repeated efforts of compassion He has for His creation. He continuously provides redemption. He never tires of pursuing us.

Throughout the Old Testament, His provision of grace is obvious but comes to an ultimate climax when He presents the perfect sacrifice. It is in the New Testament He ushers in the long-awaited Savior that brings with Him the promise of eternal life. Old, imperfect sacrifices that needed repeating are removed and, in their place, Jesus.

The entire word of God points us to eternity with Him. It prepares us to live with Him. He gives us the knowledge we need to seek and know Him. It is the greatest treasure.

Let's Pray

Holy Father, thank You for Your Word. I want to write it on my heart so that when pressed, it is the thing that pours out of me. In Jesus' name. Amen.

Call to Action

Many think the Bible is hard to understand. Reading it opens the vast magnificence of God. It reveals the heart of God toward His creation. His love displayed on the pages of His love letter to you. Do you have a reading plan? If not, make one today. Write it out.

February 3

"For God so loved the world, that He gave His only begotten Son, that whoever believes in Him shall not perish, but have eternal life."
John 3:16

God knew the repetitious sacrifices were not sufficient to redeem all humankind. In the precision He gave for the act of sacrifice for His people as they lived in a desert for forty years, He knew a temporary solution would need a permanent replacement. So, He gave His Son.

In desperate need of a Savior, all humankind wanders in desert places where we are parched and perish without the living water of God's perfect Son. He brings an eternal spring of life. He brings love so deep and desperate to save you and me through the sacrifice of Jesus.

And He allows us to choose Him. He allows us to believe in Him or not. He allows us to perish or have eternal life. It is our choice.

Let's Pray

Holy Father, You sent Your perfect Son to die in my place and experience hell on my behalf so that I could have eternal life with You. Please forgive me for my sins. I need Jesus. I need Your love. Thank You for loving me. In Jesus' name. Amen.

Call to Action

Do you believe in Jesus? Have you confessed Jesus as Lord of your life? Write it out.

February 4

Apply your heart to discipline
And your ears to words of knowledge.
Proverbs 23:12

The world tells you to follow your heart. Meaning whatever you may be feeling now, just go with it. No matter what it is, follow it. Even if it will lead you into a place you don't need to be, follow your heart.

This is contrary to what God wants from you. He knows our hearts because He made them. He knows they can easily be influenced by temptation. He knows we crave stuff. He also knows the only thing that fulfills any craving we desire is Him.

This is why we are to discipline our hearts. We are to guard our hearts for the purpose of loving God. He filled us with emotion but also knowledge through His Word. We can bring our heart into subjection to Him when we draw near Him and study His Word.

Let's Pray

Holy Father, You are Lord of my heart. When temptation tries to pull me away from You, please pull me back. You are the holder of my heart. I trust You. In Jesus' name. Amen.

Call to Action

Do you know God cares about what you care about? He wants your heart. He desires to fill it so that you can be His witness to His goodness. How will you discipline your heart? Write it out.

February 5

In this is love, not that we loved God, but that He loved us and sent His Son to be the propitiation for our sins.
1 John 4:10

Our love cannot accomplish what the love of God accomplished. It wasn't our love of God that forgave our sins but His love for us. It isn't our love that causes Him to love us.

He lavishes us with His love. It is a fierce love that far surpasses anything our imaginations can hold. His love provides the way for us to return to Him again and again.

He saw the condition of our minds and hearts and knew we had been enticed by evil. He knew we had no hope. He knew He had to provide for our redemption.

His plan was completed on the cross. The perfect Lamb of God slaughtered, sacrificed to satisfy the blood requirement for the atonement of sin. Not just one but all. All sin covered by the perfect sacrifice of Jesus. This is the love of God.

Let's Pray

Holy Father, I need You. I need Your love for me. I need Your forgiveness. I need the blood of Jesus. Thank You for the perfect sacrifice for my sin. I love You. In Jesus' name. Amen.

Call to Action

He loves you. Do you recognize His love for you? How? Write it out.

February 6

"for where your treasure is, there your heart will be also."
Matthew 6:21

I have heard people say to look at your spending and that is where you will find what matters most to you. This is where you find your treasure. Where are you spending money?

My grandson picks up rocks and acorns. He stuffs them into his pockets. He pulls them out in his tiny hands and holds them out to me and shows me his treasure. His eyes wide with the wonder of the treasure he found. Always looking for more.

God wants to be your treasure. He wants you to seek Him. He wants to be found by you. He wants your eyes to be wide with wonder just like that four-year old boy holding out his little hands full of rocks and acorns

---

Let's Pray

Holy Father, there is no price, except the life of Jesus, which could be paid to find our treasure in You. You give us access to the greatest treasure by allowing us to come to You. May we never take the treasure of You for granted. Thank You for the greatest treasure. In Jesus' name. Amen.

Call to Action

Is there earthly treasure in your life that has attempted to steal your treasure in God? Do you need to clean out that treasure to make room for eternal treasure? Write it out.

February 7

By this we know that we abide in Him and He in us, because He has given us of His Spirit.
1 John 4:13

In John 14, Jesus told His disciples that He would ask the Father to give them another Helper. This Helper abides in those who believe the truth of Jesus Christ. This Helper is Holy Spirit. The very Spirit of God dwelling in and with those that accept Him and believe Him.

A constant presence of help from God dwells in you if you only believe. Are you aware of His presence? Do you know He is always with you? You are not orphaned. You are not left alone.

Closer than your spouse. Closer than your parents. Closer than your children. Holy Spirit dwelling in you, moving where you move, seeing what you see, reading what you read, listening to what you say. Always with you. He is your constant help.

Let's Pray

Holy Father, You are worthy of all praise. You know our deepest need and are faithful to dwell with us. You help in ways we do not even comprehend. Help us to recognize Your presence. Help us to stay alert so that we can walk in the freedom You provide. In Jesus' name. Amen.

Call to Action

My attention can easily be interrupted. I am not always focused on His presence with me. Do you have the same tendency? What do you do to keep your focus on God? Write it out.

February 8

Bind them continually on your heart;
Tie them around your neck.
Proverbs 6:21

Your heart craves more of God. Don't miss this. There isn't any replacement for the filling from God. What you pour into your heart will seep out of you.

Anything you use to satisfy or comfort or depend upon other than God is an idol. It is a pathetic substitution for perfect, worship-worthy God. Do you have any idols you need to remove from your heart? Is there something occupying God's space in your heart?

Let me encourage you to fill-up with God. Open His Word every day. Allow Him to pour into you so that you will pour out for Him.

Let's Pray

Holy Father, fill us with more of You. Keep us from attempting to replace that grace-filled love You give us with any inferior substitute. In Jesus' name. Amen.

Call to Action

Take time today to fill-up with Him. Consider those things that need to be removed so you can make room for Him. What is it that keeps you from filling up with Him? Make a list of what needs to be removed and take action to remove it from your life. Next make a commitment to Him. Keep that commitment in writing in a place you see frequently. Write it out.

February 9

Whoever confesses that Jesus is the Son of God, God abides in him, and he in God.
1 John 4:15

Speak it aloud. Go ahead. Do it. "Jesus is Lord." "Jesus is the Son of God." Do it again. When I speak it aloud, a smile spreads across my face. I feel like I can breathe deeper. Peace fills my soul. I feel lighter.

Confessing Jesus is the Son of God is celebrating, praising, declaring, agreeing, speaking out, taking a stand for Him. Connecting yourself to Him and declaring Him as Savior of your soul. You invite Him as He invites you to dwell together.

You abide with God. God abides with you. You remain with Him. He remains with you. You are held by Him. You hold Him. You keep Him. He keeps you.

Confess it again. "Jesus is the Son of God."

Let's Pray

Holy Father, You invite me into a dwelling place with You. It is the space held deep within me where You fill with Your goodness. You created this space just for me. In Jesus' name. Amen.

Call to Action

Create a decorative banner with your confession. Make it as big as you want. Write it out.

February 10

"For where your treasure is, there your heart will be also."
Luke 12:34

Where is your treasure? How do you define treasure? Do you have a cabinet or room or building full of collected items from years of seeking and searching? Is this your treasure? Is this where your heart dwells?

I am full of questions for you today. Does this treasure treat you well? Do you find peace and rest in this treasure, or do you find toil and labor and dust? Does your treasure go with you wherever you go? Does it provide help when you are in hard circumstances?

These are questions only you can answer. You know where your heart resides. And if it resides anywhere but in the perfect grasp of God, consider relinquishing possession of that false treasure and instead relinquish possession of your heart to Him.

Let's Pray

Holy Father, You are my treasure. You hold my heart in Your hands. I want to dwell safely in Your grasp. I lay down everything in this world and surrender to You. In Jesus' name. Amen.

Call to Action

Take time to think about your treasure. What is it that you hold dear to your heart? What is it that you would have a tough time giving up? Will you, can you give it up for Him? Write it out.

February 11

There is no fear in love; but perfect love casts out fear, because fear involves punishment, and the one who fears is not perfected in love.
1 John 4:18

Cradling the head and body of the fresh-from-God gift of a newborn baby reveals a tiny glimpse of the great love of God. A soul wrapped in flesh that has just been sent into this world to face sin and death. Peaceful sleep is an indication of perfect love casting out fear.

Born a sinner but intrinsically drawn to Love. Seeking Love to dispel fear. Fear realized in the depths of sin. Fear and sin irradicated by perfect Love. There it is. Perfect Love is the answer.

When I consider the love of God, fear runs away. Held by Him, nothing can destroy my relationship with Him. I have full assurance of His protection. He is my refuge.

Let's Pray

Holy Father, fear must leave in Your presence. So, I want to stay in Your presence. Fully knowing that no matter what comes my way, You hold me. In Jesus' name. Amen.

Call to Action

Fear likes to insert itself when I take my focus off the cross of Jesus. Fear doesn't belong in my life. It doesn't belong in your life. Fear will lie to you. Will you commit to keeping Love front and center in your life so that fear has no hold on you? Write it out.

February 12

in whatever our heart condemns us; for God is greater than our heart and knows all things.
1 John 3:20

I am my own worst critic. You too? I come face to face with constant faults. They are never-ending. When one is found, more will surely pop up. Then it becomes a barrage of faults being revealed. My heart can be harsh with me.

But God gives grace I don't. Holy Spirit teaches me grace. He takes hold of my heart and softens it toward myself and shows me all those faults point only to my humanity and not to my ruin. In my human form, faults will exist. God sees through them all and sees me and loves me anyway.

I turn to Him instead of my faults. I give Him my faults, and He gave me grace. I give Him my heart because He already gave me His.

Let's Pray

Holy Father, You have not condemned me to death because of my faults. Instead, You are the grace-giver. You lavish grace upon me in all my messes. Thank You. In Jesus' name. Amen.

Call to Action

Do you offer grace to yourself and others by the same measure God gives it to you? God knows our hearts and sees the grace we offer. Are there areas of your life that you find difficult to offer grace? What will you do with those areas of your life? Write it out.

February 13

if someone says, "I love God," and hates his brother, he is a liar; for the one who does not love his brother whom he has seen, cannot love God whom he has not seen.
1 John 4:20

Loving others becomes proof of my love for God. To have love and compassion for everyone is the goal. Finding it inside me because God placed it there. Love. For others. For all. To have compassion for those that have offended. Understanding everyone deals with sin and hurt.

Asking God to forgive me for having hatred in my heart toward anyone. Asking Him to remove it from me. I want to love God. And I want God to show me, to teach me how to love others. I want Him to help me to meet them where they are and lavish love onto them.

Wanting love to be my natural language. Wanting love to spill out of me and be the proof of God's love in me. Wanting my life to be evidence of His love.

Let's Pray

Holy Father, without You I am incapable of loving anyone. Your love and forgiveness lavished on me turns my stony, hard heart into soft, pliable flesh. Thank You for your love for me. Help me love others. Shape my heart to look like Yours. In Jesus' name. Amen.

Call to Action

What are some practical ways you can display love? Write it out.

February 14

"Moreover, I will give you a new heart and put a new spirit within you; and I will remove the heart of stone from your flesh and give you a heart of flesh."
Ezekiel 36:26

The earliest declaration of a heart transplant is recorded by Ezekiel. Removing what is cold, hard, and unfeeling and replacing it with warm, soft, blood pumping flesh. Blood pumping flesh recirculating life.

Jesus took my heart and removed the callouses. It took a hammer and nails. He chiseled away all the hard edges, leaving fresh life. Pulsing life filled with Him.

There is no room for Him in a cold, stony cavern. Without His hammer and nails, my heart would still be cold and hard and void of His life-giving blood. But because of His hammer and nails my heart comes alive with His Spirit filling my veins.

Let's Pray

Holy Father, You took the build-up of plaque from my heart and laid it upon Jesus. All the rocks I tried to hoard inside shattered at the swinging of that hammer. In place of those lumps of coal, You gave me shimmering diamonds in the form of life-giving blood. In Jesus' name. Amen.

Call to Action

Do you need a heart transplant? There is only One source. Will you ask Him? Write it out.

February 15

For this is the love of God, that we keep His commandments; and His commandments are not burdensome.
1 John 5:3

Drawing near to God brings with it the desire to know His commandments and to live within their boundaries. The boundaries are set to separate us from eternal darkness. His protection lies within those boundaries.

Loving God is easy within the boundaries. Step out of them and loving God becomes difficult. He doesn't dwell outside the markers of His commandments. He isn't found there. He makes it easy to stay within the markers. His faithfulness through the blood of Jesus makes it easy to dwell there with Him.

When you are tempted to step out of His boundaries, His commandments, remember the sacrifice Jesus made for you. His body marked with the boundary lines of His love. He removed your guilty wretchedness and replaced it with His gracious wellness.

Let's Pray

Holy Father, You make it well with my soul. Your love captivates. In Jesus' name. Amen.

Call to Action

How does He make your relationship with Him easy? Write it out.

February 16

The LORD is my strength and my shield;
My heart trusts in Him, and I am helped;
Therefore my heart exults,
And with my song I shall thank Him.
Psalm 28:7

He is my strength. He is my shield. He is trustworthy. He helps me in ways I didn't even know I needed help. Which is in every way! Hallelujah!

My heart wallows in Him. I am soft clay in His hands. He molds me into the shape of His fingertips. There is great strength in His hands. Under His strength I bend and conform to the imprint of Him.

He is worthy of my song. Lifting my voice to Him in an offering of thanksgiving. Praising Him for His strength. Worshipping Him for His trustworthiness.

Let's Pray

Holy Father, You alone are worthy of all praise. Your strength grasps me and keeps me. You shield me when fiery arrows are aimed at me. My heart is Yours. You are my constant help. Holy Father, I worship You. In Jesus' name. Amen.

Call to Action

His faithfulness is never-ending. Looking back can you see times when He helped you? Maybe an unexpected word of encouragement? Or a way out of a difficult situation? Write it out.

February 17

If I speak with the tongues of men and of angels, but do not have love, I have become a noisy gong or a clanging cymbal.
1 Corinthians 13:1

The utterances of the heart resemble either a divine symphony or a trash truck dumping your garbage. They spring forth from your heart through your mouth. God's presence or lack of is evident in what comes out.

Trash spewing from your mouth only resembles word vomit. Daggers thrown from a loveless heart. Dry and suffocating gasps of air from a dying heart. This is the picture of a heart outside the presence of God, outside the presence of love.

A symphonic oasis of life springs forth from the heart of the one filled with the presence of God. Love drips like honey from the lips of a heart shrouded in the light of God's love. Pleasant are the words from a loved-filled heart.

Let's Pray

Holy Father may the words of my mouth reflect a heart filled with Your love. Allow me to hear my words and seek Your transforming love for my heart. In Jesus' name. Amen.

Call to Action

Have you heard the words of your heart? Do you need a heart adjustment? Ask God. Write it out.

February 18

"Moreover the LORD your God will circumcise your heart and the heart of your descendants, to love the LORD your God with all your heart and with all your soul, so that you may live."
Deuteronomy 30:6

God wants your whole heart. Not just when you need something or when something is going wrong. He desires a relationship with you. When you give your whole heart to God, He removes what is not needed and replaces it with a longing for Him that only He can satisfy.

Life truly begins when your heart belongs to Your Creator. Opening Your heart for only God makes room to love others. Sounds strange, I know. But without placing your love on the source of love, all other recipients become idols. Idols pull us away from God, therefore, pulling us away from true love.

God's love displayed through your life can continue for generations. Your life is an example for others to imitate. What legacy do you want to leave for your family, faith and love or idolatry?

Let's Pray

Holy Father, thank You for Your example of love. Thank You for the love You place in us. We need Your guidance in loving others well. In Jesus' name. Amen.

Call to Action

Do you have someone in your life that left a legacy of faith for you? Write it out.

February 19

If I have the gift of prophecy, and know all mysteries and all knowledge; and if I have all faith, so as to remove mountains, but do not have love, I am nothing.
1 Corinthians 13:2

All the gifts given by God, sitting inside vessels with vacant hearts are wasted. God-given gifts waiting to be put to work for His kingdom. But the work of His kingdom begins in our hearts. The work begins by removing the hard stone walls of cynicism and hurt and replacing them with warm beating lively flesh ready to share His love through the administering of His gifts.

Connecting the love of God with the gifts and abilities that only come from Him is faith in action. Helping a neighbor, not from obligation but from love. Going on a mission trip, not because others are going but because God has called you to it and your heart is pulled to help. Love fulfills the gifts God placed in us.

Let the love of God drive your purpose. When you do, things happen. Joy will be your evidence.

Let's Pray

Holy Father, put us to work for Your kingdom through the love and gifts You give us. In Jesus' name. Amen.

Call to Action

Do you know the gift He has given you? Are you using it in His love? Write it out.

February 20

But Mary treasured all these things, pondering them in her heart.
Luke 2:19

Mary had an up close and personal view of God in flesh. She gave birth to Him. She raised Him. She loved Him both as a mother and a child. She was His mother. He was her Father.

She witnessed His life on earth and knew His ways. She knew His face and hands and toes. She knew His scent. She knew His voice. She held Him. He held her.

She was thrust into motherhood and equipped with all she needed to do the job. Love came down to reside in her house and in her heart. Will you invite Him into your house and your heart?

Let's Pray

Holy Father, You are worthy of all praise. We ask You to equip our hearts and homes so that they are acceptable for Your dwelling place. Jesus made it known before His crucifixion that He would be leaving a Helper. We need Holy Spirit to dwell in us. We need His help and guidance. Without His teaching we cannot understand and know all that You have for us. In Jesus' name. Amen.

Call to Action

Have you considered how God equipped Mary? Have you considered how He has equipped you? Do you love others through your equipping? Write it out.

February 21

And if I give all my possessions to feed the poor, and if I surrender my body to be burned, but do not have love, it profits me nothing.
1 Corinthians 13:3

Vanity drags us into conceit. The reason for doing whatever it is you are doing matters more than what you are doing. Are you doing it for your glory? Or are you doing it for God's glory?

There is a significant difference between doing work for your glory and for His glory. Efforts fall flat and are empty when done for the attention you seek. But when done for His glory, imagine fireworks going off in heaven.

His glory shines on you and your profit increases exponentially when your actions are sincerely directed at Him. Let Him be the target of your efforts. All the good and perfect gifts He gives are to be lavished back for His glory.

Let's Pray

Holy Father, You are the perfect giver of all good things. May You find the return from Your children acceptable and pleasing. Give us clean hands and pure hearts. In Jesus' name. Amen.

Call to Action

Not from pride but from a thankful heart, recall a time when your efforts blessed you as much as they did the intended recipient. Where do you think that blessing came from? Write it out.

February 22

"The good man out of the good treasure of his heart brings forth what is good; and the evil man out of the evil treasure brings forth what is evil; for his mouth speaks from that which fills his heart."
Luke 6:45

Listen to the conversations around you. What do you hear? Spoken words carry great indication of the condition of the heart. What words are you speaking?

Blessing or cursing. Life or death. Beauty or trash. Humility or pride. Justice or injustice.

Listen. What do you hear? What do you hear from others? What do you hear from yourself?

Will you ask God to help you clean up the conversations around you by allowing you to reflect His good treasure? Your words are heard by others. Pray that they hear the words of God when they listen to your voice.

Let's Pray

Holy Father, allow only good to come from our mouths. Transform our hearts and minds to be full of Your treasure so that we can pour out blessings on others. In Jesus' name. Amen.

Call to Action

How have you heard blessing or cursing in conversations? Have you heard yourself spout cursing and afterward regretted it? It is not too late to confess and repent. Write it out.

February 23

Love is patient, love is kind and is not jealous; love does not brag and is not arrogant,
1 Corinthians 13:4

Patience means there is something you must endure. Have you heard someone say they don't pray for patience? Doing so would be inviting some hardship to endure with perseverance. And that is exactly what love does, endures with perseverance through difficulties.

Love does not get wrapped up in fits of jealousy. It is free and trusting. Unencumbered devotion with no traces of suspicion. Love is completely trustworthy.

Love is not about you but about others. Love directs itself outward. Love is applied by opening your hands and heart for service to others with no expectation of return.

Let's Pray

Holy Father, You are the definition of love. You offer it to us. You engrave it in our hearts. And You give us room to grow in it or allow it to waste away. God, keep us from mistreating what You have given us. God, help us to direct the love You have placed in us onto others, so Your glory is known. In Jesus' name. Amen.

Call to Action

In what ways do you express love? What are some ways you can increase your display of God's love, with patience, without jealousy, without bragging, and without arrogance? Write it out.

February 24

"Since I know, O my God, that You try the heart and delight in uprightness, I, in the integrity of my heart, have willingly offered all these things; so now with joy I have seen Your people, who are present here, make their offerings willingly to You."
1 Chronicles 29:17

Willing submission to God. Stripping away all the junk that weighs down. Standing straight in a right place. Pouring out from the filling received. Seeking Him and His direction. And doing it again and again.

He pours into us if we are willing to receive the measure of faith He offers. When we receive it the scales on our eyes are removed and we are open to receiving more of His goodness. He is faithful to provide all we need. He keeps pouring from His never-ending supply of love.

From His abundance, we get to reciprocate. From His pouring out, we get to pour out. Sweet offerings of life dripped from our overflowing cup filling the cups of others.

Let's Pray

Holy Father, You fill my heart and mind with joy. Unspeakable joy that spills over onto others is the desire of my heart. Offerings made from the fullness You gave to me. In Jesus' name. Amen.

Call to Action

Joy seeps out from those that have filled up with God. Do you know someone that drips with joy? Would you give them an encouraging note of thanks? Write it out.

65

February 25

does not act unbecomingly; it does not seek its own, is not provoked, does not take into account a wrong suffered,
1 Corinthians 13:5

Falling onto fresh waxy petals, the rain beads and rolls off. A shiny surface of green remains, unaffected by the heavy drops. They bounce back to take in more sunshine.

Hardships fall hard on us. Situations overwhelm and confuse. The struggle is real. There is One greater than all our struggles.

Like the waxy petals, shedding water, readying to take on new light, we also are continually readying for fresh opportunities. We are setting aside hurts and deciding nothing will hinder us from the love we find in God. In sincere humility, we open our eyes to see the grace and mercy we have received and offer the same.

Let's Pray

Holy Father, sometimes it is hard to move past offenses. But we know that staying in that condition only hurts us. It keeps us separated from knowing full fellowship with You. Give us the capacity to love others. In Jesus' name. Amen.

Call to Action

Are you holding on to hurt? Is it worth it? Will you let it go? Write it out.

February 26

"If you do not listen, and if you do not take it to heart to give honor to My name," says the LORD of hosts, "then I will send the curse upon you and I will curse your blessings; and indeed, I have cursed them already, because you are not taking it to heart."
Malachi 2:2

All the worries of the world sitting on your heart can be replaced by the One who gave you your heart. Taking to heart what matters in place of what doesn't matter. Giving to God the heart He gave to You. Give Him all the honor He is due.

His Word is clear concerning your heart. The allegiance you give from your heart proves your loyalty. Circumstances attempt to pull us away from Him. He accepts our return repeatedly. He is faithful to allow our return.

But His name is holy. His name is high and lifted. He is worthy of all honor and praise. Worship belongs to Him alone. His name is to be reverenced always.

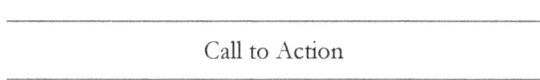

Let's Pray

Holy Father, correct us when our loyalty is misdirected. Keep us in Your will so that we can give acceptable honor to Your holy name. In Jesus' name. Amen.

Call to Action

What is your offering of praise today? Will you bless His name in worship? Call out to Him in honor. Write it out.

February 27

does not rejoice in unrighteousness, but rejoices with the truth; bears all things, believes all things, hopes all things, endures all things.
1 Corinthians 13:6-7

In our highly volatile political and cultural society, it is important to know who to trust. Talking heads want your attention to convince you that what they are saying is the truth. Attitudes and opinions are forced and hatred spews if conformation doesn't happen.

Love sets everything into a proper perspective. As believers, we were not promised an easy road. But we are promised a Helper who resides in and with us so that we can rejoice as we stand on the truth of love.

Life may be hard. Situations and circumstances may seem impossible. Be assured that your faith is not in what this life throws at you. Place your faith in the Author of righteousness. This is where you find truth and endurance to face anything.

Let's Pray

Holy Father, we are inundated with junk. It presses down on us so hard and makes us want to give up on people. But God, Your love is greater. Thank You. In Jesus' name. Amen.

Call to Action

Name your hardship and declare over it that God's love covers it. Write it out.

February 28

We lift up our heart and hands
Toward God in heaven;
Lamentations 3:41

Turn on your favorite worship music. Lyrics that point to God. Think about the lyrics. Are they leading you into a posture of praise? Are they bringing you to a place of worship?

God is worthy of all praise. He deserves our worship. Nothing else is worthy. Sporting events and concerts get more praise than God. This is misplaced worship.

Make worship of God a daily practice. Set your intentions fully on Him as you begin your day. Lift your hands and heart to Him. No one needs to see or know what you are doing, only God.

Let's Pray

Holy Father, You alone are worthy of all praise. I give You, my heart. You captivate me with Your majestic sovereignty. I cannot comprehend the wondrousness of You. You are too vast to contain. I worship You. I lift my hands and heart to You because You alone are worthy of my praise. I trust You with my heart. I open my hands for You to remove whatever may be keeping me from sincere worship of You. I keep them open so that You can give me the desires of Your heart. In Jesus' name. Amen.

Call to Action

What words of praise do you have for God? Write it out.

February 29

But now faith, hope, love, abide these three; but the greatest of these is love.
1 Corinthians 13:13

The love of God is the dwelling place for faith and hope. Faith and hope reside on the rock of love. Love is the foundation for faith and hope. Love encompasses faith and hope.

They come together as the driving force of living for Christ. Feelings can interrupt that force and cause you to believe otherwise. But the love of Christ was so great that He paid the perfect sacrifice for you and me and eliminated the impact of fickle feelings.

Love covers feelings and sets them in a vertical position in view of the cross of Christ. Love is the posture of faith and hope. Love always considers the cross.

Let's Pray

Holy Father, we lay at Your feet with faces to the ground in worship of You. Your love was and is and always will be perfect. It is just and righteous. It is not based on emotions but on the sincere compassion poured out on the cross for us. That cross ushering in faith and hope. Faith to always know Your perfect provision for all things. Hope for what You are doing and will continue to do for our good. Thank You, God. In Jesus' name. Amen.

Call to Action

Have you flipped that switch? The one that allows love to override feelings. Write it out.

*THEREFORE I URGE YOU,
BRETHREN, BY THE MERCIES OF
GOD, TO PRESENT YOUR BODIES
A LIVING AND HOLY SACRIFICE,
ACCEPTABLE TO GOD, WHICH IS
YOUR SPIRITUAL SERVICE OF
WORSHIP. AND DO NOT BE
CONFORMED TO THIS WORLD, BUT
BE TRANSFORMED BY THE
RENEWING OF YOUR MIND, SO
THAT YOU MAY PROVE WHAT
THE WILL OF GOD IS, THAT
WHICH IS GOOD AND
ACCEPTABLE AND PERFECT.
ROMANS 12:1-2*

March

Therefore I urge you, brethren, by the mercies of God, to present your bodies a living and holy sacrifice, acceptable to God, which is your spiritual service of worship. And do not be conformed to this world, but be transformed by the renewing of your mind, so that you may prove what the will of God is, that which is good and acceptable and perfect.
Romans 12:1-2

Your life, and mine, are our sacrifices of praise to our Creator. Our daily interactions point to what we hold dear. The world either sees us as part of them or some strange phenomenon of righteousness. Hopefully, we act like aliens in a foreign land.

Living transformed is a daily practice. God has given us control over our thoughts. He desires our attention in seeking Him for the renewing of our minds. As we walk with Him, as living testimonies of His love, we are proving His goodness. Our bodies are His vessels of presentation to the world of mercy available to all.

My prayer is for you to seek Him in all that you do. That the work of your hands is done for His glory. That you are on mission to share the love of God with everyone you encounter. That His sacrifice of Jesus would not be betrayed by you or your loved ones.

Now go share His love!

March 1

And the testimony is this, that God has given us eternal life, and this life is in His Son.
1 John 5:11

You are walking and talking a testimony. Your language carries the word that is in your heart. You are sharing your testimony with everyone. What testimony is seen and heard from you?

Testify of love. Testify of joy. Testify of peace. Testify of patience. Testify of kindness. Testify of goodness. Testify of faithfulness. Testify of gentleness. Testify of self-control.

The evidence of eternal life in you will come from your daily testimony. As you share it, you will be offering the same to those around you. God gave you the gift of eternal life. Go share it.

Let's Pray

Holy Father, we are living eternally now. It isn't saved for the moment we take our final breath but instead, You have us here to share You in a fallen world. Our intentions are to worship and praise You in every moment of every day with every ounce of strength within us. With You, we are spreading the name of Jesus so that others will know eternal life and have testimony of the same. In Jesus' name. Amen.

Call to Action

What is your testimony? What can you share with others? What evidence is there in your life of the hand of God? Are you sharing it with others or keeping it to yourself? Write it out.

March 2

"LORD, make me to know my end
And what is the extent of my days;
Let me know how transient I am."
Psalm 39:4

Time is just vapor. Here one moment and gone the next. It passes so quickly. And yet time is limitless for God. He alone knows the boundary of time.

How do you spend your days? Moment by moment you are doing something. Staring at a screen. Raising babies. Cooking meals. Cleaning messes. Communicating with clients. Visiting patients. Constructing buildings. Creating art. Singing. Driving. You are doing something with your time.

Time is short. Use it well. Make good use of the time you are given. Make an impact on this world. Be intentional. Find the passion God placed in your mind and heart and use it for His kingdom. This is your opportunity to make a difference for Him. Do it.

Let's Pray

Holy Father, thank You for the gift of time. It is a precious gift that can be wasted without intentionally setting our hearts and minds on You. The world grabs our attention on the latest and greatest entertainment. Keep us from wasting the time You have given. In Jesus' name. Amen.

Call to Action

What is the intention of your heart? How do you spend your time? Write it out.

March 3

"Yet even now," declares the LORD,
"Return to Me with all your heart,
And with fasting, weeping and mourning;"
Joel 2:12

Removing anything that causes us to think we rely on anything other than God brings our focus back fully onto Him. He sustains and provides for all our needs. Without Him we have nothing.

Fasting is practiced for spiritual and health purposes. Throughout the Bible, fasting is called to seek God, removing food so that your body enters a state of reliance on God. This is a humbling time of devotion to Him.

Allow your mind to focus on God, seeking Him with all your heart, asking Him to remove impurities and replace with His goodness. Ask Him what this looks like for you. Enter a fast fully aware of His presence.

Let's Pray

Holy Father, You call us to fast so that we can seek You. Keep us from mindless rituals that do more harm than good. Humble us in our fast. Speak to us in our fast. In Jesus' name. Amen.

Call to Action

Have you fasted for spiritual purposes? Did you allow God to speak to you through the fast? Did He humble you in the fast? Would you do it again? Write it out.

March 4

"Truly, truly, I say to you, he who hears My word, and believes Him who sent Me, has eternal life, and does not come into judgment, but has passed out of death into life."
John 5:24

The voice of God is heard every time I read the Bible. If I ask God for an audible expression of His Word, I read it aloud. Listening to and reading His Word is listening to and reading His love letter to me.

Without Him there is no life. The absence of life is death. Without Him I am dead. With Him I am living eternally with Him. He brings me into life out of death.

Recognizing His sovereignty. Realizing the ultimate sacrifice was paid by His Son on the cross. Understanding His Son paid the penalty for all my sins allows me to live with Him.

Let's Pray

Holy Father, You give life. Through the blood of Jesus You took my sin and paid the debt I accumulated with the sacrifice that came at the cost of Your Son's life. His blood offering for my sin. You are worthy of all worship. You did what I could not. Thank You. In Jesus' name. Amen.

Call to Action

Do you know Him? Have you read His letter to you recently? Will you open it even now and read the verses before and after John 5:24? What does it say to you? Write it out.

March 5

To You I shall offer a sacrifice of thanksgiving,
And call upon the name of the LORD.
Psalm 116:17

Thanksgiving is not just a holiday celebrated on the fourth Thursday every November. Thanksgiving is a daily reminder of the provision of God. Thanksgiving is a daily offering of praise to God.

Ann Voskamp gave the challenge in "One Thousand Gifts" to document your gratitude. Innumerable lists have followed with moments of gratitude found in the ordinary of everyday living. Journals full of pages chronicling gratitude. Perhaps you have filled in a few journals.

Keep filling. Your offering of thanksgiving opens your eyes and heart to receive more from Him. Pouring out your offering makes room for more filling.

Let's Pray

Holy Father, thank You for those who stir and inspire us to draw closer to You. Our list of gratitude is endless. Each list contains secret, intimate reflections of the writer. Glimpses of Your glory found in the mundane. God, You are not mundane. Your glory radiates with brilliance in the life of each person. Thank You for Your distinctive touch in us. In Jesus' name. Amen.

Call to Action

Will you grab a blank journal and start writing? Begin your offer of thanksgiving. Write it out.

March 6

In Him was life, and the life was the Light of men.
John 1:4

Close your eyes for a moment and think about what you see. Come back and speak it aloud. I would guess you say "Nothing." Or maybe you say "Darkness." Without light, darkness prevails.

Opening your eyes reveals light. If you are sitting outside on a sunny day, even with your eyes closed you sense the light. You feel its warmth on your skin. Your eyelids may seem to give a red glow to your sense of vision.

If you believe in God and have submitted to His lordship over your life, you carry His light. You are a beacon of light in a dark world. You have the radiance of the Father bringing His warmth wherever you go. Shine His light so others can see it.

Let's Pray

Holy Father, thank You for the warmth of Your love and compassion. Thank You for the gift of Jesus. Thank You for trusting us with Your message of love. Thank You for Your faithfulness. In Jesus' name. Amen.

Call to Action

On cloudy days do you feel different than you do on sunny days? Have you noticed how a bright sunny day after prolonged cloudiness can change your mood? Write it out.

March 7

Therefore, He had to be made like His brethren in all things, so that He might become a merciful and faithful high priest in things pertaining to God, to make propitiation for the sins of the people.
Hebrews 2:17

He stepped into an earthly body as a baby. A helpless, innocent baby in need of everything from His mother. He couldn't feed Himself. He couldn't walk or talk. He couldn't bathe or change His clothes.

As He grew, He faced the angry, doubting world. Instead of succumbing to the temptations, He submitted to the will of His Father. He knew every temptation known to man. He faced them all. But He did not fall victim to their strangling grasp.

Instead, He approached the wrath of God in my place. The perfect, sinless Savior satisfied the blood requirement of sacrifice on my behalf. He overcame the world so that I could be redeemed.

Let's Pray

Holy Father, Your redemption through the spotless Lamb of God of all sin must be recognized to be claimed. God, thank You for my redemption. In Jesus' name. Amen.

Call to Action

Has God made His redemption known to you? Have you accepted it? Through His strength, you too, can overcome temptation. Will you seek Him for His power? Write it out.

March 8

The sacrifice of the wicked is an abomination to the LORD,
But the prayer of the upright is His delight.
Proverbs 15:8

The heart of sacrifice determines its intention. God knows the difference. He knows your heart. He knows if a sacrifice is made to gain attention. He knows if a sacrifice is made in humility.

The sweet delight of a sacrifice made in humility is what God desires. Submission to Him delights Him. He doesn't desire a sacrifice that is made for your benefit. He desires a sacrifice that is made from love for Him.

Anything done from conceited purposes ruins the intention of sacrifice. Laying down your desires in submission to Him is giving Him your whole heart. This becomes compassion for Him. This is His delight.

Let's Pray

Holy Father, thank You for listening to my prayers. You are faithful to hear my petitions and answer according to Your will. May any sacrifice I offer be found acceptable and pleasing to You. In Jesus' name. Amen.

Call to Action

Lay face down and seek God's will for your sacrifice. Name your sacrifice. Write it out.

March 9

"But if you had known what this means, 'I DESIRE COMPASSION, AND NOT A SACRIFICE,' you would not have condemned the innocent."
Matthew 12:7

Sacrifices are needed for the remission of sin or as an act of worship to God. Before the perfect sacrifice of Jesus, sacrifices were made to atone for sin. These sacrifices were the recognition of God and His desire to have fellowship with His creation. Sin separated that fellowship, so sacrifices returned the sinner to a right relationship with God.

Commitment to God in compassion, following His commands, is keeping fellowship with Him. Where fellowship and righteousness exist, there no longer needs to be sacrifices. Jesus paved the road for continual fellowship with God.

This is God's will for us. He wants us to stay in continual fellowship with Him. He provided the unblemished Lamb so that we can remain in His fellowship.

Let's Pray

Holy Father, the spotless Lamb became the final sacrifice of blood for the remission of all sin. Proclaiming the finality of it, Jesus spoke it aloud. It is finished. In Jesus' name. Amen.

Call to Action

Is there anything keeping you from fellowship with God? Confess it. Write it out.

March 10

"He who loves his life loses it, and he who hates his life in this world will keep it to life eternal."
John 12:25

What is most important in your life? Think about it. Where do you spend the most time and money? Where are your thoughts focused most of your waking hours?

Loving God more than anything or anyone brings everything else into proper perspective. Living with the realization that God is your source of life allows you to see your life as His. Your complete devotion to Him is your life.

Lay aside everything that gets in your way of complete devotion to Him. Bring Him with you into every relationship so that you can love like Him. He is your life.

Let's Pray

Holy Father, You are the Creator of all life. It is only by Your hand that we live and breathe. We lay all that we have at Your feet. It is all Yours. Thank You for life. Thank You for breath. You are the joy of our life. Your will be done. In Jesus' name. Amen.

Call to Action

Jesus wants your life. He wants to love you through it all. Will you allow Him to be Lord of your life? What steps do you need to take to make that happen? Does your heart need spring cleaning? Ask Him to help you. He is faithful. Will you trust Him with your life? Write it out.

March 11

"He who believes in the Son has eternal life; but he who does not obey the Son will not see life, but the wrath of God abides on him."
John 3:36

I know it is not a popular topic. I realize March 11 may be the last entry you read in this book. If you have made it this far, though, I doubt you are ready to lay it down for good.

The wrath of God is real. Denying the lordship of Jesus brings the wrath of God. This wrath is not a one-time punishment. The wrath of God is eternal separation from God. Exiled from His presence. Banished from fellowship with Him.

It is heavy. It isn't pretty. You don't want to experience it. You don't want your family to experience it. You don't want your friends to experience it. So, share the love of Jesus with them. Do everything you can to make sure your loved ones will not experience the wrath of God.

Let's Pray

Holy Father, it is fearful to consider my loved ones eternally separated from You. God, help me to be faithful in sharing Jesus with them. But God, the work of the Holy Spirit in hearts and minds is what is needed. Thank You for Your faithfulness. In Jesus' name. Amen.

Call to Action

Make a list of those you love. What will you do to help them know Jesus? Write it out.

March 12

So I gave my attention to the Lord God to seek Him by prayer and supplications, with fasting,
sackcloth and ashes.
Daniel 9:3

Daniel knew the source of His strength. It wasn't in the food he ate but he certainly had a careful nutrition plan. It wasn't in physical exercise. It wasn't in the position of influence he held.

His attention was focused on seeking God. He knew that only through prayer and making requests to God could his life be used for God's intended purpose. Without that communication he would not have been able to share the messages proclaimed by God.

By humbling himself, he was found to be in high esteem. Bowing low to the Most High brought him understanding. He postured himself low in reverential fear of God.

Let's Pray

Holy Father, let us all take Daniel's lead in bowing low before Your throne of grace to seek You. Thank You for answering and caring about our every need. In Jesus' name. Amen.

Call to Action

The answers to your prayers may not come like Daniel's but when you seek God earnestly, consistently, He will answer. They may not be the answers you expect but He is faithful to provide what we need, when we need it most. How has he answered you? Write it out.

March 13

for bodily discipline is only of little profit, but godliness is profitable for all things, since it holds promise for the present life and also for the life to come.
1 Timothy 4:8

My workout routine is haphazard. I may exercise consistently for weeks and then have a period of stagnation. Then it will hit me, and I will begin again. On and off the cycle continues. Consistent exercise becomes most beneficial for my physical body. But my physical body will not stay with me in eternity.

My soul, on the other hand, will remain. The exercise of godliness will provide eternal benefits. And it is eternity now!

The discipline of growing in knowledge of God is a life-long journey. He provides wisdom. Studying His Word with others and privately provides a foundation that cannot be shaken.

Let's Pray

Holy Father, thank You for Your Word. Help us to learn more so that we can take Your message and accurately share it with others. In Jesus' name. Amen.

Call to Action

Are you actively participating in a Bible study? I encourage you to participate in a local body of Christ followers. Study God's word together. Make a commitment to doing so. Write it out.

March 14

Then the disciples of John came to Him, asking, "Why do we and the Pharisees fast, but Your disciples do not fast?"
Matthew 9:14

The disciples had the ready resource of the Savior in their physical presence. How much closer could they get? They were in active engagement of learning in preparation for the day when He would no longer be in their midst. They were being stretched and pulled to levels they had never known as they walked with Him.

Fasting depletes resources to engage dependence on God. They already had God with them. He was in their face. They touched Him. They smelled Him. They ate with Him. They were first-hand witnesses to miracles.

They were being poured into by Jesus Himself. Jesus was preparing them for ministry after His ascension. Their full attention was already on God.

Let's Pray

Holy Father, we are in Your presence, but we do not have Your physical presence like the disciples. As we fast, allow us to draw closer to You. In Jesus' name. Amen.

Call to Action

Have you made a commitment to fast? Seek God when you do. Write it out.

March 15

but He, having offered one sacrifice for sins for all time, SAT DOWN AT THE RIGHT HAND OF GOD,
Hebrews 10:12

One sacrifice. That is all He had to make to satisfy the sacrifice needed for sins for all time. Not just some sins. Not just for a certain time. All sins. All time. He accomplished what no priest could. His sacrifice was sufficient for all.

When He had completed the sacrifice and declared it finished and ascended to the Father, He sat down at God's right hand. Now He intercedes on our behalf with the Father. He is preparing a place for us.

He will return. He is waiting for the Father to give Him marching orders. Will you be ready?

Let's Pray

Holy Father, I do not doubt the sufficiency of that one for all sacrifice of Jesus. He satisfied the payment of my sin-debt. Holy is His Name. He is worthy of all praise. In Jesus' name. Amen.

Call to Action

If you have recognized Jesus as your Savior, when was it? Do you remember the details? Have you shared those details with anyone? I encourage you to do so. Write it out.

March 16

"But I will sacrifice to You
With the voice of thanksgiving.
That which I have vowed I will pay.
Salvation is from the LORD.*"*
Jonah 2:9

Sometimes we must hit the very bottom of the ocean before we cry out for help. Jonah was there. And at the bottom of the ocean, he knew the salvation of God and what disobedience could bring. So, he repented and vowed to keep the instructions he had received from God.

Have you been there? Desperately running away from that which God entrusted to you. Not wanting to do that which is in front of you. In running, you find despair. Nothing goes right. Everything you attempt fails because you are running away from God's assignment.

Then, when you confess your disobedience and make it right with God, the water burial of despair spews you into life renewed.

Let's Pray

Holy Father, the death burial of baptism signifies we have died to our old ways. Coming up out of that water grave, we find resurrection in You. You give new life. Thank You for the cleansing power of the Living Water. In Jesus' name. Amen.

Call to Action

How does it make you feel to witness baptism? Write it out.

March 17

"When you sacrifice a sacrifice of thanksgiving to the LORD, you shall sacrifice it so that you may be accepted."
Leviticus 22:29

The recipient of thanksgiving is the One to whom gratitude is given. Recognition fully placed on the One who deserves all praise. Laying aside any presumption of ownership due self and placing all where it is rightly due.

This is a sacrifice. Taking what is in your possession and laying it down on the altar as an acceptable offering to God. Pouring out what He has given back to Him. Giving back the gifts from Him. Because it is all His.

Then the benefit becomes yours again and again. Thanksgiving repeated throughout time because all comes from Him and returns to Him. Living full of thanksgiving.

Let's Pray

Holy Father, the words seem so inadequate, but we say them. Thank You. Please accept our lives as sacrifices of thanksgiving and may we continually live gratitude for all You have done, are doing and will do. You are the giver of life. In Jesus' name. Amen.

Call to Action

What sacrifice of thanksgiving will you offer God? Write it out.

March 18

"It is the Spirit who gives life; the flesh profits nothing; the words that I have spoken to you are spirit and are life."
John 6:63

Getting caught up in a crowd, enthusiastic about the event, being pulled along in a rush of excitement. Not even knowing the headliner. You bounce along with the crowd. Is that where you are in your relationship with Christ? Just bouncing along without fully knowing the One you are following.

Hard statements from Jesus caused some of His followers to leave. They weren't there for Him but for the excitement that came along with Him. When lessons got hard, they hit the road.

His statements gave directions for His followers. Instructions to follow when He wasn't with them in person any longer. He knew what was coming and He knew who would be there. He knows today who His true followers are.

Let's Pray

Holy Father, thank You for giving us hard statements. Thank You for telling us truth. We confess that we are sinners and in need of You, our Savior. Please forgive us. In Jesus' name. Amen.

Call to Action

Examine your heart to determine if you are truly a follower of Jesus. Write it out.

March 19

"Is it a fast like this which I choose, a day for a man to humble himself?
Is it for bowing one's head like a reed
And for spreading out sackcloth and ashes as a bed?
Will you call this a fast, even an acceptable day to the LORD?"
Isaiah 58:5

Pride cannot exist in an acceptable fast. Bowing low in humble submission to God to remove bonds of strongholds results in drawing closer to Him. Denying pleasure for the purpose of drawing near to the heart of God.

Sweet fellowship comes in giving up anything that may hinder access to the Father. He is always there waiting for you to draw near. He even comes to meet you on the floor.

Let Him speak over you. Listen to His voice. You are His beloved. You are a child of the King. He takes delight in You. You are the apple of His eye. His love for you is greater than any sin. He formed you. He created you. He knows everything there is to know about you. He cares for you.

Let's Pray

Holy Father, hot tears form when I think about the love You have for me. Undeserved. But given still. Thank You for Your endless grace and mercy. In Jesus' name. Amen.

Call to Action

What other truths can you list? What else does He call you? You are His good creation. Continue the list. Write it out.

March 20

For if we go on sinning willfully after receiving the knowledge of the truth, there no longer remains a sacrifice for sins,
Hebrews 10:26

Repentance is turning away from the bond of sin. Leaving behind that which enslaves you to evil. Call it what it is. Sin is evil.

Returning to that sin, once you have turned away from it, means you have doubts about the sufficiency of the sacrifice of Jesus. Think about that! You don't believe His sacrifice was sufficient, so you return to being a slave to sin. Wallow in that mud pit a little longer.

Sounds harsh? It is harsh to call the perfect Lamb of God and the sufficiency of His sacrifice as incapable of irradicating the stronghold of sin in your life. You know the truth. Now walk in it.

Let's Pray

Holy Father, please forgive our doubt. Forgive our continued return to that which is evil. Holy Father, reveal any hidden sins in our lives so that we can repent and run back to You. Keep us from temptation. Thank You for the perfect solution to our sin problem. We need Your continued provision of grace and mercy. Thank You, Father. In Jesus' name. Amen.

Call to Action

Does doubt cause you to live in a pit of despair? Ask God to pull you out. Write it out.

March 21

"He who offers a sacrifice of thanksgiving honors Me;
And to him who orders his way aright
I shall show the salvation of God."
Psalm 50:23

Gratitude no matter the circumstances. Setting your heart open to what God is doing. Even in the hard, counting all joy, for the glory of God. Looking beyond the here and now, understanding what is in the here and now leads into eternity with God.

Stepping intentionally into this day with thanksgiving first. Offering gratitude to God for what you can see and what you cannot see. Offering gratitude to God for what you hear, smell, touch, and taste.

Colorful flowers blooming outside my front door. Rain gently falling on the metal roof. Coffee brewing. The keys wore smoothly underneath my fingertips. Blueberry compote over French toast.

Let's Pray

Holy Father, we are thankful for all that You give. We desire to order our steps so that we are found acceptable to You. Let all honor You. Thank You for salvation. In Jesus' name. Amen.

Call to Action

Will you take time to make a list of five things for which you are thankful, one for each of your five senses: vision, hearing, smell, touch, and taste? Write it out.

March 22

"But go and learn what this means: 'I DESIRE COMPASSION, AND NOT SACRIFICE,' for
I did not come to call the righteous, but sinners."
Matthew 9:13

That thief on the cross beside Jesus didn't come to that place in right standing. A criminal hanging for the deeds done. He had not performed any sacrificial offering for the sins committed. His sins were on display for all.

He saw the Man. He observed the God of the universe hanging beside him. He recognized Him. He knew Him without being told Who He was. It was evident. And he knew He was the source of life, both now and after the earthly vessel is finished.

So, he asked. And Jesus answered. And in compassion, because He is Compassion, Jesus granted that criminal entry into Paradise.

Let's Pray

Holy Father, thank You for forgiveness. Thank You for the example of the thief and the promises You provide. Thank You for the redemption of my sins. In Jesus' name. Amen.

Call to Action

Do you find yourself in the place of the thief beside Jesus? Neck deep about to go under when just in time Jesus reaches out and saves you. Have you thanked Him? Write it out.

March 23

Through Him then, let us continually offer up a sacrifice of praise to God, that is, the fruit of lips that give thanks to His name.
Hebrews 13:15

Take a bite of your favorite fruit. Savor the juice on your tongue. Sense the burst of flavor as you bite down. Smell the sweet aroma. Enjoy every bite.

Now think about the fruit that comes from your lips. The fruit you enjoyed gave you satisfaction and pleasure. Do the words of your mouth do the same for God? Are your words giving Him praise? Your lips are praising something. Listen. What do you hear? What are you praising?

Each word that passes from us expresses our heart for God. We are either honoring and praising Him or not. Words cannot be gathered back up. Once they come out, they stay out.

Let's Pray

Holy Father, please forgive the mindless slips of my tongue. Allow my words to be transformed into praises to You. Allow my heart and mind to come into agreement so that what comes out of my mouth is a pleasing aroma for You. In Jesus' name. Amen.

Call to Action

Do you continually use praise-worthy speech? Do you know someone where the exact opposite is true? Will you commit to speak only words that are pleasing to God? Write it out.

March 24

To do righteousness and justice
Is desired by the LORD more than sacrifice.
Proverbs 21:3

Two choices staring you in the face. One is exciting, daring. Something you have never done and is even questionable to your moral compass. The other is secure and safe. Still, something you have never done but you are drawn to it in peace. The decision may seem obvious to some.

At the crossroads of a decision, there is a Counselor that will never guide you wrong. The choices you make beside Him may feel hard but with Him as your leader, you can rest in the assurance of His righteousness. This is His desire for you: righteousness.

His sacrifice was abundantly sufficient to cover any unrighteousness. But once you have the knowledge of righteousness, straying from it betrays His sacrifice. He has your back. Make righteous choices.

Let's Pray

Holy Father, with the knowledge of Your righteousness and the compass You give, may we never betray Your Son's sacrifice. Thank You for discernment. In Jesus' name. Amen.

Call to Action

Gray areas pop up. Sometimes it is not a matter of righteousness between two choices. God will still provide counsel. Will you commit to seeking Him in your choices? Write it out.

March 25

"But you, when you fast, anoint your head and wash your face"
Matthew 6:17

If you have ever fasted, you know in the first twelve hours or so, you may begin to feel the effects of not having food in your body. Even if you had an early dinner and late breakfast the next day, your body may send signs of hunger. You may experience a headache or grumbling noises from your belly. It doesn't always feel holy. But feelings are fickle!

When entering a time of fasting for spiritual reasons, you are entering an intimate time with God. You may still need to go to work and care for your family. There may be errands to run. Your countenance can speak volumes. Your outside should carry the same degree of joy that you carry on a non-fasting day. Wash your face. Do something with your hair. Put on clean clothes.

Present yourself as if you are presenting yourself to God. Seek Him for the endurance and word you need during the fast. He will honor your efforts and meet you there.

Let's Pray

Holy Father, You are faithful to provide our every need. Thank You. In Jesus' name. Amen.

Call to Action

What is the first physical feeling you experience when fasting? Write it out.

March 26

whom God displayed publicly as a propitiation in His blood through faith. This was to demonstrate His righteousness, because in the forbearance of God He passed over the sins previously committed;
Romans 3:25

All my past mistakes are erased. Unbelievably thankful as the realization hits. He accomplished the unimaginable on my behalf. Jesus faced the wrath of God so I wouldn't have to face it myself.

In His perfect condition, He removed the filth on and in me and replaced it with a robe of white. The filth still dripping from His hands, I stand blameless before His presence. The love in His eyes matches the brilliance of the white in my robe.

He did it once. Only once. When He removed my filth, He removed yours. He finished it for us. Now we are adopted as His children. We are heirs of the King. Children of the Most High. We are members of the royal family.

Let's Pray

Holy Father, thank You for washing me clean. Help me to walk worthy of being a member of Your family. Thank You for mercy and grace. In Jesus' name. Amen.

Call to Action

His goodness is abundantly beyond anything we could imagine. Thank Him. Write it out.

March 27

Be silent before the Lord GOD!
For the day of the LORD is near,
For the LORD has prepared a sacrifice,
He has consecrated His guests.
Zephaniah 1:7

Silence calls for reverence. Holy fear of God in anticipation of His nearness. Solemn posture of preparation before His sacrifice. Preparation for His coming.

Entering His presence, only those consecrated and prepared by Him. Set apart from those to be cast out. Two distinct groups: those who believe and are adopted as children of the Father and those who have denied themselves of the Father.

Which group will you choose? Prepare for His coming. Know He is returning.

Let's Pray

Holy Father, bowing low with face to the ground doesn't feel low enough to submit to Your presence. It is only by the blood of Jesus that I can escape Your wrath. My heart wants to explode out of my chest when I consider anyone choosing separation in place of fellowship with You. God, help me to share the message of salvation to others. Thank You. In Jesus' name. Amen.

Call to Action

I pray your salvation is sealed. I also pray that you are actively engaged in sharing the message of salvation with others. It is an active choice we get to make. Are you sharing? Write it out.

March 28

and walk in love, just as Christ also loved you and gave Himself up for us, an offering and a sacrifice to God as a fragrant aroma.
Ephesians 5:2

The moment I held them in my arms, my heart changed. Even carrying them in my womb for nine months and loving them the whole time, having them in my hands, breathing in fresh skin, the love became an inseparable bond. Christ loves you even more.

Walking in that love, for Him, is the pleasing aroma of sacrifice. Righteousness lived out by His children is His delight. The sacrifice being honored by those it served to redeem is beautiful.

No greater love exists than the love of the Father. It washes all the filth away. It removes my sin. It covers all sin. His love is greater than your sin.

Let's Pray

Holy Father, the expression of love You gave for us cannot be measured. Our gratitude and offerings of thanksgiving are inadequate. Yet we give them, and You graciously accept them. You are holy. May we be a pleasing aroma to You. In Jesus' name. Amen.

Call to Action

What expression of love can you share with your Savior? Think of the most wonderful thing you could do for Him. Now share it with Him. Write it out.

March 29

But even if I am being poured out as a drink offering upon the sacrifice and service of your faith,
I rejoice and share my joy with you all.
Philippians 2:17

Joy shared is joy multiplied. Paul found a filling of joy as he served the Philippians. He rejoiced because his pouring out resulted in their faith. The proof of their faith was in their service.

I have been in a place of service that became drudgery. My perspective shifted somewhere in the service and continuing became hard and eventually stopped. Looking back, I see that my service lacked joy. It had become hard because I allowed myself to feel isolated and fearful.

Joining in the service of faith requires keeping your eyes on the prize. The gift of joy is worth rejoicing. God will be faithful to fill, if we are faithful to keep our focus on Him and honor Him with our service.

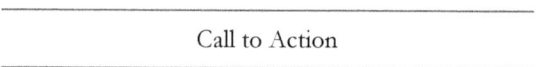

Let's Pray

Holy Father, please accept our service of faith. Please find it honoring and pleasing to You. Thank You for filling us with joy as we work in service for You. In Jesus' name. Amen.

Call to Action

What is your act of service for the kingdom of God? Have you experienced times where the work was hard? What did you do? Write it out.

March 30

"Go, assemble all the Jews who are found in Susa, and fast for me; do not eat or drink for three days, night or day. I and my maidens also will fast in the same way. And thus I will go in to the king, which is not according to the law; and if I perish, I perish."
Esther 4:16

Esther's willingness to sacrifice for her people relied on the confidence of God. She knew the history of her people. She knew the promises of God for her people. Yet, here she stood, placed in a position to do something about the situation facing them.

You hold a position to do something for the kingdom of God. Whether you realize it, you have influence. Perhaps you are not approaching the seat of authority in direct defiance of the law with the possibility of death, but you are positioned here and now for your calling from God.

Esther was willing to die for her people. She realized her position held major influence with the king and could be used for the glory of God. So, she prepared and entered her calling with the full power of God.

Let's Pray

Holy Father, You have positioned each of us at this moment in time for Your glory alone. May we fulfill Your calling as confidently as Esther. In Jesus' name. Amen.

Call to Action

Seek God for your calling. His peace will direct your path. Write it out.

March 31

"Offer to God a sacrifice of thanksgiving
And pay your vows to the Most High;"
Psalm 50:14

Scents of warm summer blooms wafting through the air. Sun sinking low on the horizon. Guests whispering below the melody softly playing. Flickers of candles dancing with the wind. A wedding celebration is about to commence.

The groom anticipates his bride's arrival. His cheeks are wet from the dripping of emotion coming from his eyes. The melody changes heralding guests to rise for the entrance of the bride. In a gown of white she glides toward her groom. She sees no one except him. Vows spoken to God and each other. Their union is their sacrifice of thanksgiving.

The vows to God coming first. His love explains the love between the groom and bride. His love defines all love.

Let's Pray

Holy Father, we look forward to the wedding feast of Jesus. Find our vows acceptable. Thank You for defining love. Thank You for Your love toward us. In Jesus' name. Amen.

Call to Action

When was the last time you attended a wedding? I pray that it felt like a worship service for you. Remember the event and pray for the couple. Write it out.

I PLANTED, APOLLOS WATERED,
BUT GOD WAS CAUSING THE
GROWTH.
1 CORINTHIANS 3:6

April

I planted, Apollos watered, but God was causing the growth.
1 Corinthians 3:6

The work of your hands is important to the kingdom of God. His message is shared through the testimonies of those who have walked through hard stuff knowing God through it. Promises of hope spread to those that have no hope. You are a beacon of light when you share His love.

The life of Jesus is recorded for us to study. The Holy Spirit teaches us as we open the Word of God, seeking Him with all our heart, mind, soul, and body. He is faithful to teach those who diligently seek Him.

I encourage you to stay in His Word. Pray as you read for God to open your eyes, mind, and heart to know Him more fully. Continually seek Him in all that you do. He is always there willing to listen and communicate with you. You just need to listen as you read and pray.

Find a group of believers to study together. God's Word tells us in separate locations that friends are beneficial to our faith-walk. They encourage us. They hold us accountable. They help us through struggles.

I pray you find encouragement and inspiration during the month of April.

April 1

So then neither the one who plants nor the one who waters is anything, but God who causes the growth.
1 Corinthians 3:7

Hiding in the dark fertile soil, soaking in the moisture, softening that hard outer shell, the seed waits until it is called out of hiding. Light calls its name. Slowly life expands the shell. The shell cracks open with life peeking out, seeking the Light that is calling its name. Reaching hard and high, stretching through the soil, it finds the Light.

The Light continues to call as life grows taller and fuller. Leaves erupt catching more Light. Buds form with the hope of flowers and fruit, expanding, waiting for the moment color erupts. Petals unfold for a splendid display. The heart of the flower beckons bees to share its sweetness.

As the petals begin to fade, fruit begins to form. The fruit also expands, reaching for the Light. Bitterness turns to sweetness as flesh softens and new seeds form within the deep. Until the day the fruit is tasted and the seed saved and dried to ready it to begin again.

Let's Pray

Holy Father, thank You for life and growth. To You is all glory. In Jesus' name. Amen.

Call to Action

Plant a seed and document what you observe. Write it out.

April 2

To grant those who mourn in Zion,
Giving them a garland instead of ashes,
The oil of gladness instead of mourning,
The mantle of praise instead of a spirit of fainting.
So they will be called oaks of righteousness,
The planting of the LORD, that He may be glorified.

Isaiah 61:3

Through our circumstances, God remains faithful. He provides all that we need. Provision comes in many forms. Food is a primary provision. He provides beauty to behold. He provides comfort, peace, joy, love, strength, healing, grace, and mercy. He provides everything for good.

There is nothing that God will withhold from those who earnestly seek Him in righteousness. But to come in righteousness, fully aware of His bountiful provision, not wanting from a place of greed. Seeking His will and Him providing from His goodness.

He knows our hearts. He knows our needs. He knows our desires. He is faithful.

Let's Pray

Holy Father, You are so faithful to provide for all our needs. In our sorrow, You bring joy. In our hunger, You bring food. In our weakness, You bring strength. In our sin, You bring forgiveness. Thank You. You alone are worthy of all praise. In Jesus' name. Amen.

Call to Action

What are the provisions God has supplied for you? Will you give Him praise? Write it out.

April 3

'Now a man who is clean shall gather up the ashes of the heifer and deposit them outside the camp in a clean place, and the congregation of the sons of Israel shall keep it as water to remove impurity; it is purification from sin.'
Numbers 19:9

Where sin exists, there is a need for purification. There needs to be cleansing. There needs to be removal of the impurity. Without cleansing, fellowship with God cannot exist.

Through Moses, God gave the Israelites instructions for sacrifices. This was their only way to return to a right standing with the Father. Consequences were known for those that disobeyed.

Jesus stepped in and removed the need for continual sacrifice. He provided the perfect sacrifice for all people, for all time. You and I are not required to sacrifice animals because the spotless Lamb of God stood in our place and satisfied the cleansing and purification on our behalf.

Let's Pray

Holy Father, Your ways are higher, and Your thoughts are greater than ours. God, thank You for the sacrifice of Jesus, Your only Son. Your loving kindness to us is incomprehensible. You allowed Him to take my place in hell so I can dwell in Your presence. Thank You, Holy Father for Your mercy and grace and provision of my Savior. In Jesus' name. Amen.

Call to Action

It never gets old. Give Him praise for your salvation. Write it out.

April 4

and will come forth; those who did the good deeds to a resurrection of life, those who committed the evil deeds to a resurrection of judgment.
John 5:29

Look outside. What do you see? Depending on your location, you may see buildings or desert or trees. Look for a tree. Look for green leaves.

In September 2024, hurricane Helene came through Valdosta, Georgia. Trees, houses, and lives were ripped apart. At the time of this writing, April 4, 2025, the remaining trees have burst forth with leaves. What looked dead for the past six months has come to life.

Not unlike the trees that have weathered storms and winter, those who seek God with all their heart will know life. Those trees that were ripped apart have been removed and cleaned up. Life for those that stand firm. Death for those that crumbled in the storm.

Let's Pray

Holy Father, thank You for bringing us through storms. Thank You, for giving us the strength, when we lean on You, to know life and to stand firm. Thank You for the resurrection to life. You are the giver of life. You resurrect us from our death bed of sin into life. In Jesus' name. Amen.

Call to Action

What storm has tossed you about, but you stood firm because of God? Write it out.

April 5

But they were insistent, with loud voices asking that He be crucified. And their voices began to prevail.
Luke 23:23

The noise was deafening. Evil chanting for blood. Wickedness waiting to devour the unblemished Lamb. The purity was too much for such depravity. It revealed too much of their sin, so the solution seemed to be death. Do away with Him who was Light on their darkness.

To darkness they sent Him. Flesh splitting nails into splintered wood. Gush of blood and water. Raised up for all to see the spectacle of dripping life. Great drops of life from Life. His life for mine. His life for yours.

Ears ringing as the crowd grows quiet with His final words. His Word is final. His Word is exponentially greater than the wicked cry for blood. His blood satisfying any further need for my blood. He willingly took what I deserved.

Let's Pray

Holy Father, we cry, not for Your blood again, but for Your life in us. We long to sit at Your feet and recognize You as Savior. Thank You for this opportunity. In Jesus' name. Amen.

Call to Action

He will provide. He is faithful. Have you cried out for life with Him? Write it out.

April 6

And Mary Magdalene was there, and the other Mary, sitting opposite the grave.
Matthew 27:61

Weak and weary, they could not remember the last time they had slept or eaten. Watching as the body of their Savior was placed in a borrowed tomb. Cold stone was no place for the King.

But there they were, witnessing the unimaginable. What were they to do now? Their lives had been wrapped up in following this Man for years. They had ministered to Him and He had ministered to them. Their lives were completely different because of this Man laying in the cold rock behind a large stone.

Dark was coming. What bed could give rest after witnessing this brutal execution? Sorrow stole comfort. The blood could not be washed from their sight. Fileted flesh embedded in their memories. But something in the back of their minds kept them from despair. Hope was not dead.

Let's Pray

Holy Father, You gave Your Son to be our Savior. He taught us what living looks like. Lovely, just, kind, merciful, compassionate, forgiving. Help us. Thank You. In Jesus' name. Amen.

Call to Action

Can you put yourself in the place of these women? Losing not only the Savior but a well-loved friend. Maybe you have lost a friend. What would you do? Write it out.

April 7

Jesus said to her, "I am the resurrection and the life; he who believes in Me will live even if he dies,"
John 11:25

Martha had been mourning and wondered why Jesus took so long to come to them. She wondered why He had not saved Lazarus. But Jesus had. Martha just didn't understand yet.

Here and now, we have the very same promise Jesus gave to Martha. Even in the physical death we all face, there is life. If we believe in Jesus, that He is the Son of God, that He is Savior, then we will have life after these physical bodies run out of breath.

Jesus wasn't finished with this story of Lazarus. He wasn't finished, and isn't now, with the story of Lazarus. The dead will come to life in Jesus. Life in Him is now and forever.

Let's Pray

Holy Father, You give life everlasting. The breath in our lungs will run out but the life in You will not. Thank You for the gift of Jesus, Who provides the way for us into the eternity with You. Thank You for Your Word so that we can know You. In Jesus' name. Amen.

Call to Action

Can you testify of a life walking with God? Can you claim the promise of everlasting life with the Father? Are you living your eternity now? Trust in Him and tell Him. Write it out.

April 8

When the grass disappears, the new growth is seen,
And the herbs of the mountains are gathered in,
Proverbs 27:25

Sometimes the layers we accumulate only serve to hide a precious gift waiting to be uncovered. When the layers are removed the gift emerges to be gathered in and enjoyed. The layers can be provisions or hindrances to the gift waiting underneath.

God gently keeps well protected those who believe in Him. But for those who doubt and keep up the walls of hindrance, any perceived provision is a shallow imitation of the perfect provision of faith. Opening the layers of doubt, of hindrance, to receive the faith of God, opens the precious gift for His glory.

Do you have layers that need to be peeled back? Do you have grass covering the beginnings of flowers waiting to bloom? Is your heart and mind ready to take the next step in faith with God?

Let's Pray

Holy Father, thank You for the gifts and talents You have given us. Help us know them. Help us uncover them. Help us use them for Your honor and glory. In Jesus' name. Amen.

Call to Action

Do you know your gift, your talent? What brings passion to your life? Write it out.

April 9

"I will establish for them a renowned planting place, and they will not again be victims of famine in the land, and they will not endure the insults of the nations anymore."
Ezekiel 34:29

Every morsel, every bite, every taste, every sip, every slurp, every chomp, every gulp, provisions from God. Lifting a fork full of savory yumminess and placing it in the mouth to chew slowly, enjoying the flavor of the spices infused throughout delectable, palate-pleasing nourishment. Praising God for another mouth full of sustenance.

Rows upon rows of green, speckled with peeks of yellow. Rows upon rows of bushy silver-green leaves and branches dripping with drops of blue. Trees full of orange and yellow and red spheres of juice and pulp. All provisions from God.

Proof of abundance and not famine. God provides for the nourishment of your body. He gives good life-giving gifts. To be used for His glory. To be enjoyed in His delight.

Let's Pray

Holy Father, Your abundance for me is exceedingly beyond anything I could imagine or ask. Your provisions are constant. All glory be to You. Thank You, God. In Jesus' name. Amen.

Call to Action

Think of your favorite food or meal. Will you thank God for it? Write it out.

April 10

In each and every province where the command and decree of the king came, there was great mourning among the Jews, with fasting, weeping and wailing; and many lay on sackcloth and ashes.
Esther 4:3

Stepping away from food and comfort to express a heart contrite in despair. Considering what is good compared to what is evil and setting aside the good so that returning to it is sweeter. Stripping away any trapping that may distract from placing committed attention to the One that can rectify any situation and turn it around for His glory.

Either complete annihilation at the hands of the world or placing it in the hands of God. Which results would you want? I want God's hands wrapped around every situation I face. The world doesn't have my best interest in mind. God does.

So here I am God. All the messes I make lay open at Your feet. I commit to stripping them away so that all remains is my bare heart for You to mold and make into the masterpiece of Your desire. The ashes of my messes, fertilizing the soil of my heart for Your purpose.

Let's Pray

Holy Father, You take what I can't and turn it into beauty. Thank You. In Jesus' name. Amen.

Call to Action

What mess have you seen God turn into an amazing work? Write it out.

117

April 11

But if there is no resurrection of the dead, not even Christ has been raised;
1 Corinthians 15:13

The completed work of God raised Jesus from the dead. Without God bringing back to life that which has died, our eternity becomes uncertain. The former law would reinstitute the demand for sacrifices only offered by Levitical priests. Without God bringing back to life the Savior of the world, the completed work through Jesus Christ becomes void.

Oh, but He did raise Jesus from the dead. His resurrection ushered in Jesus as High Priest for all time, for all sin, for all people. He gave life to all mankind, for the second time. Through Adam, we are born into this world to live. Through Jesus, we are born into eternity to live.

Have you received a second life? Have you accepted the completed work of God through Jesus Christ? Have you been raised from death into life?

Let's Pray

Holy Father, thank You for Your work on my behalf. Thank You for allowing Your Son to take my place and receive the wrath I deserve. Thank You for resurrecting to life Jesus and me. In Jesus' name. Amen.

Call to Action

If you have been raised to life, will you give God praise? Write it out.

April 12

Wishing to satisfy the crowd, Pilate released Barabbas for them, and after having Jesus scourged, he handed Him over to be crucified.
Mark 15:15

You and I are Barabbas. We deserve crucifixion. We deserve scourging. Instead, Jesus stood in our place. He satisfied what we could not. His blood is the only blood that could satisfy the necessary sacrifice for all humanity to be released from the prison of sin.

His motive? Love.

His love kept Him there. The love that He has for you is so great that He stayed in that place until it was finished. No greater love exists. That God would provide His Son. That His Son would provide Himself. For you. For me.

Let's Pray

Holy Father, words seem so inadequate to express gratitude for the death of Jesus in my place. He accepted my punishment and paid the debt I owed for all sin I ever committed or will commit. And He did it willingly. Thank You for loving me. In Jesus' name. Amen.

Call to Action

Is there someone in your life that needs Jesus? What action would you take to keep that person from experiencing the wrath of God? Write it out.

April 13

And they went and made the grave secure, and along with the guard they set a seal on the stone.
Matthew 27:66

The enemy will always try to prevent victory. Taking measures to ensure success is not achieved. Obvious or hidden, obstacles will be placed strategically to deter triumph. Be watchful.

The stone. The guard. The seal. No match for the One inside the grave. The enemy didn't have a chance. The enemy underestimated the One inside the grave. The enemy doubted the ability of their foe.

The One inside the grave only moved that stone to give proof to those outside the grave that the grave was empty. The enemy couldn't hold Him. The grave couldn't keep Him. His work on the cross was finished for you and for me but His work for eternity continues. He got up out of that grave so that we could get up out of our graves of sin.

Let's Pray

Holy Father, holy, holy, holy is the Lord God Almighty. Who is and was and is to come. Thank You for the work on the cross. Thank You for the empty grave. Thank You for defeating the enemy. Help us to walk in the truth of Your complete victory. In Jesus' name. Amen.

Call to Action

Is the enemy attacking you? Will you cry out to God for victory? Write it out.

April 14

So also is the resurrection of the dead. It is sown a perishable body, it is raised an imperishable body;
1 Corinthians 15:42

Plant what looks like a dead vessel. Farmers do it every year. They bury multitudes of dead looking vessels just deep enough in the dirt to feel the light. Water, air, light working together pulling life from that dead vessel. Birthing new life from that which was dead.

And so, it is with our mortal bodies. These bodies are only good for so long. They were designed to keep us for just a little while. They provide temporary shelter for our spirit and soul. We care for them while we have them and then we need them no more.

But God will provide a new body. One free from the trappings of the mortal flesh we wear now. New bodies that won't wear out and break down.

Let's Pray

Holy Father, You are faithful to provide in this life and the one to come. You wrap us in flesh while we are here. Help us to care for the bodies you gave us. Thank You for our bodies and we look forward to the new body You prepare for us. In Jesus' name. Amen.

Call to Action

Are you taking care of the body you have? Will you commit to doing so? Write it out.

April 15

and not holding fast to the head, from whom the entire body, being supplied and held together by the joints and ligaments, grows with a growth which is from God.
Colossians 2:19

Your brain tells your body what to do. Even the heart should be mastered by the brain and not the other way around. Movements are triggered by the brain. The brain tells you when to breathe. Learning doesn't end with formal education. Your brain continues to learn.

Your brain is also where distractions can come to lead you away from the path with God. But He gave you the ability to recognize them so you can turn away from them. Through prayer and studying His Word, we have the tools with Holy Spirit to keep going with Him.

Are you making good choices? Decisions based on His direction. Begin now.

Let's Pray

Holy Father, You fashioned our brains to control our bodies. You gave us the ability to think and move and to make the decision to follow You. God, keep us from following the world and instead keep us on the path for Your glory. In Jesus' name. Amen.

Call to Action

What are you doing with your brain? Learning something new? Studying the Bible? Seeking God? Making conscious decisions to work for His glory? Write it out.

April 16

'Build houses and live in them; and plant gardens and eat their produce.'
Jeremiah 29:5

Live where you are. God has placed you right there for right now and He intends for you to be productive right there. That productivity looks different for each one. Maybe for you it is getting up and going to work, taking kids to school, cooking, cleaning, caring for an aging parent, homeschooling, or being cared for by someone else.

In whatever circumstance you find yourself in, are you sowing seeds? Is the house you live in teeming with life? If I came to visit, would I see evidence of a life well lived? Would I see evidence of God splattered all over the place?

Unpack those boxes. Eliminate the unnecessary. Enjoy what you have. Share with others. Host dinners. Show hospitality to whoever comes into your space.

Let's Pray

Holy Father, thank You for the provision of a space to live. For a roof over my head and bed to sleep in. For food. For the ability to share. Your provisions are exceedingly abundantly more than I could ask. In Jesus' name. Amen.

Call to Action

Will you commit to sharing what God has blessed you with? Write it out.

April 17

Tamar put ashes on her head and tore her long-sleeved garment which was on her; and she put her hand on her head and went away, crying aloud as she went.
2 Samuel 13:19

Grief shows up on my face. I can't hide it. It becomes tight eyebrows and frowned lips. The heavy weight of a wrong done obvious for anyone to see just by seeing my appearance.

Tamar's wrong may look different than mine. But wrong is wrong. It hurts. I carry it like heavy baggage. Tears flood my eyes. The pain takes my breath.

But God. In His measure of comfort, He reaches and holds my heart. He soothes my mind. He catches and holds my tears. He cares and sees the pain. In Him, is my only peace.

Let's Pray

Holy Father, sometimes there are no words to express the grief we experience. But You know and care enough to gently comfort my pain. You are not a stranger to pain. Please forgive me for not seeing the pain Jesus endured on the cross in my place. Forgive me for not running to You for my comfort and trying to replace Your perfect provision with a cheap imitation. Thank You for Jesus. Thank You for caring. Thank You for loving me. In Jesus' name. Amen.

Call to Action

Do you carry grief? Will you ask God to comfort you through it? Write it out.

April 18

Martha said to Him, "I know that he will rise again in the resurrection on the last day."
John 11:24

Eternal life begins the moment of surrender to belief in the cleansing power of the blood of Jesus. Jesus did what you and I cannot. We have no power on our own to overcome the plague of sin that grips us so tightly. It is only by the power of the death and resurrection of Jesus that we can have the assurance of salvation from the depth of hell.

Claiming the promise of salvation transforms the path from a dead-end road to a never-ending journey with the Almighty God. Trading that which brings eternal death for that which breathes life for eternity. Accepting His gift of salvation brings hope to the hopeless.

Is there evidence in your life that you are living for eternity with God? Or do you still have one foot in the world? Will you claim His promise today?

Let's Pray

Holy Father may there be evidence in my life that I am living fully for and with You even now. Keep me from straddling the fence. Place me fully in Your will. In Jesus' name. Amen.

Call to Action

Do you recognize family, friends or coworkers who are on fire for Jesus? What characteristics of their lives cause you to know they walk with Him? Write it out.

April 19

The angel said to the women, "Do not be afraid; for I know that you are looking for Jesus who has been crucified."
Matthew 28:8

Grave sitting. Seeking the living among the dead. Faithful women arriving early, getting up before the sun preparing to seek that One whom they thought they had lost. Going to His grave to find Him. Going to His grave, expecting it to be sealed. Making sure His final resting place was secure. They had been separated from Him since Friday. It was Sunday.

Pain filling their hearts. Wanting to touch the stone that had been rolled in the entrance. They just needed to touch the stone, to grave sit for just a while. Hoping to find some measure of comfort.

Hearts pounding. Eyes wide open in disbelief. Words unable to form, just open-mouthed wonder. The grave, open. The grave, empty. With a fearsome sight explaining the One they were looking for wasn't in that grave. He is risen.

Let's Pray

Holy Father, through the resurrection of Jesus, we also find resurrection to live. Thank You, Holy Father for that empty tomb. In Jesus' name. Amen.

Call to Action

Imagine the sight after such weariness. Tears? Laughter? Confusion? Write it out.

April 20

"Go quickly and tell His disciples that He has risen from the dead; and behold, He is going ahead of you into Galilee, there you will see Him; behold, I have told you."
Matthew 28:7

Go. Tell. He has risen. With urgency the message was shared that Jesus was no longer in that tomb but had come out of the place where He conquered death on our behalf. And He lives.

And not only is He alive but we can see Him. He is ahead of us. Moving, preparing, making the way for us to follow Him into the place He has prepared.

Elated anticipation for what He is doing. Excited expectation to join the work of His kingdom. Living intentional so that others can see evidence of Him living in me.

Let's Pray

Holy Father, it is only by the resurrection of Jesus that we can also conquer death and the grave. God, You gave us the same power to be raised to life through the blood of Jesus. Give us confidence in studying Your Word so that we can boldly share the good news that Jesus has finished the defeat of evil and redeems us to You. In Jesus' name. Amen.

Call to Action

Are you excited about what Jesus did for you on the cross and in that grave? Are you sharing your redemption story with others? If not, why? Write it out.

April 21

And with great power the apostles were giving testimony to the resurrection of the Lord Jesus, and abundant grace was upon them all.
Acts 4:33

They were doing life together. The tying binds of Jesus knit them together with fierce love. Possessions recognized as belonging to God and used for His glory to help all. Resurrected living with grace falling on all who came to life.

The testimony of the early church reminds us to love one another. It shows us what generous, sacrificial living is all about. Jesus gave the perfect sacrifice. We can devote our lives sacrificially to giving what we have so that others will know Him.

What resources can you share? Is there anything you can do to help others? What is your testimony of generosity? What are you willing to sacrifice to live resurrected?

Let's Pray

Holy Father, thank You for the blood of Jesus. Thank You for Your perfect love. Help us to live fully resurrected in the power of Your Son's sacrifice. In Jesus' name. Amen.

Call to Action

What does resurrected living look like for you? Do you need to change anything to live fully resurrected? What change can you make right now to make it happen? Write it out.

April 22

from whom the whole body, being fitted and held together by what every joint supplies, according to the proper working of each individual part, causes the growth of the body for the building up of itself in love.
Ephesians 4:16

The spectator remarked that we looked like we worked well together. Each one had their job to do, and we did it efficiently. Not crossing over into the others lane but staying the course and lending a hand when needed.

It was a simple campsite. Tent camping. All the necessities were placed for a weekend birthday celebration for a little boy. Nothing grand, just a well-appointed campsite.

And so, God orchestrates our bodies and His body. Our bodies work by the creation of His hand so that we fit into His body of believers. Each of us formed and fitted into the role He has for us. When all is done for the glory of God, love is built with growth in the body.

Let's Pray

Holy Father, You are the Light that we grow toward. We long to be productive members of Your kingdom. Lead us in the work You have for us so that we are honoring You. Thank You for the ability to work. Thank You for the growth. Thank You for love. In Jesus' name. Amen.

Call to Action

Recall a time where you saw Christ-centered collaboration. Write it out.

April 23

So the LORD God appointed a plant and it grew up over Jonah to be a shade over his head to deliver him from his discomfort. And Jonah was extremely happy about the plant.
Jonah 4:6

The sun is beating down hard and hot. Spring in the South has already brought temperatures in the 90's. It feels more like July than April. Working outside is slightly unbearable. Then a cloud moves in front of the sun and welcomed shade gives relief.

Jonah had experienced more than just the hot sun. He was running from God. He didn't want to help obstinate and rebellious people. But it was the assignment God had given him. God was faithful to provide what Jonah needed. He does the same for us.

Your assignment may look different than Jonah's. Hopefully, your assignment doesn't cause you to run and be swallowed by a great fish. But are you running? Is there something God has given to you, and you are avoiding it? An assignment He fashioned just for you. Don't run from it!

Let's Pray

Holy Father, thank You for appointing us to work for Your glory. Help us to be intentional in the work You have for us. Keep us dedicated to the mission in front of us. In Jesus' name. Amen.

Call to Action

Are you running from the assignment God gave you? Why? Write it out.

April 24

When Mordecai learned all that had been done, he tore his clothes, put on sackcloth and ashes, and went out into the midst of the city and wailed loudly and bitterly.
Esther 4:1

Sometimes anguish is written all over your face. Sometimes it is too great a weight to bear alone so you take it to the streets and share it with anyone willing to hear your cries. Your gut-wrenching wails become other-worldly aches.

God didn't leave Mordecai in the streets of the city vainly crying out from despair. Oh, no! God heard his cries just as He hears yours. He listens. He cares and He acts.

On your behalf, He reaches down to orchestrate your rescue. He already had it planned. Sometimes it takes us reaching the bottom before we can look up to see our help is already there.

Let's Pray

Holy Father, You are our constant source of refuge and strength. You continually save Your people from despair. And yet, in our sinful nature, we return to the same old places of despair. But You still hear our cries. You still rescue. You still save. Thank You for our constant source of refuge. Thank You for Your Mighty Hand. In Jesus' name. Amen.

Call to Action

Have you met Him at the bottom of despair? Did you cry out to Him? Did He hear? Write it out.

April 25

and coming out of the tombs after His resurrection they entered the holy city and appeared to many.
Matthew 27:53

Walking down the street, you think you see a familiar face but can't place it. Who is that? The familiarity seems so real, but you struggle to remember. Reminds you of that old friend that has been gone for a while, but it couldn't be. She gets closer. Your eyes can't understand.

She brought you along beside her when you struggled. She showed you scripture passages that caused your faith to increase. She was always helping others. Her faith spilled out onto others. Your memories of her flood your eyes.

Passing by you smell the familiar scent. The smile is unmistakable. But something is different. Untouchable love envelopes you in a warm embrace. Then she is gone. But her essence stays.

Let's Pray

Holy Father, thank You for placing faithful brothers and sisters in our path. Thank You for Your Holy Spirit teaching us and using others to lead us in studying Your Word. Help us to lead those that come behind us. Thank You for using us for such a time as this. In Jesus' name. Amen.

Call to Action

Who has been instrumental in your faith walk? Send them a note of thanks. Write it out.

April 26

Now those who belong to Christ Jesus have crucified the flesh with its passions and desires.
Galatians 5:24

Christ takes what the world offers you and replaces it with devotion to Him. The sinful ways leading to death become repulsive in a mind fixed on Christ. Thoughts shift to goodness and righteousness. Transformed thinking renewing your life.

My favorite time of day is early morning when the house is quiet, and it is still dark outside. I slip out of bed and start my day. I need that hour or more to wake-up and spend time with God. Just me with Him. No interruptions. It sets the tone of my heart and mind on Him.

Do you have habits that help you to focus on God? Do you set aside time to spend alone with Him? Will you commit to give Him your attention in quiet prayer, study, and praise?

Let's Pray

Holy Father, Your work on the cross, in the grave and resurrection finished what was needed for our redemption. Through Christ we are transformed into Your children. Thank You for the presence of Holy Spirit in us to be our constant teacher. In Jesus' name. Amen.

Call to Action

Does the world try to take over in your thoughts? What do you do to stay focused on Christ? I write in a journal. Here is your opportunity. Write it out.

April 27

"Go therefore and make disciples of all the nations, baptizing them in the name of the Father and the Son and the Holy Spirit,"
Matthew 28:19

Are you going? Are you making disciples? Are you a disciple bringing others into discipleship with you? If not, why?

Does life get in your way? Do your own thoughts of insecurity keep you from being and making disciples? Discipleship is coming along with others, side by side, learning and living the message of Christ. Discipleship is being devoted to that message and sharing it so that all who hear grow and learn the heart of God.

Jesus didn't keep His message to Himself. He shared it. He gathered people to walk along beside Him and gave them the message so they could take it and spread it. He has gathered us to do the same. Go now! Keep sharing the message of Christ.

Let's Pray

Holy Father, thank You for Your Word. Thank You for the calling and equipping to share the message of salvation with a lost world. Thank You for salvation. In Jesus' name. Amen.

Call to Action

Will you commit to come along side others for discipleship? Write it out.

April 28

For if we have become united with Him in the likeness of His death, certainly we shall also be in the likeness of His resurrection,
Romans 6:5

Giving up the old. Doing away with the sin that weighs us down and keeps us in the grave. Knowing and living with the truth that Jesus took care of all that ugly sin once and for all. He called it done. He called it finished. If He says it is finished, so should we.

Accepting the transformation of being a grave-dweller to being a raised-to-life believer is freedom-living. Sin no longer has a grip on you. Jesus took the weight of death off you and placed it on Himself so you can live in His love. Redeemed. Transformed. Resurrected.

You are united with Him. He is right there with you. Sin no longer belongs to you. Give it no more attention. Turn your attention to your Redeemer.

Let's Pray

Holy Father, there are not enough words to express the gratitude I have for the resurrection power of Jesus. Thank You for pulling me out of the wretched death that sin had claimed was mine but replaced it with life with You. I love You, Lord. In Jesus' name. Amen.

Call to Action

Are you living a resurrected life? Will you begin right now? Write it out.

April 29

You water its furrows abundantly,
You settle its ridges,
You soften it with showers,
You bless its growth.
Psalm 65:10

Dry parched earth devours the rain that falls. Streams of mud form, moving earth, transforming it into different shapes. The rain fingers stretch out to create a web of soaking life. Saturated earth grows green again.

I open my Bible. Dry bones drink from the life-sustaining words. Sweeter than honey to my lips. Panting heavily for the water that pours from the pages. Satiated from the stream of goodness.

Transformed as the words flow through my mind. God taking and molding me into the shape He wants. Me, willingly drinking from His fountain.

Let's Pray

Holy Father, I need You more than water and air. You are the life-sustaining source for all people. Your provisions are exceedingly abundant. Please forgive me when I do not find indulgence in You. Forgive me for looking for that indulgence from things that are incapable of satiating. Thank You for returning me to Your righteous provision. In Jesus' name. Amen.

Call to Action

Find a passage of scripture that brings life back to your dry bones. Write it out.

April 30

A time to give birth and a time to die;
A time to plant and a time to uproot what is planted.
Ecclesiastes 3:2

What is in your garden? Is it fresh with the promise of harvest? Are there weeds trying to kill what you have planted? Is it time to pull the roots of weeds out from the soil so the nutrients can supply energy and growth for your expected harvest?

Will you spend a few minutes today evaluating time-wasting thoughts and actions in your life that cause you distraction and frustration? Decide to eliminate one harmful habit so you can devote energy to good habits. Maybe it is social media. Maybe it is shopping. Maybe it is overeating. What good can you use to replace the harmful?

It will take practice. It will require focus. It will take determination. But most importantly it will require you to seek God's help in replacing the bad for the good He has for you.

Let's Pray

Holy Father, forgive us for allowing weeds to creep up and overtake our lives. Help us to uproot the life-sucking habits that try to steal our joy in You. You are the provider of our joy. Thank You for always bringing us back. In Jesus' name. Amen.

Call to Action

What weeds are you pulling today? Write it out.

SO THE WORD OF THE LORD WAS
GROWING MIGHTILY AND
PREVAILING.
ACTS 19:20

May

So the word of the Lord was growing mightily and prevailing.
Acts 19:20

May becomes a busy month in the Martin household. As I write this, I have one son about to graduate from high school. Another son is on the verge of proposing marriage and planning a wedding. My daughter has two of the biggest blessings of my life; the oldest of the two has been in t-ball for several weeks and the youngest is desperately trying to walk and has been in swimming lessons. Not to mention, she is wrapping up another year of teaching. My husband is also wrapping up another year of teaching while working in real estate.

Through all the busyness, flowers are blooming, the garden is growing, aging parents need attention, this book calls for my attention, my full-time job is demanding. All the stuff can try to consume me. But I come back to these pages and find stillness in the scripture and promises from God for spiritual growth and understanding. Through all of life's demands He is my constant. I can, at any and every moment of my day, seek Him. He is always willing to be found in the middle of whatever I am in.

My prayer for you as you enter the pages for May is that you will seek Him. That you will pull weeds out of the garden of life you are in at this moment so that your life will not be consumed by junk but that you will prepare for a bountiful harvest. I pray that you find yourself surrounded by believers who are willing to hold you up and walk along life's road with you while you all seek God earnestly.

Be blessed!

May 1

"When anyone hears the word of the kingdom and does not understand it, the evil one comes and snatches away what has been sown in his heart. This is the one on whom seed was sown beside the road."
Matthew 13:19

Sitting in the sanctuary, struggling to keep eyes open, wanting to listen but being pulled into slumber. Have you been there? I am sure you have. The week has caught up with you and sitting still in silences causes your body to think: REST. So, your eyes become heavy, and your breathing relaxes, and sleep is calling your name.

You miss all the goodness from the pastor's sermon. Or if you happen to hear small nuggets, they land flat. Words wasted on your ears because you couldn't fight off demanding sleep. A missed opportunity for understanding.

Be alert. Come to the sanctuary rested and ready for worship and knowledge. Come prepared to hear the Word preached for application and understanding.

Let's Pray

Holy Father, please forgive us when we come into times of worship unprepared. God, You know our flesh is so weak. Please strengthen us. Cause our spirit to be stronger. In Jesus' name. Amen.

Call to Action

What can you do to prepare for worship? Write it out.

May 2

"The one on whom seed was sown on the rocky places, this is the man who hears the word and immediately receives it with joy; yet he has no firm root in himself, but is only temporary, and when affliction or persecution arises because of the word, immediately he falls away."
Matthew 13:20-21

I recently heard someone sharing about this very passage of scripture. They explained that plants have a tough time growing in rocky places because the rocks heat up from the sun and dries the soil. Creates an inhospitable environment for growth.

When I was about ten years old, our class was on an outdoor basketball court. Girls on one end and boys on the other. A boy decided it would be fun to throw a rock into the group of girls. The rock met the back of my head with a hard thud. Reaching up, I pulled back a bloody hand. That rock brought harm to my head and sent me to the office away from my friends.

Inhospitable environments can cause us to doubt and shrink back from absorbing the Word of God. Heated debates or harsh words thrown your way can drive you away from the goodness of His Word. He will give you the strength you need to stay on the course if you persevere.

Let's Pray

Holy Father, help us to stand firm in Your Word when persecuted for it. In Jesus' name. Amen.

Call to Action

Has there been a time in your life when you were ridiculed for your faith? Write it out.

May 3

"And the one on whom seed was sown among the thorns, this is the man who hears the word, and the worry of the world and the deceitfulness of wealth choke the word, and it becomes unfruitful."
Matthew 13:22

Late yesterday evening, I grabbed the hoe and started removing weeds from the garden. The soil is fertile, and I want all the nutrients to go to the expected harvest. The weeds have no place, taking up the goodness of the space intended for the plants intentionally placed there.

If I left the weeds there, the tomatoes would suffer. I have proven it. Weeds left to overtake plantings will choke out and bring harm. Removing the weeds gives space for the tomatoes to thrive in the rich soil and brings a bountiful harvest.

What about the space in your heart and mind? Is the soil fertile to accept the Word of God? Are there any weeds that are taking up space that need to be removed? Is there anything that is choking out your acceptance of the Word of God?

Let's Pray

Holy Father, thank You for Your Word and how Your Holy Spirit instructs as we study. Reveal to me anything that hinders my growth so that I can remove it. In Jesus' name. Amen.

Call to Action

What do you do to keep the weeds from overtaking your study of God's Word? Write it out.

May 4

"And the one on whom seed was sown on the good soil, this is the man who hears the word and understands it; who indeed bears fruit and brings forth, some a hundredfold, some sixty, and some thirty."
Matthew 13:23

Billy Graham will always be remembered for the many people who flocked to events around the world to hear the good news he preached. I remember as a young child, watching him on television. His messages were passionately leading people to believe in the One that could save souls from eternal wrath. And many accepted what he spoke and entered relationships with God.

God had prepared him to speak those messages and prepared the people to hear and make decisions to accept God's redemption. God prepares people today to share His good news. He also prepares people to receive it.

Which one are you? Are you in the position of needing to hear (which we all are) and accept the redemption from the Savior? Or are you in the position of sharing that message with others?

Let's Pray

Holy Father, wherever we are at this moment, speak into our hearts and minds so that we can move in faith to follow You where You lead. We want to live for You. In Jesus' name. Amen.

Call to Action

Where are you? Need to accept or already out there sharing? You decide. Write it out.

May 5

"But while his men were sleeping, his enemy came and sowed tares among the wheat, and went away. But when the wheat sprouted and bore grain, then the tares became evident also."
Matthew 13:25-26

Has the enemy been in your garden? Did you leave the gate open so he could slip in and wreak havoc? Now there is a mess of weeds with thorns intertwined with your expected harvest. But maybe it is hard to distinguish between the good and the bad. The harvest is coming though and will prove what needs to be ripped out.

Open your eyes to view your life through the lens of God's Word. Thoughts and activities that you have always had may be producing nutrient-sapping weeds that steal your fellowship with God. Evidence may come in the form of attention being pulled away from prayer, church attendance, Bible study, or fellowship with other believers.

Close the gate so the enemy won't come in to steal and destroy your fellowship with God. Remove anything that keeps you from intentional worship. Ask God for His help.

Let's Pray

Holy Father, give us discernment between righteousness and evil. In Jesus' name. Amen.

Call to Action

What steps will you take to weed the garden of your life? Write it out.

May 6

"Allow both to grow together until the harvest; and in the time of the harvest I will say to the reapers, "First gather up the tares and bind them in bundles to burn them up; but gather the wheat into my barn.""
Matthew 13:30

This is not an easy thing to tell you. It is not fun or cute. You may find it offensive and decide this is the final page you will read. I hope and pray instead it will give you encouragement to continue and even find the desire to share with others.

Jesus was sharing with His disciples after speaking to large crowds. He was laying down lessons for His followers so that the lessons could be taken and shared. This lesson pointed to a time where believers and non-believers will be separated.

Gathered into the presence of God will be those who have placed faith in the gift of Jesus as Savior. Those who have no connection with Jesus will be turned away and exiled into eternal fire. Where do you stand? What about your loved ones? What will you do to share the message of salvation?

Let's Pray

Holy Father, thank You for the sacrifice of Jesus and the salvation given. In Jesus' name. Amen.

Call to Action

Are you following Jesus to share with others the message of salvation? Write it out.

May 7

"The Son of Man will send forth His angels, and they will gather out of His kingdom all stumbling blocks, and those who commit lawlessness, and will throw them into the furnace of fire; in that place there will be weeping and gnashing of teeth."
Matthew 13:41-42

I told you yesterday that you may not want to continue. Know that these passages of scripture only display the truth. As you read God's Word, there are some hard truths to accept. This is the hardest for me. To know that there are people walking around me that will not join me in heaven is the most devastating reality to accept.

This is why I write. This is the reason I share Jesus with others. For others to know Him.

His mercy and grace are gifts He gives, but they must be accepted and recognized. Through the acceptance, we proclaim that we are sinners in need of a Savior. We make decisions moment by moment to recognize temptations for what they are and avoid following through with anything that will cause us to be sinful. We look to know God so that we can walk in a manner worthy of His precious sacrifice. Then we take the love He gave us and share it with others.

Let's Pray

Holy Father, help us to share what You have given us. In Jesus' name. Amen.

Call to Action

Is there someone you need to share Jesus with? Write it out.

May 8

"Woe to you, scribes and Pharisees, hypocrites! For you clean the outside of the cup and of the dish, but inside they are full of robbery and self-indulgence. You blind Pharisee, first clean the inside of the cup and of the dish, so that the outside of it may become clean also."
Matthew 23:25-26

It starts with me. In my heart. In my mind. The clutter of temptation and sin litters my thinking. The piles of rubbish can stack up high unless I am diligent in taking out the trash. I must remove the junk, so my line of vision is clear and the path in front of me is unobstructed.

On the outside you may never know the junk I carry around. I can look the part of the righteous believer sharing Jesus with the people I meet, but if my heart and mind are not right with God I will trip and my ugly secrets will come out. Those thoughts of jealousy and hatred will become evident.

I am unable to clean it up alone. I must seek Jesus to help me clean up the mess in my heart and mind. He is the only One with the proper cleaning solution.

Let's Pray

Holy Father, wash me clean from the inside out. Thank You for the precious blood of Jesus that washes me white as snow. You take all the evil in me and remove it. In Jesus' name. Amen.

Call to Action

What do you need to ask Jesus to remove from your heart and mind? Write it out.

May 9

"I will vindicate the holiness of My great name which has been profaned among the nations, which you have profaned in their midst. Then the nations will know that I am the LORD," declares the Lord GOD, "when I prove Myself holy among you in their sight."
Ezekiel 36:23

Precious is the name of the One who created the earth and all it holds. Wonderful is His name. Worthy to be exalted above all. Almighty God worthy of all praise and worship. Praise Him.

Holy is the name of the One who created mankind in His image. He placed a heart of flesh in my chest for compassion. He fills my lungs with the breath of His lungs. I am breathing His air.

His name is worthy to be spoken intentionally in praise. His name is worthy to be used in cries of desperation with devotion to His will. His name is worthy of me prostrate on the ground in submission to Him. His name is worthy of my complete surrender to His Majesty.

Let's Pray

Holy Father, forgive mindless slips of the tongue that profane Your precious name. Let my tongue only have praise and adoration for Your name. The mention of Your name makes my heart soar in my chest. My chest wants to explode. I praise Your precious name. You alone are worthy of all praise. I love You, Lord. In Jesus' name. Amen.

Call to Action

Do you need to repent and ask forgiveness for using God's name inappropriately? Write it out.

May 10

"Then I will sprinkle clean water on you, and you will be clean; I will cleanse you from all your filthiness and from all your idols."
Ezekiel 36:25

Laying bare before the Lord. Available for His work. Available for His pleasure. A willing vessel desperately wanting to be cleansed and made right in His holiness. Desiring nothing but Him.

Asking Him to cultivate my life. Turn the soil fresh and ready to accept the seeds that will grow deep and take root for a mighty harvest. Placing my foundation on Him because He is the cornerstone that will provide the stability to keep me standing firm.

Leaning on Him for understanding and wisdom. His living water washes me clean. He removes all my filthiness and replaces it with His holiness.

Let's Pray

Holy Father, words seem so inadequate for praise to You. Find my heart and mind and body an acceptable offering of praise to You. Accept my worship as fragrant incense. Help me to pour it out for Your exaltation. Holy Father, thank You for Your lovingkindness to me. Your compassion never fails. I love You, Lord. In Jesus' name. Amen.

Call to Action

What is your praise to God today? How will you express your love for Him? Write it out.

May 11

"I will put My Spirit within you and cause you to walk in My statutes, and you will be careful to observe My ordinances."
Ezekiel 36:27

He took my sin and replaced it with grace. Mercy is given for me to dwell in the presence of the Most High. Giving me Himself. Love so great that He would turn His face away from the One who willing took my place in hell, giving me access to the Father, giving me relationship with God. He wants me. He sings over me. He rejoices over me.

My desire is turned to Him. The longing of my heart is in His presence. These dry bones are desperately searching for the living water He provides.

When He turns on the faucet, I drink hard. Gulping whatever He gives. He is kind to give me exactly what I need.

Let's Pray

Holy Father, it is only by the blood of Jesus that I dwell in Your presence. I am in awe of You. I want to stand and shout and fall face down on the floor all at the same time in worship of You. Teach me Your ordinances. Keep me within Your will. In Jesus' name. Amen.

Call to Action

Spend time considering God's ordinances. What do they mean to you? Write it out.

May 12

"You will live in the land that I gave to your forefathers; so you will be My people, and I will be your God."
Ezekiel 36:28

The faithfulness of God endures. Man's faithfulness, on the other hand, is not so consistent. Like the Israelites, my heart and mind wander away from God. I allow the cares of this world to come in and consume my thoughts and actions. Temporal trappings try to steal my attention.

But God is always there to remind me of His provision for eternity. He comes in softly and gives another chance for walking in obedience to Him. He holds out His hand and offers me another opportunity to join Him for the purpose He has called me into. He is gentle with me.

Living in the land He gave me by being intentional to walk out His calling is the most fulfilling action I can take. It far surpasses any of the worldly activities that only wastefully consume resources. But walking in intentional obedience is claiming what He gave for His glory.

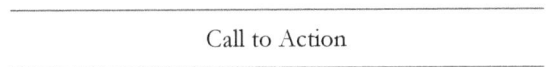

Let's Pray

Holy Father, thank You for the provisions You have given me. Thank You for faithfulness toward me. You are patient and kind. Help me to be obedient. In Jesus' name. Amen.

Call to Action

Do you get side-tracked? Ask God to bring you back. Write it out.

May 13

"Moreover, I will save you from all your uncleanness; and I will call for the grain and multiply it, and I will not bring a famine on you."
Ezekiel 36:29

Dirt accumulates fast. I sweep and by the time the broom is back in its place, there is more grit on the floor. The window left clean gathers fingerprints. Empty laundry containers collect dirty clothing. Dishes appear in the clean kitchen. It never ends.

I wonder if God feels the same way about me. Each time He corrects and sets things back into rightness in me, something interferes and smears my face with dirt. Needing His constant attention to bring me back again.

When He brings me back, He gives a fresh supply of provisions. He sets things into perspective. He scrubs my face and floors so that I walk in the radiance of His glory. He is the best cleaner.

Let's Pray

Holy Father, thank You for washing me white as snow. Forgive my poor housekeeping. Forgive my slop and filth. Create in me a clean and pure heart that walks in fellowship with You. Keep me and restore me. You are worthy of all praise. In Jesus' name. Amen.

Call to Action

What housekeeping do you need for your heart and mind? Ask God to help. Write it out.

May 14

"I will multiply the fruit of the tree and the produce of the field, so that you will not receive again the disgrace of famine among the nations."
Ezekiel 36:30

The garden is beginning to show promise of harvest. Small green tomatoes hang. Watermelon vines are spreading. Corn is reaching high toward the heavens. All the leaves face up to catch all the sunlight possible.

The longer I sit in His light the more I grow. Like the plants in the garden, time and light strengthen my roots. His promise of harvest ripens the fruit of my life.

He removes the fear of famine. He supplies fruit in abundance. His provision multiplies and spreads through each of us.

Let's Pray

Holy Father, thank You for the abundance You provide. Through Your grace and mercy, You call us to work to further Your kingdom. Through furthering it Your sufficiency proves to be exceedingly great. God, there is no other work worthy of doing but that which You ordain in us. Find the work of our hands and hearts acceptable. In Jesus' name. Amen.

Call to Action

Is there a harvest in front of you? Can you see it? Ask God for it. Write it out.

May 15

"The desolate land will be cultivated instead of being a desolation in the sight of everyone who passes by."
Ezekiel 36:34

My husband and I have bought four pieces of property over the years that have been left to grow wild. Two have had dwellings that were left damaged. All four properties took work to bring to a useful state. We left them better than when we found them.

When we meet Jesus and allow Him to cultivate the soil of our hearts, He makes us better than before. Just like the work we put into those properties, Jesus removes the trash and the weeds and develops the space in us for purposeful work.

The transformation is clear to all who pass by. You view the property, and it is unrecognizable from its former condition. And so, it is with our hearts. Jesus takes the mess of us and creates a renewed mind and heart ready to be used for His glory.

Let's Pray

Holy Father, thank You for the cultivation in my heart and mind. Your transforming power is clear in the lives of those who draw near to You. In Jesus' name. Amen.

Call to Action

Have you seen God transform someone? What was the evidence? Write it out.

May 16

Create in me a clean heart, O God,
And renew a steadfast spirit within me.
Psalm 51:10

I am a morning person. My best thinking happens in early mornings. But some mornings it is hard to get out of bed. Sometimes it depends on how late I stayed up the night before. Other times it doesn't matter how much I sleep; my body doesn't want to cooperate with my mind.

When I have trouble getting up, I can generally point back to where my thoughts have been hanging out. If I have been focused on the world and all the tugging on me, then I want to pull the covers over my head and stay in the comfort of my bed. I don't want to face the day and what might pummel me.

But if I turn my attention back to where it belongs and ask God to set my perspective straight, He will. I can get out of bed in excited anticipation of what God has in store for me. He is faithful to renew me and provides a clean start.

Let's Pray

Holy Father, thank You for faithfully renewing me. God, help me keep my focus on You so that the world doesn't pull me in so greedily. Thank You for Your renewal. In Jesus' name. Amen.

Call to Action

Are you a morning person? What time do you find renewal? Write it out.

May 17

"Wash yourselves, make yourselves clean;
Remove the evil of your deeds from My sight. Cease to do evil,"
Isaiah 1:16

Am I the only one that has the exact same things pop up in my face to tempt me and side-track me? You too? It never fails. I say not again but there it is again. I can go for months at a time without any temptation and one little blip will send me into a tailspin. I will either spiral out of control into the abyss, or I will recognize it for what it is and refuse to enter that death-trap.

Making a concentrated effort to remove any hint of temptation sets me up for success. Washing clean whatever threatens to separate me from God. Removing any temptation so I can walk in a manner worthy of the love He has given me.

Temptations will continue to threaten. But God offers a way to escape. He has no desire to leave you in the middle of your mess. It is up to you to allow Him to rescue you.

Let's Pray

Holy Father, thank you for cleaning up my mess. Keep me from making more messes. Thank You for restoring to right relationship with You. In Jesus' name. Amen.

Call to Action

What messes do you need to give to God? Write it out.

May 18

"Moreover, they shall teach My people the difference between the holy and the profane, and cause them to discern between the unclean and the clean."
Ezekiel 44:23

Before Jesus came and gave us direct access to God through His Holy Spirit, Levites served as spiritual leaders and intercessors. They were the access points for learning and discernment. They served God by serving the people.

Jesus came and died and left a Helper. This Helper is His Holy Spirit. Acknowledging Jesus as Lord of Your life and following Him invites Holy Spirit to dwell in you. You have constant access to learning and discernment. He is yours. You are His.

It can be difficult sometimes to keep focus on His presence. The world wants your attention. Ask God to hold your attention so you can learn and discern His will for your life.

Let's Pray

Holy Father, it is only by the blood of Jesus that we have access to You. Thank You for the work on the cross and the presence of Holy Spirit. Help us to continually remember You are with us. Teach and direct us as we navigate life. We love You, Lord. In Jesus' name. Amen.

Call to Action

Do you seek Holy Spirit's guidance on all matters? If not, why? Write it out.

May 19

let us draw near with a sincere heart in full assurance of faith, having our hearts sprinkled clean from an evil conscience and our bodies washed with pure water.
Hebrews 10:22

God's posture never changes. I picture Him constantly bending over, in great strength, tending to His children. Always near to comfort or correct. Patiently waiting with loving anticipation for those that have yet to recognize Him.

As we draw near Him, He leans in a little closer. Always patient to allow us the space and time to make the first move. His desire is for our desire to be for Him. He could force us, but He doesn't.

His welcoming presence renews our minds and removes our old desires of sinfulness. He cleans up our heart and mind. We are made new each time we draw close to Him. Staying close to Him is where I want to be.

Let's Pray

Holy Father, thank You for Your patience with me. You know my tendency to wander away from You. Yet You are always welcoming me back. To remain in complete awareness of Your presence is my desire. Help me to always recognize You in all situations. In Jesus' name. Amen.

Call to Action

What can you do to remain aware of the presence of God? How do you draw near? Write it out.

May 20

While He was in one of the cities, behold, there was a man covered with leprosy; and when he saw Jesus, he fell on his face and implored Him, saying, "Lord, if You are willing, You can make me clean."
Luke 5:12

Have you ever wanted something so badly that you fell on your face begging God to make it so? Complete desperation took you down to the dirt, prostrate, crying out to the only One that could do anything about your situation. Sometimes laying there your heart finds a new perspective about the situation. The situation may not change but your view shifts to gain a better perception.

God never disappoints. His answer to our prayers may not be what we expect but He never fails to answer righteous requests. Faith in His sovereignty means accepting the provision of His love.

Never doubt His love. His love for you is so great that He gave you the best gift ever given, His Son. If He is willing to do that, He will be faithful to hear your righteous prayers and answer. Hold firmly to your faith in His faithfulness.

Let's Pray

Holy Father, cleanse my mind and heart to agree with the answers you provide to my prayers. Thank You for Your faithfulness to me. In Jesus' name. Amen.

Call to Action

What is heavy on your heart right now? Have you laid it before the feet of Jesus? Write it out.

May 21

"A disciple is not above his teacher, nor a slave above his master."
Matthew 10:24

You have a place. We all have our place. For some, it is to teach. For some, it is to learn. For some, it is to lead. For some, it is to follow. For some, it is to tell others what to do. For some, it is to be told what to do.

Those roles may shift through time. Learning without application isn't true learning. Observing your leader while you follow may bring you to a place of leadership eventually. Receiving instruction unbegrudgingly, sets the stage to give instruction with humility.

Do you know your place? Do you know your role? Have you experienced shifts through time? Seasons come and go. We all face them. Are you living fully present in your current season?

Let's Pray

Holy Father, Your orchestration of our lives is remarkable. You provide opportunities for us to follow You in furthering Your kingdom. Thank You for entrusting this work to us. May we be found faithful in the work You have given us to do. Reveal to us the role You would have us fill in the work of Your kingdom. In Jesus' name. Amen.

Call to Action

Spend time finding your role in God's kingdom. Write it out.

May 22

"Whoever does not carry his own cross and come after Me cannot be My disciple."
Luke 14:27

It first starts as a thought. Like a seed planted in rich soil. It may stay in the depths of dark for a while, but the light is shining, calling it out of its hidden space. The dark cannot hold onto what doesn't belong there.

Pushing aside all hindrances, the thought takes shape. Determination builds and plans are made. Allowing nothing to distract from completing the plan. Executing each step with precision. Intentionally setting resources into motion.

This is our life with God. His provision of salvation is introduced to us. We consider the cost and decide if we are willing to accept His provision and lay aside everything the world has to offer. Picking up the glorious instead of the cheap imitation. Bearing any burdens the world attempts to give us with the power and strength of the One who saved us. Following Him.

Let's Pray

Holy Father, thank You for bearing the weight of my cross. Your strength is in me. Without You I am unable to pick up my cross and follow You. In Jesus' name. Amen.

Call to Action

Are you picking up your cross daily knowing Jesus carries the weight? Write it out.

May 23

"So then, none of you can be My disciple who does not give up all his own possessions."
Luke 14:33

Tracking resources, accounting for the coming and going of money, has been my occupation for twenty-seven years. I have seen those who hoard and those who give generously. I have seen greed take people by the throat and turn them into stone-cold ravenous wolves. I have also seen God richly bless others who hold what He has given them as His and not their own.

All we have been given is to be used for the honor and glory of God. It is all His. Nothing has been obtained without God allowing it. My revenue comes because of the work God allows me to do and I can do nothing without Him. Your bank account belongs to God.

Instead of holding tightly to what we think is ours, we need to relinquish control to God. It is all His anyway. He allows us to use His provisions. Are we using them for His glory?

Let's Pray

Holy Father, please forgive my greed and selfish possession of the resources You have entrusted to me. Thank You for the abundance You provide. Help me steward it well. May my hands be loose when it comes to giving back for Your kingdom growth. In Jesus' name. Amen.

Call to Action

What possessions do you need to relinquish control of to God? Write it out.

May 24

Now in Joppa there was a disciple named Tabitha (which translated in Greek is called Dorcas); this woman was abounding with deeds of kindness and charity which she continually did.
Acts 9:36

I looked out the window and saw him on the mower. The lady next door was struggling to push her walk-behind mower through the thick grass. It had become obvious that she had not been able to have someone mow the yard as often during this growing season. Seeing a need, my husband went and helped her finish the job.

Throughout our years of marriage, he has done the same thing. If he sees a need, he doesn't wait to be asked, he gets up and does. Always willing to lend a hand. Quietly, expecting nothing in return. Making no spectacle of it, just takes care of it.

Performing the work that needs to be done. Helping others when there is an obvious need. Not waiting to be asked but seeing a need and performing what needs to be done.

Let's Pray

Holy Father, reveal to us the work that needs to be done. Find us charitable in all we do so that there is no pride in what is done, only gratitude for the ability to do. In Jesus' name. Amen.

Call to Action

Are you drawn to charitable deeds? What do you find to do? Write it out.

May 25

"If anyone comes to Me, and does not hate his own father and mother and wife and children and brothers and sisters, yes, and even his own life, he cannot be My disciple."
Luke 14:26

Jesus desires to be your first love. No other love is to come before that which you have for Him. The love you have for Him will create love for others. Without His love first, your love for others will be shallow and idolatrous.

This can seem contrary to what we live out. Because perhaps we have placed the priority of our affection on what can be seen instead of placing our love devotion on the One who gave His all for our soul. Coming to the realization of what He has done and is doing for us shifts our love.

There is no other being that has sovereignty over life. Only Jesus took what He didn't deserve to offer us His eternal provision and presence of peace. No love is greater than His.

Let's Pray

Holy Father, my heart swells when I consider the love You have for me. In my wretched state, You offered to me Your love. Gently reaching out to me in compassion, wanting my heart, You took my punishment and gave me freedom. I love You, Lord. In Jesus' name. Amen.

Call to Action

Do you need to shift your love focus? Ask God to help you. Write it out.

May 26

"And whoever in the name of a disciple gives to one of these little ones even a cup of cold water to drink, truly I say to you, he shall not lose his reward."
Matthew 10:42

Taking his cup, he knows which one he wants. Taking the top off. Ice. Always ice. He likes it cold. Then fill it with water. Replacing the top. Placing it in those little hands. Long draws from the straw. Instant satisfaction.

Did you reach for a cup? Did you sip or slurp? Was it refreshing water you reached for?

Maybe the cup of cold water looks more like a life-verse. Maybe the little hands are large hands, calloused from life. Maybe the heart behind those hands needs a refreshing dose of living water.

Will you offer water to those around you? Keeping what may be needed and offering it to those you meet. Replenish your supply so you are ready to offer.

Let's Pray

Holy Father, keep me in fresh supply of what I need to offer to others. Whether it is a kind word or a drink of water, let it all be done in Your name. In Jesus' name. Amen.

Call to Action

Friends have shared how they carry snacks and water with a passage of scripture ready to be given when the opportunity arises. Will you be prepared to fill a need? Plan. Write it out.

May 27

And Jesus said to them, "Therefore every scribe who has become a disciple of the kingdom of heaven is like a head of a household, who brings out of his treasure things new and old."
Matthew 13:52

This is my responsibility. To do the work God placed in front of me. To write this book. To share with you the words He placed in my mind and heart just for you. It is mine to do.

I can't do what you are called to do. It is your responsibility. God gave it to you. He has given you all you need or will need to complete the work in front of you. Seek Him for it. Be diligent to carry out the calling He has placed so delicately in your mind and heart.

He will surely use your experiences to coordinate whatever it is He has you doing. He will be pleased to give you new experiences to season the work. Just don't sit idle.

Let's Pray

Holy Father, the work You have given us is a sacred calling that You have appointed just for us. God, keep confusion and sin from blocking us from this work. We need Your power and strength to carry it out. We know that all things are possible with You. In Jesus' name. Amen.

Call to Action

Maybe it isn't a book for you. Maybe your calling looks completely different than mine or your neighbor's. Do you know what it is God has for you to do? Ask Him. Write it out.

May 28

The Lord GOD has given Me the tongue of disciples,
That I may know how to sustain the weary one with a word.
He awakens Me morning by morning,
He awakens My ear to listen as a disciple.
Isaiah 50:4

He wakes me up early. Most days the first number on the clock is four. My alarm is set for five, not four. But He stirs me and at once starts calling me to get up. When He does, I cannot go back to sleep. If I try, it isn't restful.

Have you been there? Do you blame it on cortisol? That is the popular thing to blame it on right now. But have you considered it may be God wanting to spend time with you before you get so distracted by everything else? Have you tried getting up to devote some time to Him before doing anything else? If you haven't, let me encourage you to try it.

In the quiet of the morning, no one demands anything from me, I can sit and listen to Him. I open His Word. Journal prayer. Set my attention on Him. Express my love for Him. Accept His love for me. It sets the tone for the day.

Let's Pray

Holy Father, thank You for new mercies each morning. In Jesus' name. Amen.

Call to Action

Do you have a routine to seek God before anything else? Write it out.

May 29

For everyone who partakes only of milk is not accustomed to the word of righteousness, for he is an infant.
Hebrews 5:13

God doesn't expect us to know everything about Him. It is impossible for us to know it all. His power and majesty would obliterate us if we were to experience the fullness of who He is. But recognizing Him as the Sovereign Lord, Creator, and Savior is the first step in knowing Him.

Stopping there, just recognizing Him for who He is, short-changes you. This is the milk that the baby drinks. Taking in only mild, soothing refreshment only touches the surface of the magnitude your relationship with God can reach.

Dig in. Plug in. Reach and seek deeper relationship. Open His word with other believers. Find community. You will find great treasures in your quest to know Him more.

Let's Pray

Holy Father, it is only through Your Holy Spirit that we can truly know You. Thank You for teaching us through Your Word. Thank You for Your constant presence to guide us through our days. Open our minds and hearts to walk close to You. In Jesus' name. Amen.

Call to Action

Make a list of people that have come alongside you on your walk. Write it out.

May 30

like newborn babies, long for the pure milk of the word, so that by it you may grow in respect to salvation,
1 Peter 2:2

The purity of God's word seeps into my soul whenever I open it. It infiltrates my thoughts so that when I need a certain reminder, there it is. It is my priceless companion. There is no better treasure than to open God's word and drink in what He has to say.

I don't know about you, but I like paper pages to turn and mark. I have a Bible app on my phone that I will use but nothing beats holding my worn Bible and flipping pages, remembering the notes I have made in the margins. Sometimes I just like to hug it close to my chest.

Do you have a favorite version? The passages within this book are from the New American Standard Bible. That happens to be the version I use and hold in my personal studies. I enjoy comparing versions, allowing His words to give me a proper perspective. The Bible app on my phone allows me to view different versions. Let me encourage you to find one you love.

Let's Pray

Holy Father, thank You for Your word. Help us to grow in it. In Jesus' name. Amen.

Call to Action

What is your favorite version? Why? Do you compare versions? Write it out.

May 31

For though by this time you ought to be teachers, you have need again for someone to teach you the elementary principles of the oracles of God, and you have come to need milk and not solid food.
Hebrews 5:12

Getting back to the basics is sometimes necessary. Shifting your priorities to remember the foundation on which your faith is built. Everyone is on their own journey with God. Everyone is at different timelines and degrees of knowledge in relationship with God. Even the most seasoned veterans of faith will tell you they have to step back every now and then to regroup.

Even Jesus got away from the crowds.

But don't stay on the sidelines. Get in the game. God has a special purpose for each of us. As members of the body of Christ, we each have been given attributes to use in His kingdom. Staying out of the game deprives you and others of blessings God is waiting to bestow.

Let's Pray

Holy Father, Your richness of life far surpasses anything my brain can comprehend. I do not understand the magnitude of Your love but am so thankful for it. Help me to know the calling You have placed on my life and to accomplish Your purpose for me. In Jesus' name. Amen.

Call to Action

What are the principles of your faith? Are you ready to go deeper? Write it out.

*"THE KINGDOM OF HEAVEN IS
LIKE A TREASURE HIDDEN IN
THE FIELD, WHICH A MAN
FOUND AND HID AGAIN; AND
FROM JOY OVER IT HE GOES AND
SELLS ALL THAT HE HAS AND
BUYS THAT FIELD."*
MATTHEW 13:44

June

"The kingdom of heaven is like a treasure hidden in the field, which a man found and hid again; and from joy over it he goes and sells all that he has and buys that field."
Matthew 13:44

Are you going to the beach this summer? Maybe the mountains? What adventures await? What will you be seeking during your travels? Great treasure?

The greatest treasure you will seek and find is a relationship with Jesus Christ. Search the world and all the heavens and no treasure can compare or fill with joy as the Savior filling you with His Holy Spirit. All other treasure pales in comparison.

Whether you are a seasoned believer or a new believer, each one of us needs to cultivate the soil of our hearts and minds for greater growth. The field can become overgrown with weeds. Scorching heat can dehydrate our intentions and leave us parched. Cloudy skies can leave us pale and weak.

Through tough times we learn to pull the weeds and discern what treasures we should keep. We learn to make Jesus our Son-screen from the scorching heat and make Him our living water supply. Gloom and fatigue are lessened when we seek the Light of the world.

As you venture into the summer months, take Jesus with you. Enjoy the blessings He pours out on you. Bring others along with you. Pour out on them from your overflow.

June 1

"If you consent and obey,
You will eat the best of the land;"
Isaiah 1:19

Our travels have been limited mostly to the southeastern United States. We live in South Georgia, so we stay close to home for vacations. Four to six hours drive is enough for us.

During those trips we discover delightful places to eat. They aren't large chains, but small mom and pop places tucked into small towns. Local food with local people that are doing what they love, and it shows up in the tastes they share. They are using their God-given talents to provide tasty food and friendly atmospheres for anyone willing to walk into their establishments.

God is doing the same thing. He provides only the best for those who are willing to enter His courts of praise. He welcomes you with open arms. It is up to you to enter. You can't taste and see without going in and taking a seat to enjoy His goodness.

Let's Pray

Holy Father, Your blessings are too numerous to count. You provide only the best and we are lavished in Your goodness. Your words are sweeter than honey and it is well with my soul to enjoy Your provisions. In Jesus' name. Amen.

Call to Action

Do you have a favorite vacation spot? Is there a local restaurant you enjoy? Write it out.

June 2

Trust in the LORD and do good;
Dwell in the land and cultivate faithfulness.
Psalm 37:3

She called me early in the morning. Heart pounding in anticipation of a breakfast meeting with other ladies from her church. Ideas flow freely from observation and interacting with like-minded believers. One decision to accept the responsibility of leadership was in front of her.

Her desire is to bring fellowship with all the women of the church. She has witnessed what it looks like for women to come along side each other to encourage and give a helping hand. She just wants everyone to experience the same. She knows opinions and attitudes can offer disruption, but she knows her God is bigger and mightier than that.

She accepts, with a willing heart, the leadership role. She knows it takes a team. God has placed her where she is for such a time as this. He will provide for willing minds and hearts.

Let's Pray

Holy Father, thank You for women who will step into leadership roles. Protect them and their families from pride, from flaming arrows of attack, from fatigue. Grow faithfulness because of their leadership. Allow the work of their hands to glorify You. In Jesus' name. Amen.

Call to Action

Where do you serve? Is there a leader you can join? Are you the leader? Write it out.

June 3

"Some of those who have insight will fall, in order to refine, purge and make them pure until the end time; because it is still to come at the appointed time."
Daniel 11:35

I fell. It was a hard fall. My heart shattered into a million pieces, and it has yet to recover fully. I didn't know what I had until I no longer had it.

I don't understand why I was pulled away from the church I loved. In full confession, I have not been able to pick-up and rejoin a fellowship of believers with the same intensity. The work was deeply personal for me. I felt defined by the work.

The falling away from one body sent me to another. Time to observe and notice the needs around me. Time to dive into scripture and prayer. Time to talk with God and work some things out of me. His work is in me, preparing me for what is to come.

Let's Pray

Holy Father, thank You for purging. Thank You for moving us to different places. Help us to be willing workers in the capacity for which You have called us. Keep us in that calling. Let us know what it is so that we glorify You. In Jesus' name. Amen.

Call to Action

Have you had a fall? What did you do? Did you pick up somewhere else? Write it out.

June 4

Therefore the people quarreled with Moses and said, "Give us water that we may drink." And Moses said to them, "Why do you quarrel with me? Why do you test the LORD?"
Exodus 17:2

A drastic change brought out the grumbling. Lack of faith showed up in complaining. Instead of resting in the faithfulness of God, doubt set in and disturbed my focus on the One who provides for every need. He is faithful even when I am not.

He doesn't need my testing to prove His faithfulness. He just wants me to rest in the goodness of His faithfulness. He doesn't want me to sit back and wait for someone else to do what He gave me to do though. He desires my dependency on Him.

In a dry desert, He gives water. In famine, He gives food. In loneliness, He gives friendship. In pain, He gives comfort. In sadness, He gives joy. In confusion, He gives clarity.

Let's Pray

Holy Father, You provide for my every need. You make it personal. You work out all the details so that Your provision fits me perfectly. You alone are worthy of all praise. Thank You for Your faithfulness to me. Help me to walk in faithfulness to You. In Jesus' name. Amen.

Call to Action

Have you experienced God's faithfulness in big and small ways? Write it out.

June 5

Then the LORD God took the man and put him into the garden of Eden to cultivate it and keep it.
Genesis 2:15

As a young mother, I left my babies in the care of other people so I could go to work. Looking back, I remember sobbing as I drove from the daycare center to my office. Callouses formed in my heart during those years. I rationalized that I was doing the best thing for my children. It sounds absurd now. It sounds dreadful. Even now I am sorrowful at the thought of what I did.

God gave me beautiful lives to care for. He gave me three precious gifts. Little humans that needed me, not someone else.

Young mama, may I encourage you to prayerfully consider with your husband, if this is your situation, to understand those little humans are not little for very long. You will come to a new season of time where those littles are not completely dependent on you. While they are, be there for them. Nurture them as you seek God's direction for your family.

Let's Pray

Holy Father, thank You for being the perfect Father. We need Your help in discerning what is best for our families. Give us wisdom and knowledge to raise them well. In Jesus' name. Amen.

Call to Action

What are you cultivating? Is it a young family? Is it an empty nest? Write it out.

June 6

*And in their heart they put God to the test
By asking food according to their desire.*
Psalm 78:18

I wasn't hungry. My belly was full of dinner. I didn't need that bowl of ice cream. But I had it.

My food cravings get me in trouble. Digestive discomfort. Headaches. Swelling. My desires lead me away from the best choices. The sweetness calls my name, and I give in. My palate knows the feel of cool, creamy deliciousness and it wins over the eventual regret.

I know the best choices will bring health and not regret. I know what I should wait for and in gratitude find satisfaction in the morsels God designed for me. It always makes me feel better.

Let's Pray

Holy Father, please forgive me for allowing junk into this vessel. God, You give good choices that honor my body so that I can be fueled well to accomplish Your purpose for me. Help me to eliminate anything that brings harm to Your good design. You created me to work for You. I desire to take care of what You have provided so that my life honors You. In Jesus' name. Amen.

Call to Action

Do you have a health plan? No, I do not mean insurance. A plan to live healthily. Food plans. Exercise plans. It is so easy to get busy and ignore our bodies. I am guilty. So today I begin again. I need to be intentional! What about you? Will you plan to be healthy? Write it out.

June 7

'Is as the light of the morning when the sun rises,
A morning without clouds,
When the tender grass springs out of the earth,
Through sunshine after rain.'
2 Samuel 23:4

Dripping off the eaves of the house in the early morning hours, the remains of a summer shower run off the roof. The eastern sky is beginning to brighten. Peeks of lavender and pink streaked with red and gray from the clouds. The promise of a new day. The offering laid out in a brilliant array. Sleep shaken off and replaced by an alert sense of renewal.

Preparing for a new day anticipating the activities to be as vivid as the colors in the morning sky. Looking ahead and not behind. I couldn't go back and change yesterday but today is here and now. A fresh start again.

The possibilities are endless. What will you choose?

Let's Pray

Holy Father, Your mercies are new every morning. Thank You for the rest of sleep. Thank You for renewing my energy. Help me to make holy choices today. Please find my offering of sacrifice pleasing and honoring. I am Yours. In Jesus' name. Amen.

Call to Action

Have you thanked God for your sleep? Have you given Him reign over your day? Write it out.

June 8

"I, the LORD, search the heart,
I test the mind,
Even to give to each man according to his ways,
According to the results of his deeds."
Jeremiah 17:10

You would not want to see behind the curtain I keep erected covering my heart. I wouldn't want you to see me back there. I may let you see glimpses but not all of me. There is some ugly stuff back there. To fully open the curtain or even tear it down completely would expose stuff that would embarrass me and appall you.

But God sees it all. There is no hiding what resides in the recesses of my heart. Yours too. He knows and sees everything there is to know about each one of us. He knows your junk and mine.

He is in the business of cleaning hearts and minds. He knows the world wants to infiltrate and fill all those recesses so there is no space left for Him. He is waiting for you to allow His cleaning service to enter in and remove all that junk for you.

Let's Pray

Holy Father, thank You for Your patience. Thank You for seeing all my junk and still loving me. I give You full access to my heart and mind. Mold me and make me new. In Jesus' name. Amen.

Call to Action

Here is a new daily practice for you. Give God your heart and mind each morning. Write it out.

June 9

Praise Him, sun and moon;
Praise Him, all stars of light!
Psalm 148:3

Each Sunday, I stand with many other people as we sing praises to God. I look around and see some thoroughly involved in praise as if no one else existed. I see some with heads bowed and eyes closed in quiet worship, softly singing their praise in prayer. I see some who look as if they dread even being in the place. I see some with blank stares.

All praise belongs to God. Praise is a verb. Physical or mental action may be present in praise. The sun shines brightly in praise. The moon reflects the sun's rays in praise. Stars shine in praise.

Do you sing praise? Do you bow low in praise? Do you lift your hands high in praise? Do you allow your mind and heart to be fully involved in praise?

Let's Pray

Holy Father, You alone are worthy of all praise. As I come to praise You, help me to place everything aside so that I can be attentive to You alone. May my praise be for You and not an obstacle for anyone else. Allow my posture to be evidence of my mind and heart toward You. What an honor to praise You! Thank You for this privilege. In Jesus' name. Amen.

Call to Action

Praising God can change your perspective. How do you praise Him? Write it out.

June 10

"You and your sons and your servants shall cultivate the land for him, and you shall bring in the produce so that your master's grandson may have food; nevertheless Mephibosheth your master's grandson shall eat at my table regularly." Now Ziba had fifteen sons and twenty servants.
2 Samuel 9:10

The goal of cultivating land isn't always just about the harvest. Sometimes the care it takes in cultivating develops relationships, bringing a long-lasting harvest in the form of life-time friendships. Shared work bringing shared food bringing shared lives.

Go to a local farm any day in June that offers fresh produce harvesting and you will find conversations down rows of beans and peas. Relationships in cultivation. The hunger for companionship and for food satisfied at one time.

Find a local farm. It may be a roadside stand. Strike up a conversation over a basket of tomatoes. You may find your new best friend.

Let's Pray

Holy Father, thank You for the fresh vegetables from gardens. Cultivate in our hearts and minds the willingness to share with others from the bounty you provide. In Jesus' name. Amen.

Call to Action

Farmers work hard to provide produce. Will you write a note of thanks today? Write it out.

June 11

Examine me, O LORD, and try me;
Test my mind and my heart.
Psalm 26:2

As I ask God to examine me, I begin to examine myself. Comparing me to God's Word instead of the world is the best way for this self-examination. God's Word gives me truth as my measuring stick. The world gives me lies.

Studying scripture to know how to measure properly is important. Like building a house or sewing a garment, you must know what the finished product should look like before beginning the work. Once you know what you are working toward, taking necessary action becomes easier.

God already knows what the finished product looks like. He has it all planned out. The execution will be precise. He knows the work it will take, and the tools needed to do the job.

To join Him in His work, open His Word and know His plan.

Let's Pray

Holy Father, show me the condition of my heart and mind considering Your precepts. Create in me a pure heart so that I can be used for Your glory. Equip me. In Jesus' name. Amen.

Call to Action

Is there something you need to work on? Or maybe you are working on it now. Write it out.

June 12

Yet, O LORD of hosts, You who test the righteous,
Who see the mind and the heart;
Let me see Your vengeance on them;
For to You I have set forth my cause.
Jeremiah 20:12

My anger wants to have its own vengeance. It boils up inside me to the point it wants to erupt with spewing lava. And it has at times. The eruptions vomited from my mouth with harsh words. But vengeance wasn't and isn't mine. My outbursts accomplished nothing but embarrassment.

No wonder embarrassment comes after moments of rage. The anger that boils up inside me may be a natural response to a situation but what I do with that anger will tell a story about where my mind and heart are set. My outbursts have not been righteous. My mind and heart always tell me so afterward.

The outbursts have lessened through the years. God gently interrupts the anger and reminds me that vengeance is His and I can turn over all that anger to Him. In gratitude, I trust Him with it.

Let's Pray

Holy Father, thank You for taking the anger I experience over hurtful situations into Your hands so that I can stay calm and trust You to take care of it all. In Jesus' name. Amen.

Call to Action

Road rage? Injustice? Insults? Betrayal? Do you need to give it to God? Write it out.

June 13

The refining pot is for silver and the furnace for gold,
But the LORD tests hearts.
Proverbs 17:3

Still dark outside. The kettle gets filled with water and placed on the stove. While it heats, I grab a mug and a tea bag. The tea bag is of no use to me without the hot water.

I pour steamy water over the tea bag inside my mug. Anticipating the warmth in my hands, I still must wait. Waiting for the water to pull all the flavor from the leaves inside the bag. Waiting for it to cool enough to take that first sip.

We go through heated situations and learn how to navigate steamy waters. We can either burst and spill all the tea leaves leaving a mess or we can allow the heat to refine us and allow a pleasant flavor to fill our life. God produces great tea!

Let's Pray

Holy Father, thank You for a warm mug of tea. Thank You for refining me and teaching me through tough times. Your favor is upon me and there are no words adequate to express my gratitude. I praise You. I love You, Lord. In Jesus' name. Amen.

Call to Action

Have you walked through a refining fire? Maybe you are walking through one right now. Will you ask God to show you His direction for you in it? What flavor will remain? Write it out.

June 14

The light is pleasant, and it is good for the eyes to see the sun.
Ecclesiastes 11:7

There is a window above my shower. If I time it right, sun pours through on my face as water streams down over me. I close my eyes and drink in the brightness. It is an instant mood booster. I could stand there until the hot water turns cold or until the sun is no longer on my face.

It reminds me of lying on the beach with the sun warming my skin. The pleasure of it slows my pounding heart and gives me room to breathe deeply. It refreshes my soul.

Have you stepped out into the sun lately for the sole purpose of refreshing your soul? Take time today to find a sunny window or go outside and enjoy the warmth of light. If it is cloudy, try again another day.

Let's Pray

Holy Father, thank You for the light of the sun. In the fullness of that light, everything else fades away. My focus shifts to You and the warmth You wrap me in when I stand there enjoying Your presence. Holy Father, wash me in Your light forever. Thank You for Your presence. Thank You for giving me that window. In Jesus' name. Amen.

Call to Action

How does sunshine make you feel when you consider it a gift from God? Write it out.

June 15

Beloved, do not believe every spirit, but test the spirits to see whether they are from God, because many false prophets have gone out into the world.
1 John 4:1

Eyes and ears wide open. It is pitch black. No amount of straining will produce vision until the switch is flipped, and light floods the space revealing obstacles. With a clear view, with light streaming all around, navigation becomes easier.

While it was still dark, imaginary images waiting to devour lurk about. Without light, you don't know what is right in front of you. Obstructions will trip you and cause you to fall.

God sheds light on the obstacles in your path. His Word charts the course for you to take. He gives you what you need to know to discern those things that will bring harm. Follow His path. Seek His light. Know His Word and carry it with you. Apply it to every situation.

Let's Pray

Holy Father, Your Word is a light unto my feet. Thank You for illuminating my path. Your direction sets me on the course that is right and good for me. Thank You for discernment. You are Lord of my life and will show me Your way. In Jesus' name. Amen.

Call to Action

Do you trust and know God's Word? Do you depend on it for direction? Write it out.

June 16

therefore the LORD God sent him out from the garden of Eden, to cultivate the ground from which he was taken.
Genesis 3:23

When I find myself overwhelmed with life, I need to get back to my roots. I don't want to be sent out of Eden the way Adam was, but I need to go back to simpler times. In my greenhouse, I can reset and find time to breathe.

Getting my hands dirty. Repotting. Clipping herbs. Checking on new growth. Looking for dead foliage to remove. Planting new seeds. Sweeping off the dirt on the potting table.

Sometimes my heart and mind need the same attention as my greenhouse. Allowing God to take the shears and the spade and trim and plant. In Him, I get fertilized. He cultivates the soil of my heart. He prepares me for His plans.

Let's Pray

Holy Father, I am Your vessel and willing for You to cultivate my life to be used for Your glory. Plant me where You desire. Prune me and water me. Grow me into a living, breathing witness for Your kingdom purposes. I love You, Lord. In Jesus' name. Amen.

Call to Action

Get your hands dirty. Connect with your roots. Express your heart to God. Write it out.

June 17

"Please test your servants for ten days, and let us be given some vegetables to eat and water to drink."
Daniel 1:12

Nutrition and exercise have become major economic industries. Google diet or exercise and you will find a plethora of information. Interestingly, they all claim to be the best. How can they all be the best? I am guilty of jumping on the bandwagon for some of these self-proclaimed best nutrition or exercise programs.

I am not an expert, but I do know that consistently eating healthy options and regular physical activity makes me feel better. I can have a better quality of life. When I break my consistency, it shows up in aches and pains and bad attitudes.

What works for you? Have you tested the best plans available only to find false advertising? Allow me to encourage you to ask God for guidance. Be intentional in making choices that honor Him. He has provided the best plan. Healthy food and hopefully a body that can still move.

Let's Pray

Holy Father, Your design of our physical bodies is amazing. Thank You. In Jesus' name. Amen.

Call to Action

Will you commit to eating healthy options and getting regular activity? Write it out.

June 18

"Bring the whole tithe into the storehouse, so that there may be food in My house, and test Me now in this," says the LORD of hosts, "if I will not open for you the windows of heaven and pour out for you a blessing until it overflows."
Malachi 3:10

I have witnessed testimonies of God's faithfulness both in my own life and the lives of others. Stories and experiences of God's provision at just the right time. Undeserved favor bestowed on unexpecting followers of Christ. Recipients humbled in gratitude for the overflow of His riches.

Imagine the windows of heaven pouring out blessings upon you. God's measure so abundant it overflows in your life so that it spills over onto others. His faithfulness perfectly placed on you.

Will you give back to God? Are you already giving back from the overflow? Maybe you think there isn't enough to go around. I have been there. You just can't spare any resources. Let me encourage you to understand all the resources you have belong to God. He has provided for you and desires your worshipful return to Him.

Let's Pray

Holy Father, help our unbelief. Strengthen our faith to be faithful to You in all things. You abundantly provide and call us to give back to You. Accept our offerings. In Jesus' name. Amen.

Call to Action

Your resources belong to God. How are you giving back for His kingdom? Write it out.

June 19

"He will sit as a smelter and purifier of silver, and He will purify the sons of Levi and refine them like gold and silver, so that they may present to the LORD offerings in righteousness."
Malachi 3:3

What does righteous offering look like to you? Is it given begrudgingly? Doubt filled offering is not righteous. A righteous offering is done from a pure heart. From one who has walked through the purification found in the blood of Jesus. Oh, that my offering be found pleasing to God!

Sometimes the refining is painful. Always humbling. Always compassionate. Never hopeless.

Ask God to refine you. Do not fear His purification process. His faithfulness to you will never leave you defeated and destroyed. He will never leave you. He will bring you through the fire.

Let's Pray

Holy Father, continue to refine me. The dross in my life is still being uncovered and removed. God, Your love for me brings me through the refining fire. With care and precision, You examine me. Your exacting eye plucks the junk out of me. Thank You for Your tenderness. Thank You for Your compassion. I am Your vessel. Use me for Your purpose. In Jesus' name. Amen.

Call to Action

Have you had any junk removed lately from your life? What happened? What fruitfulness came from God's purification process in your life? Are you giving Him thanksgiving? Write it out.

June 20

"Then THE RIGHTEOUS WILL SHINE FORTH AS THE SUN in the kingdom of their Father. He who has ears, let him hear."
Matthew 13:43

Your radiance is striking. Your head held high in confidence. That slight smile on your face like you have a secret you would love to share. Your heart about to burst open from sitting in the presence of God. His righteousness poured out on you has left you basking in His glory.

You listen to His voice. He whispers sweet notes of love and tenderness in your ear. You are the apple of His eye, and He lavishes you with His love. His words are sweeter than honey.

You recline into Him. Releasing all tension. He carries the weight of you with ease. Everything You give to Him, He takes. He won't put it back on you. Leave it with Him.

Let's Pray

Holy Father, Your strength is perfect in my weakness. I can't carry the weight, but You can. I lay my burdens down at Your feet and leave them there. Your righteousness sets things right in me. You will not forsake me or leave me. You hold me closely in Your loving embrace. I want to stay here. I want to inhale Your fragrance. I love You, Lord. In Jesus' name. Amen.

Call to Action

Sit with Him a while longer. Tell Him you love Him. Listen to what He tells you. Write it out.

June 21

Test yourselves to see if you are in the faith; examine yourselves! Or do you not recognize this about yourselves, that Jesus Christ is in you-unless indeed you fail the test?
2 Corinthians 13:5

The most difficult test to face is the test you fail in the face of faith in Christ. Realization of that magnitude of failure is catastrophic. Knowing the passage of that test is the singular path to eternal salvation and knowing failure of the same shakes the earth under your feet.

Perhaps that is the very moment faith meets the sinner on their knees. The moment of utter failure cripples the throat of sobs of conviction. Heart-gripping surrender, throwing all the repressed condemnation at the foot of the cross, at the feet of Jesus.

And He, in His infinite love, reaches down and touches your face, raises you to your feet, searches your eyes for the repentance dripping down your nose and He wipes it all away. All the transgressions piled up pouring from the guttural groanings. He marks the test passing.

Let's Pray

Holy Father, Your forgiveness is all I need. For the sin that comes so naturally, I ask Your forgiveness. Repulse me from it to keep me from it. Thank You, Lord. In Jesus' name. Amen.

Call to Action

It is hard to express those groanings. The Holy Spirit intercedes. Know Him. Write it out.

June 22

May his name endure forever;
May his name increase as long as the sun shines;
And let men bless themselves by him;
Let all nations call him blessed.
Psalm 72:17

Stop and think about how your name will be remembered. We don't always go around speaking eulogies before they are needed. What if we did? Would it sound like empty flattery instead of gut-honest truth? Or would we have honest assessments that encouraged us to improve?

Do you have friends and family that can give you an honest assessment that is free of condemnation or vain flattering? How well can you make a self-assessment? Sometimes we can't see ourselves through honest lens because we have believed lies about ourselves for so long.

You are loved. You are chosen. You have the exact attributes God needs for you to have. He has great plans to bless you. He will accomplish His purpose for you.

Let's Pray

Holy Father, thank You for seeing who we really are and still loving us. In the depravity of my sin, You chose me. You called me by name; poured Your favor out on me. Help me to walk in a manner worthy of You and to have my name associated with only You. In Jesus' name. Amen.

Call to Action

What would your eulogy sound like today? What do you want it to sound like? Write it out.

June 23

"Now therefore why do you put God to the test by placing upon the neck of the disciples a yoke which neither our fathers nor we have been able to bear?"
Acts 15:10

A trusted mentor would ask others not to place her on a pedestal. She didn't want to fall off. Placing another on an elevated status will eventually bring pain to the one up high and disappointment to the ones below.

All people need the grace and mercy of the Lord Jesus Christ. No one has achieved a status superior to that need. No act of physical or mental exertion can bring on exemption from needing His gifts. It is a need, a want, an innate desire to dwell with our Creator. No one is above Him.

To attempt a higher status is futile. Customs and traditions do not create the grace and mercy found in Him. Only minds and hearts fully surrendered to His Lordship, with Him high and lifted, find the peace of everlasting love.

Let's Pray

Holy Father, You are high and lifted above us all. Keep us in right relationship with You and others. Help us to consider others according to Your command. In Jesus' name. Amen.

Call to Action

Ask God to show you if you place people into classifications. Talk with Him. Write it out.

June 24

The bellows blow fiercely,
The lead is consumed by the fire;
In vain the refining goes on,
But the wicked are not separated.
Jeremiah 6:29

The cycle seems to never end. Like the Israelites wandering around a desert for forty years, the cycle of rebellion and turning back to God in the face of His wrath and then returning to rebellion. We are just like the Israelites wandering around a desert. Like playing cat and mouse with God. The Israelites eventually came to the Jordan. But the rebellion didn't stop there.

If you and I could sit down to chat, we could share cycles of our own. We could look back and see our repeated offenses and reconciliation. Then we could recount the cycle recurring. Are you tired of the cycle? Are you ready to break it and find the path God made for you?

It ends here. If you are ready to jump off the wheel that is making you dizzy and exhausted, you can end that vicious cycle now. Will you drop to your knees and ask God to navigate you through breaking the cycle of sin that keeps you spinning in the opposite direction of Him?

Let's Pray

Holy Father, You are our way off the cycle of sin. Remove it from us. In Jesus' name. Amen.

Call to Action

God is waiting to give you freedom. Will you accept His offer? Write it out.

June 25

From the rising of the sun to its setting
The name of the LORD is to be praised.
Psalm 113:3

Outside my window the sky is brightening. Clouds streak in purple and grays with highlights of cotton candy pink. Day is dawning. God's mercies are new. His provisions are waiting for me to claim. He knows what I will face today and has already orchestrated what I will need.

So, this morning I praise Him. I praise Him for His sovereignty. I praise Him for the work He completed on the cross. I praise Him for the colors I see painted in the sky. I praise Him for the voices of birds singing melodies of praise and add mine to their selection.

I raise my cup and sip the warmth while my hands grip the comfort of its shape. I drink in the blessings He is giving me at this moment. I thank Him for what has been and for what will be. In humility, I ask for continued provisions and direction.

Let's Pray

Holy Father, all praise to You. Your mercies are fresh for the taking this morning. I accept them in gratitude for them. You alone are worthy of all praise. Thank You for a new day and new opportunities to share You with others. In Jesus' name. Amen.

Call to Action

What is your song of praise today? Sing it aloud to God. Write it out.

June 26

each man's work will become evident; for the day will show it because it is to be revealed with fire, and the fire itself will test the quality of each man's work.
1 Corinthians 3:13

The day started early, long before those cotton candy streaks began to appear. It felt good to be up and starting the day fresh, refreshed. New mercies met me in the early dark hours. More refreshing to be found in those early moments. Gratitude poured out on the Source.

But before too many moments had passed, the attacks began during the workday. An onslaught of arrows pointed straight in my direction. Each time I began to reflect on that early refreshing refresh the attacks became more intense. But the work stayed steady. Productivity unwavering.

Without those early morning moments, the time under attack may have looked different. Facing a barrage of arrows could have led me to faulter on the work at hand. But they didn't. Pressing on in the face of adversity is the only thing to do after a morning of praise.

Let's Pray

Holy Father, thank You for remaining steadfast as my strength and armor during attacks. You are my shield and refuge in the storm. You shelter me. Thank You for You. In Jesus' name. Amen.

Call to Action

After sitting on a mountaintop, do you come down and get attacked? Write it out.

June 27

"Simon, Simon, behold, Satan has demanded permission to sift you like wheat;"
Luke 22:31

He was warned. He was given the very word that attack was coming. Jesus told him. Peter should have been on the alert for what was coming. Maybe he was more focused on strengthening his brothers after the fact and gave little thought to the sifting. Read the rest of Luke 22 to see what happens.

I don't get that kind of warning. Do you? Do you always know when the sifting is about to come? Do you know when the enemy is about to attack?

I suppose we do know. If we are children of the Most High, then we should expect major assaults at frequent intervals, sometimes without a break. Count it all joy my brothers and sisters!

Let's Pray

Holy Father, Your Word gives us hope to know that in the middle of every assault is the victory that was won by Jesus Christ. The enemy was defeated, and Jesus sits triumphal over the grave. You allowed Peter to continue in Your service, and we ask to be able to do the same. Allow us to strengthen and encourage others in our walk with You. In Jesus' name. Amen.

Call to Action

Sifting is hard. Have you been there? Are you there now? Write it out.

June 28

He made the moon for the seasons;
The sun knows the place of its setting.
Psalm 104:19

According to our calendar, it is summer. In the southern hemisphere it is winter. We are almost halfway through this calendar year. Midway. What season are you in right now? How would you describe it?

This season finds me with three grown children. One, married with two children. One, about to get married this fall. One, just graduated high school. I have an accounting business that keeps me busy. My husband teaches and works in real estate. We are busy. Oh, and I am writing this.

God has been faithful to us throughout our thirty-five years of marriage. He knew what we didn't. He had our seasons planned out. He has orchestrated a full life. He knows the remainder of our days and I trust He will continue to be faithful.

Let's Pray

Holy Father, You are worthy of all trust. You have proven Your faithfulness to me through so many seasons of life. Thank You for Your constant presence even when I wasn't aware of You being there. Keep me fully aware now and in the future. In Jesus' name. Amen.

Call to Action

How have your seasons of life been? Can you trace the hand of God in them? Write it out.

June 29

"You shall not put the LORD your God to the test, as you tested Him at Massah."
Deuteronomy 6:16

I must admit my faith has wavered countless times. I am no different than the Israelites when they were in the desert facing thirst. In the heat of struggles, I have tried to do things my way eventually falling flat and being left with a mess. When, if I would have followed God, the outcome could have been different. But I won't know now. Because of my impatience.

God reminds me when I fail to listen to Him. When I fail to wait in patience for the blessing He wants to give me, I begin grumbling and searching for my own solution. My solutions fall miserably short of what God can do. Instead of impatience, He desires for me to wait for Him.

I always love seeing His outcomes. I am still learning to wait for Him. Still learning that my rushed, chaotic pushing is doing nothing but bringing me stress. My nagging becomes irritating to me. I imagine it is to God, too.

Let's Pray

Holy Father, please forgive my nagging. Forgive my doubt. I trust You. You are faithful. Thank You for Your patience with me. I love You, Lord. In Jesus' name. Amen.

Call to Action

Do you ever hear yourself nagging, repulsed by your own voice? Write it out.

June 30

Then the LORD said to Moses, "Behold, I will rain bread from heaven for you; and the people shall go out and gather a day's portion every day, that I may test them, whether or not they will walk in My instruction."
Exodus 16:4

I slept soundly last night with no hunger pains. There is food waiting for me to eat this morning. I am not fearful of going without. I am blessed to have provisions available to me. Are you?

If you are reading this, I would like to think that you have the same abundance of food that I have. I pray you have used the resources God has provided to prioritize accordingly. I would certainly not want you to choose a book over food. But thank you for reading this book.

The provisions we have today may look different than those given to the Israelites, but they are still provisions from God. He still provides today. Will you take time to thank Him for all He provides for you and your family?

Let's Pray

Holy Father, You are faithful to provide for my every need. I have a roof over my head. I am clothed in comfort. My waistline is proof that I have more than enough food. My comforts are exceedingly beyond what I deserve. Thank You, Lord. In Jesus' name. Amen.

Call to Action

It may seem simple but think of the extravagance in your life. Are you thankful? Write it out.

"For he will be like a tree
planted by the water,
That extends its roots by a
stream
And will not fear when the
heat comes;
But its leaves will be green,
And it will not be anxious in
a year of drought
Nor cease to yield fruit."
Jeremiah 17:8

July

"For he will be like a tree planted by the water,
That extends its roots by a stream
And will not fear when the heat comes;
But its leaves will be green,
And it will not be anxious in a year of drought
Nor cease to yield fruit."
Jeremiah 17:8

The dark waters of the Suwannee River in North Florida look like coffee running from the Okefenokee Swamp to the Gulf of America. Lining the river are majestic trees hugging the bank reaching out over the river with Spanish moss dripping from heavy limbs. Kayaking the river transports you to another world where cell phones and laptops aren't welcome.

The swirling dark water is fed by ice cold springs along the route. In the summertime heat plunging into that dark water cools the skin if you are brave enough to dive in. High bluffs provide a challenging jump for those wanting the thrill of danger.

Those trees stand firm along the bank trusting the water to provide for their deep roots. Floods threaten some of the weaker trees, but the largest trees hold tight. There is a codependence between those trees and that river. The river gives the trees water while the trees line the route to contain the river. Without the river, the trees dry up. Without the trees the river knocks down the banks and changes the landscape.

God provides us markers along the path we follow. Like the trees lining the banks of the river, those markers keep us on the path God has laid out for us. His moving and working in us keeps us moving to the finish line like the river's current moving to its destination.

Are you standing firm, depending on God in your every move?

July 1

So then it does not depend on the man who wills or the man who runs, but on God who has mercy.
Romans 9:16

The words were harsh and hit with such force it felt like someone had hit me in the stomach and knocked the wind out of me. Looking back, I still don't understand what happened, but I learned a hard lesson about people. Given certain conditions anyone can turn mean.

Mercy was not offered. No explanation could suffice to calm the voice on the other end of the phone. My words were not welcomed. My point of view was not wanted. Exacting rage was all the caller wanted to pour out on me. Nothing else.

Even after apologies were offered, no extension of mercy was made, and no forgiveness was given. I don't know why I still carry the scars, but I do. They remind me that God's mercy is perfect even when the world around us has none.

Let's Pray

Holy Father, thank You for Your endless mercy. Help us to extend this priceless gift to others even when it hurts us to do so. God, help us to be merciful. In Jesus' name. Amen.

Call to Action

Do you find it difficult or easy to extend mercy to others? Write it out.

July 2

However, in the Lord, neither is woman independent of man, nor is man independent of woman.
1 Corinthians 11:11

God's design is good. He made Adam and breathed life into him. He made Eve from the rib of Adam. In creating Eve, He designed her to birth more of His good creation when the two came together as one. A masterpiece designed by the Master.

Man does not exist without woman and woman does not exist without man. Neither exists without God. Adam was God's creation setting into place the cycle of life. All the inhabitants of this planet exist because of God's initial creation from the dust and breath of life.

Adam was the first but needed a helper to continue the work God began in him. Eve was designed to accept from Adam a seed of life. Her body was fashioned to nurture and grow life. Two parts. One design. The fruit of God, multiplied.

Let's Pray

Holy Father, Your creation is amazing. In birthing three of my own children, each one miraculous in design because of Your masterful touch. Oh, God, did You feel the same way I felt when they were born? In awe of the life before me. Thank You, Lord. In Jesus' name. Amen.

Call to Action

Consider God's master design of you. Thank Him for the miracle of life. Write it out.

July 3

Who will stand up for me against evildoers?
Who will take his stand for me against those who do wickedness?
Psalm 94:16

It will come. It probably already has. You will feel the sting and realize there was nothing you could do to change it. It happened and now the gaping hole in your heart is left oozing in pain from the evil that pierced it. There is only one suitable solution to heal the wound. God.

He is the only One that can heal the wound. He is the only One that can stand in the gap between you and evil. He is the only One that can protect you from future attacks.

When faced with insurmountable evil, look full into the face of God. Open His Word and your heart to receive the peace that only He gives. You are not owned by evil. Evil has no rights over you. You are a child of God. Highly favored and loved by your Lord.

Let's Pray

Holy Father, protect us from evil. Stand in the gap for us and shelter us. Remind us to wear Your armor. God, when evil slips in and penetrates our lives, heal us. Wrap us tightly in the bandage of You. Soothe our hurts so that we can help others and not hurt them. In Jesus' name. Amen.

Call to Action

Are you carrying a hurt too deep for words? Will you give it to God? Write it out.

July 4

Who are you to judge the servant of another? To his own master he stands or falls; and he will stand, for the Lord is able to make him stand.
Romans 14:4

Tend to your own business and you won't be tempted to tend to someone else's. Sounds like a grandmother proverb. Stay in your own lane. Keep your opinions to yourself. If you don't have anything nice to say, don't say anything at all. Have we all heard these things? Maybe our mama or grandma knew what God's Word said about being judgmental busy bodies.

When we judge others, we set the bar for our own judgment. Creating the standard for which we will be judged. Setting up the lens of scrutiny that will magnify all our own failures.

Flip the lens. Allow God to shift your perspective so that you understand His compassion is the same for others as it is for you. Ask Him to mold your heart into the shape of compassion.

Let's Pray

Holy Father, Your compassion is far greater than I can imagine. You will make us stand in the middle of our failures. You brush us off and set us upright to move forward in grace and mercy. Thank You, Lord for Your abundant patience and compassion. In Jesus' name. Amen.

Call to Action

Do you wear judgmental lenses? Ask God to remove them. Write it out.

July 5

If You, LORD, should mark iniquities,
O Lord , who could stand?
Psalm 130:3

They pile up so quickly I feel like I need to beg forgiveness constantly. Absentmindedly ignoring the presence of my Lord, I fall into a pit. One slip of the tongue plunges me down. The weight gets heavier until I look up to the hand that is extended to bring me back out of the pit.

He is always there. Always with hand extended, arms open wide, waiting for me to return to His loving embrace. He welcomes me back, steadying my feet on the rock of His salvation. He even offers to fill in the pit, so I don't fall again.

I don't always let Him fill in my pits. Left open, they stay and grow larger making it easier to fall again. They make a muddy mess of me. But when He fills them in, I stand on level ground that is solid and firm. He may even add some fragrant flowers for me to enjoy!

Let's Pray

Holy Father, hold my hand so I don't fall. Please forgive me for returning to those pits. Fill them for good and allow me to enjoy the work of Your hands. Keep reminding me to hold on to You so I stay out of new pits. Thank You, Lord. In Jesus' name. Amen.

Call to Action

Ask God to fill in the pits you keep falling into. Tell Him your favorite flower. Write it out.

July 6

"If a kingdom is divided against itself, that kingdom cannot stand."
Mark 3:24

What images or situations come to your mind when you think about Mark 3:24? Without reading the context you still get the message. Inner turmoil and adversity left unresolved will bring the institution crumbling down. It happens in marriages, churches, businesses, and the list continues.

Resolution takes work. Reconciliation is humbling. Neither can happen without all parties participating in the process. One left dangling outside the process will stir dissention.

When everyone comes together to seek God's will through the process a beautiful thing happens. Harmony and unity replace turmoil and division. Common ground is found at the foot of the cross. Finding fellowship and friendship with fellow followers.

Let's Pray

Holy Father, reconciliation is sometimes hard to accomplish. Without You, we are unable to successfully reconcile our hearts and thoughts with others. You give us everything we need to initiate strands of unity. Help us to be agents of harmony. In Jesus' name. Amen.

Call to Action

Is there a situation that needs your efforts toward reconciliation? Will you ask God to give you the wisdom and knowledge to initiate that work? Write it out.

July 7

for now we really live, if you stand firm in the Lord.
1 Thessalonians 3:8

Today is the anniversary of a dear servant of God going home. His sixty plus years of ministry in the kingdom of God through the people he served testified at his celebration of life. He exhibited the love of Christ during his years on earth and wanted everyone to know the same.

The family shared a video of him speaking to their family during a vacation just a few years ago. His voice strong and clear as it always was, encouraging his family to enjoy the beauty God has created while they know Him as Lord and Savior. His concern was for his family to know God.

His legacy lives on in the lives that he shepherded. Those that he led to faith and encouraged in their walk with the Lord, can stand firm in the Lord because of the work God gave him to do. I am blessed to have known him and to witness the life he lived and the lives he touched.

Let's Pray

Holy Father, it is all for Your glory that Your servants do Your kingdom work. God, the joy we know in carrying out the call You placed in us causes us to exult in You. Thank You for the life of this dear one that now worships at Your feet. Let us follow his example. In Jesus' name. Amen.

Call to Action

Who has touched your life so deeply? Does it make you want to help others? Write it out.

July 8

And He said to him, "Stand up and go; your faith has made you well."
Luke 17:19

Whether on this side of eternity or the next, God is faithful to heal our infirmities. These temporary bodies we carry here on earth will break down and begin to decay but our souls are eternal. What are you doing to take care of your soul?

We eat and exercise and groom to care for our temporary bodies and become so consumed with them that sometimes we forget about the eternal condition of our essence. God cares about both, but He wants your soul and body to be devoted to Him. Allow God to lead your soul so that your body is in His service during the vapor of life you have it.

When your soul is well, there is peace that passes all understanding. My favorite hymn, "It Is Well," describes it perfectly. No matter what this world throws my way I can stand firm in saying "It is well, it is well with my soul!"

Let's Pray

Holy Father, I worship You. Your love reaches into my soul and holds it firmly. You hold me firmly. I can stand firm in faith because of Your great love. In Jesus' name. Amen.

Call to Action

Google the lyrics for "It Is Well." Let them soak into your soul. Write it out.

July 9

Many plans are in a man's heart,
But the counsel of the LORD will stand.
Proverbs 19:21

So much to do and so little time to do it. My to-do list grows every day. There is always an abundance of stuff to do. Sometimes I don't know what to do next. I get anxious just thinking about it. My palms get sweaty, and I feel the tension in my neck tightening.

That list is a self-imposed trap. It becomes a ball and chain that imprisons me in a hamster wheel. I jump into that spinning wheel and run as hard as I can and not get anywhere at all. Futility at its finest. Am I the only one here? Can I get a witness? Please help a girl out!

But praise God that He pulls me out of that wheel. He whispers in my ear that I don't have to be a slave to my to-do list, especially if my plans have not considered His counsel. The weight of that list lessens when I sit with Him seeking direction.

Let's Pray

Holy Father, clear my mind and heart of all the junk that steals my time with You. Keep me alert and aware of Your presence in all things. God, as I begin my day keep me close to You. Let me find joy in marking off that list. But let that joy come from You. In Jesus' name. Amen.

Call to Action

Take your to-do list and write God's name on the top. Make it His. Write it out.

July 10

God takes His stand in His own congregation;
He judges in the midst of the rulers.
Psalm 82:1

Supreme and Sovereign God stands in our midst. There is nowhere you can go to avoid Him. Does that thought evoke excitement or fear? Ask me that question at different times and I will give you different answers. It all depends on the condition of my heart at that moment.

Right now, it excites me to know God is right here with me. He covers the pages of this book as I type. The world temporarily disappears while I am immersed in these pages and praying for you as I type. God is here. He prompts me. He comforts me. He is my confidence.

There is no greater joy than to know that He is with you. With Him you can be assured that nothing will separate you from Him. You can know the security of His salvation and rest easily. He is faithful to never forsake you.

Let's Pray

Holy Father, thank You for the joy You share with me. Your kindness to me far surpasses anything I deserve. But You still give it to me despite my failures. Thank You, Lord, for Your unending mercy. Allow the words in this book to encourage others. In Jesus' name. Amen.

Call to Action

Your turn. Excitement or fear in His presence? Work that out with Him. Write it out.

July 11

The wicked are overthrown and are no more,
But the house of the righteous will stand.
Proverbs 12:7

We all love movies that depict good winning over evil. Our heart cry is for good to win every time. But real life doesn't always look that way. Sometimes it feels like evil wins. Sometimes innocent people are harmed, and it doesn't leave us with that warm fuzzy the way movies do.

I have good news for you. Evil never wins in the life of a child of God. The cross defeated all evil and left behind the promise of victorious living for those that choose that path. Situations may not leave you with that warm fuzzy, but you can be assured good has triumphed over evil.

Go back and read that line again. Or better yet, let me give it to you again because you need to get this in your brain and heart. The cross defeated all evil and left behind the promise of victorious living for those that choose that path. If you have chosen that path, go live in victory.

Let's Pray

Holy Father, our victory over evil is wrapped up in Jesus Christ. Hallelujah and Amen! Jesus defeated the grave so we can live victoriously with You. Thank You! God, we need Your constant presence to remind us of this fact. Keep it in front of our faces. In Jesus' name. Amen.

Call to Action

I want to shout a word of praise! How about you? As you do, write it out.

July 12

Be on the alert, stand firm in the faith, act like men, be strong.
1 Corinthians 16:13

He wasn't expecting a snake on the steps leading down off the back porch. He stepped over it, unsure of what it was. It was small, but still a snake. Markings indicated danger so he called our son to bring a hoe, and the snake was taken care of. The uncertainty of more baby snakes nearby lingered for days as we used those steps.

We were on alert. The threat of danger keeps your awareness heightened. Not knowing what is lurking in the grass on either side of the sidewalk or in the flower bed caused us to be watchful.

Sin lurks about waiting for unsuspecting prey. Lowering your awareness presents the opportunity for it to slip in and bite. Instead, our faith can stand firm in the strength of our Lord. He will keep you upright and protected when you keep your eyes on Him.

Let's Pray

Holy Father, thank You for Your protection over my husband. God, guard our minds and hearts and keep us standing firm in faith so that we find strength in You. In Jesus' name. Amen.

Call to Action

We suspect he had been bitten by a non-venomous snake weeks before this incident in the garden. What steps do you take to stay alert to predators? Write it out.

July 13

Stand firm therefore, HAVING GIRDED YOUR LOINS WITH TRUTH, and HAVING PUT ON THE BREASTPLATE OF RIGHTEOUSNESS,
Ephesians 6:14

The father of lies has no right infiltrating your thoughts. But he tries and for me he has succeeded more times than I can say, unfortunately. When planted, they grow big and multiply. Left unchecked, their grip tightens and suffocates life out of me.

They play on repeat in my brain keeping me from walking in the truth that God has given me. I return to scripture once I realize they have been playing for too long and remember they have no place in me. I must change the tune. I play something different, replacing lies with truth.

Staying rooted and grounded in God's Word eliminates the lies. Standing firm in His truth, the Word of God, sheds light on those dark places so I can navigate away from them. The truth is where righteousness resides. That is where I want to be.

Let's Pray

Holy Father, You know how prone I am to wander away from Your truth. My heart is weak, and I desperately need Your breastplate of righteousness to protect it. Help me. In Jesus' name. Amen.

Call to Action

Are you prone to wander? Will you take up the armor of God to stand firm? Write it out.

July 14

You, even You, are to be feared;
And who may stand in Your presence when once You are angry?
Psalm 76:7

Read the Old Testament and you will find examples of the anger of God. His anger is righteous and holy. It brings me both pain and satisfaction in knowing that God exacts justice. Hear me out! There are people you and I know that will never come to salvation in Christ.

God is holy. He is patient. He is just. His love covers all sins except unrepented sin. Keeping sin for yourself and not separating from it ignores the blood of Jesus, making His perfect sacrifice invalid in your life. Ouch! You can't be covered by His blood when you hold tightly to sin.

Let it go. Avoid the wrath of God. He loves you so much that He freely gave His Son to take the wrath you deserve. Jesus accepted God's anger in your place. The price has been paid. The sacrifice completed the atonement on your behalf. Sin is not worth holding on to.

Let's Pray

Holy Father, the blood of Jesus is on my hands. In my sin, I am His murderer. Please forgive me. Remove this guilt from me and allow me to walk in the Light. Your grace and mercy abound. Thank You for lifting the weight of Your anger off me. I love You, Lord. In Jesus' name. Amen.

Call to Action

Are you holding on to sin that you need to get rid of? Will you do it now? Write it out.

July 15

Let all the earth fear the LORD;
Let all the inhabitants of the world stand in awe of Him.
Psalm 33:8

God's awesome love surrounds me. He fills me so that I overflow as He pours into me allowing me to pour into you. And to think of you being filled to overflow with His goodness so you can pour into others is all due to His wonderful love. I worship Him!

Behold the goodness of God. Take on your posture of praise and worship Him. Stand with arms high and head looking to the heavens. Prostrate yourself face down on the floor in humble praise. Kneel at His feet. Whatever posture you find. place your thoughts and heart fully on Him.

Now rest in His presence. Give Him all your burdens. He is more than capable of handling whatever it is you give to Him. And leave them with Him. Don't take them back when you get up from your posture of praise. He's got them. You are a warrior, not a worrier.

Let's Pray

Holy Father, I look forward to the day when all I do is worship You. God, this world tries to steal my worship, and I don't want it to. God, protect my mind and heart so that I can live fully aware of Your presence and make my life acceptable worship to You. In Jesus' name. Amen.

Call to Action

What is your posture of praise? Where do you find connection with God? Write it out.

July 16

Quite right, they were broken off for their unbelief, but you stand by your faith. Do not be conceited, but fear;
Romans 11:20

Mocking and spitting. The very people of the same faith. Throwing insults and accusations. Unaware of the tragedy they were sealing for themselves. Spewing hate at the One that had come for their redemption. Family and friends.

An outsider. No common connection. An extraordinary one. Connected by the scarlet ribbon of blood streaming down the rough wood. Dipping the bread in the puddle, laying in the dirt. Crouching low with head bowed. Shoulders shuddering with sobs for the King hanging above.

I am adopted into the family of God. He accepted me, an outsider, into the family tree. Others may have been removed for me to be added. Others, not willing to recognize the King. I didn't belong before, but I do now. I am a child of the Most High. I am a member of the family.

Let's Pray

Holy Father, I am humbled that You would choose me. That You made a way for me to become Your child. That You accept me into Your family. Thank You, Lord. In Jesus' name. Amen.

Call to Action

Are you a member of the family? Does the thought of it humble you? Write it out.

July 17

Put on the full armor of God, so that you will be able to stand firm against the schemes of the devil.
Ephesians 6:11

Years ago, I took part in a women's conference at our church with the theme surrounding the armor of God. A talented woman made banners depicting the pieces of armor described in Ephesians 6. Still hanging, they are beautiful visual reminders to armor up.

That armor covers it all. Protects a believer from the assault of the enemy. Leaving any off leaves room for fiery arrows to slip in and do damage, knocking us off balance. Keeping it securely in place keeps us standing firm. Ready and able for the attacks of the enemy.

Go read Ephesians 6:10-17. Make a list of the armor and write out how you use each piece mentioned. Keep your list handy as a reminder to stand firm with God's armor in full battle array. Kept in place His armor is impenetrable.

Let's Pray

Holy Father, You leave no gaps in Your armor. When the enemy finds an opening, it is because we have allowed space for his attack. Forgive us and close the gap. In Jesus' name. Amen.

Call to Action

Did you make that list? If not, do so now. Embellish it and keep it handy. Write it out.

July 18

Therefore, my beloved brethren whom I long to see, my joy and crown, in this way stand firm in the Lord, my beloved.
Philippians 4:1

He would load up the lawn mower on the back of his truck and ride down the dirt road in front of our house. We were young and didn't have much, but he could do this. He could give this. His time and effort on behalf of an elderly lady halfway down that road.

An example of brotherly love. Of having a desire to help someone in need. The needs may look different but recognizing them and taking action to lend a hand is what love looks like. Reaching out, unasked, with nothing expected in return and doing what needs to be done.

Standing unafraid to continue doing what is right and good. Not concerned about what anyone else is doing or saying but picking up the tools and going to work for a brother or sister. In humility, bowing low to give of yourself to another person. Acts of kindness equals love.

Let's Pray

Holy Father, bless the work that we find to do. Help us keep our eyes open for needs that You equip us to meet. Then allow the work to bring You honor and glory. In Jesus' name. Amen.

Call to Action

Is God calling you to reach out to help someone in need? Write it out.

July 19

Now to Him who is able to keep you from stumbling, and to make you stand in the presence of His glory blameless with great joy,
Jude 1:24

Eyes on Him. Intentional focus placed on the presence of the One who will guide your steps. Moving in His direction. Trusting He already knows what is ahead. Follow Him. He will clear the path of obstacles as you go. You may not see it now, but He will prepare the path.

Great joy is found in the journey with Him. Unspeakable joy rising up in your chest that has no words to explain the exultation you feel as He takes you by the hand and leads you. His radiance lights the way. His glory makes you blameless. In awe, you stand amazed by Him.

Your feet are securely set. Knees slightly bent but firm and strong. Hips squarely under shoulders and directly over feet. Core held tight holding the torso upright. Shoulders down and back. Hands ready to do the work. Face fully exposed to the glory ready to accept His assignment.

Let's Pray

Holy Father, we are ready for Your direction. Ready to do the work You have for us. Lead us and give us discernment to accomplish that which You have set before us. In Jesus' name. Amen.

Call to Action

How does your posture of work look different than your posture of praise? Write it out.

July 20

"Whenever you stand praying, forgive, if you have anything against anyone, so that your Father who is in heaven will also forgive you your transgressions."
Mark 11:25

They don't deserve my forgiveness. They certainly didn't ask for it. What they did was uncalled for. It shook my world, and I am still feeling the hurt. I refuse to forgive them. I hope I don't ever see them again. They are dead to me. I am done with them. Wasting no more time on them.

Have you felt this? Have you said this? Did reading it begin to build a wall in your heart? It did mine. I could feel the resentment building. Like an infected cut oozing pus. Like turning my back on God and telling Him that His forgiveness of me isn't wanted. Oh, the pain that inflicts!

No forgiveness is deserved. The nature of forgiveness is grace. It is an unmerited favor. It is laying aside your hurt because you don't want to carry it any longer and saying I forgive you. The two-ton weight on your chest lifts. Forgiveness restores righteousness.

Let's Pray

Holy Father, Your forgiveness is undeserved. But I need it. I also need to forgive others. I need to accept others' forgiveness for me. Thank You for Your forgiveness. In Jesus' name. Amen.

Call to Action

Who do you need to forgive? Remove that weight from you. Write it out.

July 21

Therefore, take up the full armor of God, so that you will be able to resist in the evil day, and having done everything, to stand firm.
Ephesians 6:13

Take it up every day. Before you even get out of bed, get dressed in the armor of God. Sounds odd, I know. How do you get dressed before you get out of bed? God will dress you. He will clothe you in the finest garments as you seek Him in prayer. He knows what you need.

The raiment is made with love. The finest stitches of faith. Fabric woven with truth. Kindness shapes the garment. The aroma of hope filling your senses. Dressed by your Designer all before rising to start your day. Assured He will be with you no matter what you face.

When you start to feel like the garment is getting wrinkled or dirty, stop what you are doing and refocus on Him. Ask Him to iron the wrinkles and wash the dirt. You carry the best dry cleaner with you everywhere you go. He takes joy in keeping you clean.

Let's Pray

Holy Father, place your armor on me. Clothe me in Your righteousness. Keep my wardrobe fresh. Help me to wear it in a manner worthy of Your name. In Jesus' name. Amen.

Call to Action

Will you ask God to clothe you in His armor? He will if you ask. Write it out.

July 22

For a day in Your courts is better than a thousand outside.
I would rather stand at the threshold of the house of my God
Than dwell in the tents of wickedness.
Psalm 84:10

Can I make a confession to you? Promise to keep it between us? I don't want to go to work today. I want to stay right here. On this page. In this book. Thinking of how God blesses you. Thanking Him for blessing me. But wait! He will be with me as I go into my office. So, I will get up from this space and go to work, knowing His presence remains with me.

Can you relate? It isn't laziness that brings this desire but a desire to dwell in His presence. Stepping away from this space introduces a myriad of things that attempt to take my eyes off Him. Demands of the day are waiting to steal my attention and joy. Makes this time much more important. This is my preparation to face whatever comes my way.

Clothed in His righteousness, I stand before His throne. Submitted to His will for this day.

Let's Pray

Holy Father, this is Your day. I submit to You in my work. Bless it. Allow it to bless others. Help me keep my eyes on You. Remove obstacles. I love You, Lord. In Jesus' name. Amen.

Call to Action

How will you stay in His presence today? Commit to that plan. Write it out.

July 23

'Behold, I stand at the door and knock; if anyone hears My voice and opens the door, I will come in to him and will dine with him, and he with Me.'
Revelation 3:20

Come in, Lord Jesus. My door is open to You. Come in and dine with me. Sit at the head of my table and let's feast on time together. Your Word is sweeter than a honeycomb. It satisfies my hunger. Your presence fills me. My cup overflows with Your goodness.

The table is set. The lights are on. Your seat is here and ready for You. You alone hold the place of honor at my table. This is Your house. Come claim Your place here in this space. We are just caretakers. Find an abundance of hospitality for Yourself and any guests You bring along.

The morsels surpass the finest delicacies on royal tables because this is a royal table for the King of Kings and Lord of Lords. They drip from Your lips. Come in, Lord. My door is open to You. Come in and dine with me.

Let's Pray

Holy Father, each day with You is a fine feast. I am full to overflowing with You. I love to taste the sweetness of Your Word. I cannot get enough yet You are enough. In Jesus' name. Amen.

Call to Action

Have you feasted with Jesus lately? What was your favorite flavor? Joy? Hope? Write it out.

July 24

"but whoever drinks of the water that I will give him shall never thirst; but the water that I will give him will become in him a well of water springing up to eternal life."
John 4:14

We visited Yellowstone National Park in June 2020. Our trip had been planned for a year. In March 2020, we had doubts about going due to the pandemic that had the world in a panic. We went with masks and hand sanitizer, standing six feet apart. I am glad we went.

Old Faithful drew a large crowd that day despite the pandemic. Acres of land with geological wonders wooed us with their eruptions. They didn't disappoint. But their significance in my heart made more of an impact than the amazing view and sound they produced.

Like those geysers springing up high into the air, the living water Jesus gives me lifts me, encourages me, inspires me, quenches my thirst. I wouldn't want to drink from a geyser, but I want to drink from God's living water forever.

Let's Pray

Holy Father, thank You for the wonders in Your creation. More importantly thank You for the living water that You allow me to drink from. I love You, Lord. In Jesus' name. Amen.

Call to Action

Are you thirsty? Ask God to give you a drink from His living water. Write it out.

July 25

This is the One who came by water and blood, Jesus Christ; not with the water only, but with the water and with the blood. It is the Spirit who testifies, because the Spirit is the truth.
1 John 5:6

Fully human but fully God. Wrapped in the flesh of humanity, Jesus was born the same way you and I were born. The Divine Seed placed in Mary's womb to grow our Savior. Water, blood, flesh swirling around the Fetus. At just the right time and just the right place, Mary gave birth to God.

Knowing he was unworthy to even touch the feet of Jesus, Jesus came to John to be baptized. John did not have any special significance. He was prepared by God for such a time as this. The example we follow today. Buried in a water grave, signifying the cleansing of our sin and resurrection to life, John baptized Jesus.

There was only water remaining. The wine was all used up. The wedding feast was still in full swing. Mary knew her Savior already. She knew Him before He was born. She knew what He could do. She encouraged Him into His ministry. He turned water into wine. The best wine.

Let's Pray

Holy Father, our water graves birthed us into life. Thank You, Lord. In Jesus' name. Amen.

Call to Action

Spend time praising God for resurrected life. Write it out.

July 26

As in water face reflects face,
So the heart of man reflects man.
Proverbs 27:19

The ripples contort the image staring back at me. The image jumping and twisting as the water laps against the shoreline. It is my image. It is me contorting and twisting, bouncing on the waves of the water. My reflection portrays the condition of the water.

The surface is smooth as glass. Peaceful. Still. Quiet. Calm. If I touch the surface, how far will the ripples go and how big they will get, widening as they move out? The water holds peace. The water is at rest. Silent.

When my heart bounces, it feels like I am being shaken and tormented. When my heart is quiet and still, peace fills the space. I think both conditions show on my face. My face reflects the condition of my heart. What about you?

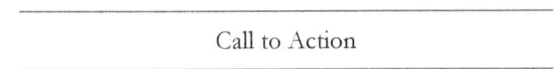

Let's Pray

Holy Father, You are the giver of my peace. When I face insurmountable waves, You can calm them when I turn my attention to You. Calm me now as the shaking wants to overtake me. Thank You for Your peace and rest. I love You, Lord. In Jesus' name. Amen.

Call to Action

Will you ask God to still the waves rocking Your heart? Write it out.

July 27

Does a fountain send out from the same opening both fresh and bitter water?
James 3:11

The mouth is a fountain. From it flows the condition of the heart. The contents of the heart get poured out and reveal the depths of conscience. It reveals integrity. Morals. Standards. Opinions. Hurt. Anger. It reveals the condition of your soul. Your words are a product of your faith.

Words cannot be taken back. Once out they are out forever. There have been times when I wanted to take them back. To erase them from the air and the ears which heard them. They can sear a soul. They can rip a heart. They can bite and bruise. They can kill relationships.

Words can also build up and encourage. Inspiration can ignite through words. Words can lead an imagination to conjure up pictures on the walls of a mind.

What are your words saying about you? Is the tone hostile or hospitable? Are they silly or sensible? Do they condemn or show compassion? Examine them. Listen to yourself.

Let's Pray

Holy Father, reveal our words to us. Forgive misuse. Thank You, Lord. In Jesus' name. Amen.

Call to Action

Do you need to clean up your words? Your heart? Ask God to help you. Write it out.

July 28

"I baptized you with water; but He will baptize you with the Holy Spirit."
Mark 1:8

I was seven. My best friend, at the time, went forward and so did I. It was the thing to do. Girls did things together. There was courage in doing things together. Girls are still doing things together. I did it because she did it. I knew it needed to be done, and I had a fear of water.

After the baptism service, as kids do after church, we were running and playing tag. The brick sign in front of the church was base. I was slow and clumsy. Reaching to get there before getting tagged, I tripped. My head met the corner of that sign. Three stitches, with a scar remaining.

Twenty-four years later, in a Sunday evening service, a speaker shared his testimony. He asked the question so many Christian speakers ask but it hit me differently that night. If you died right now, would you go to heaven? Are you 100% certain? I walked forward into my relationship with Jesus Christ and received the baptism of Holy Spirit. I followed it up with water baptism, following the example of my Savior. No stitches after that one!

Let's Pray

Holy Father, thank You for calling me into relationship with You. In Jesus' name. Amen.

Call to Action

What about you? Are you 100% certain that you will go to heaven? Write it out.

July 29

Like cold water to a weary soul,
So is good news from a distant land.
Proverbs 25:25

July is a hot month! Step outside and it feels like you opened the hot oven door. In South Georgia, it gets hard to breathe in the heat. The relief of the air conditioner cools the skin, but cold water cools the insides. I keep water close all the time. I am thankful for drinking water!

I shared with someone just yesterday that sometimes I get a little panicked if I don't have a bottle of water with me. There is normally one on my desk. There is one beside my bed. There is at least one in my car. Sometimes there is one in my purse. I like to stay hydrated.

The good news of the gospel is water for my soul. When I am parched, reading God's Word refreshes me. It quenches the thirst of my heart better than the water quenches the thirst of my mouth. It never runs out. There is no fear of not having enough. It is planted securely in me.

Let's Pray

Holy Father, thank You for Your Word. I love to sit and drink it in. As I do, help me to understand. Give knowledge and wisdom. Thank You for Holy Spirit teaching me as I study. Open Your Word for others to soak up. I love You, Lord. In Jesus' name. Amen.

Call to Action

Open God's Word. Find a verse. Any verse. Grab a pen. Write it out.

July 30

As the deer pants for the water brooks,
So my soul pants for You, O God.
Psalm 42:1

Earlier this week, one of our security cameras picked up a deer. It stood in our driveway, intent on something in our front yard. Standing still just looking. Slowly, it walked away and into the thick tree line. I wanted to warn that deer my guys are hunters! It is relatively safe in my yard because of the proximity of neighbors.

I am sure that deer wandered off to find something to nibble on. There are ponds and streams close by, so it has access to water sources. Animals will not stray far from known food and water sources. They need it. They long for it. That is what they live for to eat and drink.

For what do you live? Are you living to eat and drink? Are you living for your job? Are you living to raise kids, so they move out of your house? For what are you living?

Let's Pray

Holy Father, I can get so consumed by stuff that doesn't matter. You are my sole reason for living. You have given me everything that I have. I long to be with You. Nothing fulfills me the way You do. Thank You. I love You, Lord. In Jesus' name. Amen.

Call to Action

Do you find satisfaction in God's presence? Does He fill you up? Write it out.

July 31

And He said, "Come!" And Peter got out of the boat, and walked on the water and came toward Jesus.
Matthew 14:29

Just get out of the boat. Jesus is holding out His hand asking you to step out. Surely if He is asking you to step out of the boat, He already knows what you don't. He wants you to trust Him. He is asking you to come to Him. Put your leg over the side and step out.

How many times have you already stepped out without even knowing that is what you were doing? When you changed jobs, with uncertainty as to how it would work out. Going on that first date with the person you have been married to for thirty-five years. Think about it!

He held it together for you. He is still holding it together for you. If you are reading this, you are on this side of heaven, which means He is still working all things together for His glory. Let Him prove it to you again. Step out of the boat.

Let's Pray

Holy Father, You know the personal conviction I experience in writing this. Today. God, I trust You completely. My faith is in You and how You will work things out. In Jesus' name. Amen.

Call to Action

I am with you stepping over the side of the boat. Where are we going? Write it out.

SO THAT YOU WOULD WALK IN A MANNER WORTHY OF THE GOD WHO CALLS YOU INTO HIS OWN KINGDOM AND GLORY.
1 THESSALONIANS 2:12

August

so that you would walk in a manner worthy of the God who calls you into His own kingdom and glory.
1 Thessalonians 2:12

Back to school! It is that time of year. My husband teaches fifth grade math. By late July each year, he starts thinking about the supplies he will need to get the school year started. The teachers always distribute a supply list so the teachers can keep supplies on hand when students run out. They know it is best to keep the supplies in the classroom because the students will forget or lose their supplies. Many times, the teachers provide some of the supplies themselves.

Keeping adequate supplies makes teaching and learning a little less stressful. When the proper tools are in place everyone can be prepared to do their best. There is no stopping to search for the lost pencil. Plenty of paper is available to write out your work. Searching for supplies is not the reason for being at school. Learning is the goal. Advancing knowledge is the purpose.

And so, it is in life. Advancing our knowledge of God. Moving forward in our relationship with Him so we can walk in a manner worthy of His calling. Gaining knowledge happens through studying and seeking to know the subject matter. God's Word is our authoritative source for knowledge of Him.

Get your tools ready. Gather your supplies. Download an app on your phone. Grab a pen. Dust off your Bible. Let's gain some knowledge about God so we can draw closer to Him and know Him better. Will you join me?

August 1

The mind of the prudent acquires knowledge,
And the ear of the wise seeks knowledge.
Proverbs 18:15

This week I had a challenge which required reading and studying on a previously unknown topic. I have spoken with experts and decided that not everyone that claims to be an expert is an expert. I have learned that online research requires discernment. False information is abundant.

My challenge is not solved but I am continuing my quest to determine the best solution. People are relying on me to complete the puzzle and present an appropriate answer to the dilemma. It is time-consuming and complex but with acquiring knowledge I am confident there is a solution.

I have relied on God through this process. He answered prayers along the way. Some that I didn't even know how to pray. His faithfulness to me is constant and consistent, unwavering. Praying He continues to pave the way for a complete and appropriate solution for this challenge.

Let's Pray

Holy Father, thank You for caring about the tiny details of our lives. For seemingly insignificant issues, You still listen to our cries for help and are faithful to answer. Thank You, Lord for Your faithfulness. I commit my work to You. I love You, Lord. In Jesus' name. Amen.

Call to Action

How has God helped you with a challenge recently? Write it out.

August 2

Now concerning things sacrificed to idols, we know that we all have knowledge. Knowledge makes arrogant, but love edifies.
1 Corinthians 8:1

Discerning how to use knowledge is more important than knowledge itself. Holy Spirit, lead! Careless use of knowledge easily tears down any good that could have come about. But intentional consideration builds up and fortifies recipients of knowledge.

To learn just to learn and not apply with discretion is arrogance at its finest. Puffed up in pride spouting facts with nothing to show evidence of its usefulness is shameful. Better to keep thoughts to yourself than to make a mockery of the intelligence God gave you.

Silent knowledge applied well brings edification to all beneficiaries. Stakeholders get a front row seat to the blessings bestowed. Ask God to lead you in applying and sharing knowledge.

Let's Pray

Holy Father, Your creation of our minds is wondrous. The complexity of the human brain is amazing. It is incomprehensible for me to understand the work of Your Hands. Thank You for allowing us to think and obtain vast knowledge and in turn apply it. In Jesus' name. Amen.

Call to Action

What knowledge has amazed you and brought application in your life? Write it out.

August 3

My people are destroyed for lack of knowledge.
Because you have rejected knowledge,
I also will reject you from being My priest.
Since you have forgotten the law of your God,
I also will forget your children.
Hosea 4:6

I am afraid that we too often ignore situations. We don't want to take time to be bothered by it. It doesn't concern us so why would we stop to see about it? It is out in the open for all to see but no one wants to take care of it, so the situation continues until it brings ruin.

Ignorance is not bliss despite what some may think. The lack of knowledge causes missed opportunities. The lack of knowledge, specifically in the oracles of God, causes misunderstandings and potential separation from Him.

Know what you know and why you know it. Know enough to know you need to know more. Keep knowing the One who created you and know Him more. Open His Word and ask Holy Spirit to teach you through it. Accept the knowledge He wants to give you and grow in it.

Let's Pray

Holy Father, Your Word contains all we need for knowing You. It is a blessing to open it and have Your words enter my mind and heart. You are my greatest treasure. In Jesus' name. Amen.

Call to Action

Will you pray and ask God, through Holy Spirit, to teach you more about Him? Write it out.

August 4

Every prudent man acts with knowledge,
But a fool displays folly.
Proverbs 13:16

You've seen it. I've seen it. It is the classic theme in just about every movie and book. The good guy and the villain. Good against evil. Good portraying wisdom and understanding far deeper than anyone else. Evil portraying jealousy and anger because the good is pure and innocent.

It has been that way since the Garden. Evil, slithering its way into our path attempting to devour our blessing. Tripping us and making us fall on our faces. Mocking us and telling us lies. Tearing down relationships. Shredding hearts with hatred.

But our good God, raises us up. Knowing Him gives us victory over evil. He will brush the dirt off our faces and set us upright. His words over us show us His favor. He only speaks the truth. He builds up relationships. He repairs shredded hearts and fills them with love.

Let's Pray

Holy Father, keep us in the center of Your love. Make us permanent fixtures in Your kingdom. Thank You for blessing us and making us victorious. Cast evil away from us. Shield us and protect us. Raise us up for Your honor and glory. I love You, Lord. In Jesus' name. Amen.

Call to Action

Has evil entered your space and you need it gone? Ask God. Write it out.

August 5

The naive inherit foolishness,
But the sensible are crowned with knowledge.
Proverbs 14:18

God protects certain special people. I believe that in His infinite love and grace and mercy, those that are truly unable to obtain understanding for reasons beyond their control, are held in a special place by God. But for those of us that can gain knowledge, we don't have any excuses for not knowing Him more.

Excuses abound. I don't have time to read the Bible. You have time for what you want to have time for. It is hard to understand. Ask God to help you understand. I am not comfortable going to church. You don't go to church for your comfort you go to worship God and be a productive member of the body of Christ. It isn't for you. It is for Him.

Let me just tell you, if you are reading the words in this book, you may not be the one who struggles with desiring to know Him more. But there may be someone you know that does. Seek God's will in helping someone know Him more.

Let's Pray

Holy Father, thank You for allowing us to know You. I love You, Lord. In Jesus' name. Amen.

Call to Action

You know your assignment. Who is the one that you will come alongside to help? Write it out.

August 6

Teach me good discernment and knowledge,
For I believe in Your commandments.
Psalm 119:66

You are not alone in your studying God's Word. You have the perfect teacher. He resides in you. If you are a child of the Most High, His Holy Spirit is your teacher. He isn't like that loud obnoxious teacher that irritated you in high school. He is more like that quiet teacher that cared and showed compassion which made all the students want to be near her.

Holy Spirit is there waiting for you to notice Him. He wants to teach you. He wants to give you discernment. He intercedes on your behalf. He loves you and is closer to you than anyone else.

Hallelujah! For His presence never leaves you. Praise Him for He is good. Worship Him. Bless His holy name. Give Him honor. Listen to His voice. Ask Him to reveal Himself to You.

Let's Pray

Holy Father, thank You seems so inadequate for what You give. You have taken this sinner and saved me. You gave me Your Holy Spirit as my constant helper. You never leave me. You give me knowledge too great for words. You speak to my heart and love me. You open Your Word and teach me. I worship You alone. I love You, Lord. In Jesus' name. Amen.

Call to Action

Time to sit still. Listen. Open His love letter to you. What is He telling you? Write it out.

August 7

"Take my instruction and not silver,
And knowledge rather than choicest gold."
Proverbs 8:10

He picks up rocks and tucks them securely in his little pockets. Small sticks go in too. He is especially fond of quarters. They can be used on certain machines which produce more treasure. At the seashore, there are shells and more rocks. Small balls find their way into the collection.

He proudly shows me his treasure. "Come, look." He says, pulling me by the hand. I lean down, with eyes wide in wonder, taking in the treasure of him more than the collection of artifacts he displays. Because I know the treasure I hold is the hand in mine and the attention of this child.

I lean closer and tell him of a treasure greater than his meager collection. A treasure that can be his forever. I look him in the eyes with the excitement of a four-year old little boy so that I capture his attention and tell him how much Jesus loves him.

Let's Pray

Holy Father, simple daily moments are monumental treasures. Allow our attention to be captivated by the treasure You place in front of us. Help us to grow in Your instruction and to pass that instruction on to others. I love You, Lord. In Jesus' name. Amen.

Call to Action

Precious metals pale in comparison with some treasure. What is yours? Write it out.

August 8

Whoever loves discipline loves knowledge,
But he who hates reproof is stupid.
Proverbs 12:1

It takes intentional dedication to learn something new. Devoted attention to the subject matter. Repeated practice to get it exactly right. Setting your mind to the task. Training your body in strength and endurance. Increasing your brain power. Increasing your muscle memory.

Learning takes time and energy. Whether you are learning to paint or training for a marathon, you are experiencing something new. Some days there will be great advancement in your progress toward your goal. Other days you will find a challenge where correction is necessary.

Opening the pages of God's Word is no different. Gaining knowledge about something you care deeply about is worth the effort. The more you know, the more you want to know. God's Word is a living testament that gives you something new each time you open it.

Let's Pray

Holy Father, new glimpses of You come with each flip of a page. You weave Yourself into my heart and mind and I want more. God, keep me from selfishly hoarding what You give me. Let me share it so others will fall in love with You. I love You, Lord. In Jesus' name. Amen.

Call to Action

What have you committed to learning? Did you find struggles? Was it worth it? Write it out.

August 9

*Apply your heart to discipline
And your ears to words of knowledge.
Proverbs 23:12*

Your heart is undergoing some type of discipline or practice. Distinguishing the type will only encourage more of the same. What are you watching? What has captured your attention? Is it something you are pleased to share with others? Or is it something you wish to hide?

Certain practices can sever fellowship with God and those you love. Scrolling through social media can be one practice that distracts me from being present for the important stuff. Television can be another. Anything that removes my attention from what matters is not good for me.

Removing those things then can become discipline. Applying my attention to what matters most and not allowing mindless distractions secures my heart to those things. All the other stuff may get louder when I protest but I get to choose where my attention stays.

Let's Pray

Holy Father, saturate all of me with You so there is no distraction that can take my attention away from You. Allow me to represent You well in all the things I do. Forgive and correct when I miss the mark set by Jesus. Teach me to follow You. In Jesus' name. Amen.

Call to Action

So many things vying for our attention. Is there anything you struggle with? Write it out.

August 10

A wise man is strong,
And a man of knowledge increases power.
Proverbs 24:5

Hard decisions. Experience guiding the way through the maze of choices. Pros and cons weighed carefully. Facts gathered. Seeking God's will through each step. Praying for His guidance.

In his own strength, the decisions are insurmountable. But there is One who is stronger than he. With his knowledge alone, enough facts are inadequate. But there is One who knows it all. The wisdom and power are not his own but from the One who gives both.

On the edge of a precipice. Doing nothing is a choice. Doing something is a choice. Both choices are possible. Either choice is acceptable. God will be in the midst of whichever choice is made. In His power and strength, tough decisions bring good choices, which bring peace.

Let's Pray

Holy Father, our minds and hearts struggle with the choices in front of us. You know what is best, so we need Your wisdom and guidance. Impart knowledge so that all things are considered. Prepare the way in front of us so that the choices honor You. Thank You for Your infinite wisdom, knowledge and power. I love You, Lord. In Jesus' name. Amen.

Call to Action

Do you have a choice sitting in front of you? Ask God for guidance. Write it out.

August 11

Because they hated knowledge
And did not choose the fear of the LORD.
Proverbs 1:29

A project at work has been pushing me. It has required me to dig for knowledge. Sometimes the guidance is incomplete or ambiguous. It leaves the users to interpret for themselves instead of creating a clear-cut path. At times, the users place their own spin on the guidance for their gain.

This is where the heart of the matter comes in. Deciding what is the intention of the guidance. Considering the goal of the guidance. Considering what is the purpose.

The guidance of God has clarity. You may find yourself in peculiar situations where it feels confusing and uncertain, but be certain God is not confused. His direction is sure. His integrity never falters. He doesn't muddy the water. You can count on Him for truth. He is worthy of all reverence. He will guide you if you let Him.

Let's Pray

Holy Father, all praise to You. Thank You for Your unwavering integrity. God, draw me closer. Pull me in so that the direction You have for me is right with You. Let there be no separation. Forgive me when I pull away and pull me back to You. In Jesus' name. Amen.

Call to Action

Do you wander away from His guidance? Ask Him to pull you back. Write it out.

August 12

And by knowledge the rooms are filled
With all precious and pleasant riches.
Proverbs 24:4

Entering through the front door, the room was hidden. The greeting of the house was immediately comfortable. Like someone had just brushed past you leaving you feeling warm and welcomed. Moving through the rooms and hall, it opened.

Lining the back wall, an abundance of windows calling your eye to the back of the house. Inviting you to sit with a book and warm cup of coffee. The colors were crisp. Like a treat for your eyes. Drinking it all in, praying over the space. Welcoming God into where He already is.

His provision laid out in front of them. So completely obvious. The weeks of worry and struggle only served to bring confirmation for this one. They were home. They were standing in the place God had prepared for them. This was their house.

Let's Pray

Holy Father, the way You provide strikes me with awe. You keep us from obtaining what doesn't belong to us and then You drop what does right in front of us. You are so good to us. You fill our hearts and minds with precious and pleasant riches. Thank You, Lord. In Jesus' name. Amen.

Call to Action

Have you wanted something, and it didn't happen, but God gives something better? Write it out.

August 13

To give to His people the knowledge of salvation
By the forgiveness of their sins,
Luke 1:77

The weight lifted. Or rather set down. Removed from these weak arms. I couldn't carry it any longer. I had to set it down. So, I did. I laid it at the feet of Jesus.

I won't lie to you and say that I didn't try to pick it back up. Old habits have a way of repeating. Even when you think you are done with it, something pops into your mind, and you find yourself being drawn back into that old pattern.

But when Holy Spirit is living in you, the follow through becomes different. That old habit doesn't have the satisfaction that it used to. Now when you follow through, you are left feeling miserable. You immediately know that your salvation is in Jesus alone and not that old habit.

Let's Pray

Holy Father, Your salvation in me assures me of Your constant presence. You made a way for me to come to you when I didn't deserve to be with You. You love me despite all the old habits I keep trying to come back to. Help me kick them out for good. In Jesus' name. Amen.

Call to Action

Do you have one or more? An old habit? Ask God to help you get rid of it. Write it out.

August 14

always learning and never able to come to the knowledge of the truth.
2 Timothy 3:7

Practice what you know. Apply the knowledge you have in real ways. Seems logical. Seems like it would be easy to apply your knowledge. But is it?

If you know that sweet treat will cause physical or mental stress, put it down. Refuse it. If you know watching that show will place thoughts in your head you don't want, turn it off. If scrolling on your phone hurts your neck, eyes, shoulders, wrists, and hands, put down the phone. If you know speaking certain words in certain tones causes hurt and division, don't speak the words.

Practice what you know. Apply the knowledge you have in real ways. Use the truth of what you know to build up and not tear down. And as you learn more, apply it.

Let's Pray

Holy Father, You fill our minds with knowledge. We are constantly learning. Holy Spirit, teach us to apply the knowledge You give in real ways. Keep us from filling our minds and never using what we learn. Put us to work for Your glory and honor. We are willing vessels to be in service for furthering Your kingdom. Bless the knowledge we put into practice. In Jesus' name. Amen.

Call to Action

Have you learned anything recently you want to start applying? What will you do? Write it out.

August 15

The lips of the wise spread knowledge,
But the hearts of fools are not so.
Proverbs 15:7

Do you listen to the words you speak? There are times I hear myself spewing nothing but junk. That is a hard confession. When I hear myself in those tirades, I hush. I ask God to forgive me and to put edifying words in my mouth. I want my words to reflect the heart of God.

My words have gotten me into trouble too many times. They are a direct reflection of my heart. When I forget who I am and take my eyes off the cross, that is when my heart gets hard and vicious. I allow the world to infiltrate when I lay down the armor. And I can't take back words.

But I can ask forgiveness. I can stop the words from forming on my tongue by filling my heart and mind with the truth of God. I can reshape my words so that they sound like the goodness that has been poured into me. Then I can share that goodness with others. And good words abound.

Let's Pray

Holy Father, sometimes I need a big piece of tape over my mouth. Will you fill my heart and mind so that only good comes from my lips? You take control of my heart and mind so that the words I speak reflect Your goodness. Please forgive my hurtful words. In Jesus' name. Amen.

Call to Action

Have you spoken words that hurt? Does your speech need God's touch? Ask Him. Write it out.

August 16

Cease listening, my son, to discipline,
And you will stray from the words of knowledge.
Proverbs 19:27

When my daughter was born, I started listening to the lyrics of the music on my radio and began to realize that was not what I wanted her to hear. I felt like I was allowing what feels like a soul cry through music to give praise to something other than the One who deserves it all.

I changed stations. I turned the dial to find something I wanted her to hear. To something I needed to hear. I haven't gone back. I need all the edifying sounds I can get in my head.

I have AirPods that stay in my ears as I work at my desk now. Music or podcasts play. The lyrics and topics must be laced with Christ. I want nothing but Him. Anything that turns away from Him gets turned off. He is the keeper of my heart and mind. I only want to praise Him and fill my mind with more of Him. I want to be saturated with Him.

Let's Pray

Holy Father, thank You for music. Thank You for allowing me to worship You. Thank You for allowing me to praise You. You alone are worthy of all praise. God, protect hearts and minds from the evil that exists in the world. I love You, Lord. In Jesus' name. Amen.

Call to Action

Do you need to change the channel? Ask Him to show you what needs to go. Write it out.

August 17

Such knowledge is too wonderful for me;
It is too high, I cannot attain to it.
Psalm 139:6

The rocky ascent towers above the landscape. Magnificent heights capped with white. Reaching high. Standing firm. But the hike up is treacherous. Not for the faint of heart. There is no path. Steep steps on thin ledges require careful navigation. Trusting the rock to hold and not give way.

That is life with God. Reaching to the heights of what He has for you. The journey may seem dangerous and risky sometimes. Your heart may race, and the next step may be far away, and you feel stranded. God will never leave you. He will plant your feet on solid ground.

On the other side of the chasm, there are heights you could never imagine. The fellowship with Him surpasses anything else. His love is so great. His mercy is unending. He is unwavering in His affection for you. There is nothing that can separate you from His love.

Let's Pray

Holy Father, words seem inadequate to express my gratitude. You reach down into my miniscule life and fill it beyond comprehension. You are so good to me. Thank You. Help my lack of comprehension so that I can help others to know You. In Jesus' name. Amen.

Call to Action

Today, will you take time to just praise Him for His unfathomable love? Write it out.

August 18

that in everything you were enriched in Him, in all speech and all knowledge,
1 Corinthians 1:5

Today marks a special day for me. It is the anniversary of my entry into this world. Before that day, God had all my days numbered and accounted for. He knew everything I would do. He knew everything I would say. He knew every feeling I would feel. He knew all my failures and still He chose to bring me into this space for such a time as this.

The blessings He has poured out on me are innumerable. The experiences are too vast to contain in one book. The encounters reach beyond my memory. The relationships are as varied as fingerprints. He has enriched my life. He has watched over me all my days.

As I type this, I look at my fingers clicking over the keys and I consider this to be a gift. This book being filled with inspiration and encouragement. Prayers and admonishment. Testimonies and confessions. He has been gracious to me. I pray this gift of mine becomes a gift to you.

Let's Pray

Holy Father, forgive me for so many years of dreading the anniversary of my birth. God, I now see that You have been with me the whole time and You will continue. In Jesus' name. Amen.

Call to Action

What gift did God give the world when He made You? Write it out.

August 19

With his mouth the godless man destroys his neighbor,
But through knowledge the righteous will be delivered.
Proverbs 11:9

We don't always know the full story. We are quick to criticize another and point fingers without knowing all the details. The details may not be ours to know. The criticism may be pointing fingers back in our direction while attempting to point out shortcomings in others.

Maybe you do need more details. Maybe that one needs someone to talk to and you may be the one to listen. You may be the confidante someone needs for this very thing because maybe you have some experience and knowledge that could help instead of harming the situation.

There may be some healing waiting for you too. Lending an ear or a shoulder could be the very thing you both need. Reach out. In love. No judgment. Make an offer to listen.

Let's Pray

Holy Father, keep our eyes open for opportunities to help and not criticize. Turn our concern into compassion. Use the knowledge You have given us to walk alongside someone else who may be experiencing something we have experienced. Give us hearts to help. In Jesus' name. Amen.

Call to Action

You already have someone in mind. I know you do. Go ahead. Write it out.

August 20

For I delight in loyalty rather than sacrifice,
And in the knowledge of God rather than burnt offerings.
Hosea 6:6

Loyalty and obedience negate the need for sacrifice. But God had to make a way for this sinful race to come to Him, so sacrifice was required to make atonement and restore fellowship. He cleared the path to the foot of the cross. He planted the tree. He created the human form that held the One that would make the perfect sacrifice for my sin and for your sin.

Because of Jesus, in His perfect glory, once was all it took. One sacrifice to be sufficient for eternity. No further sacrifices for atonement ever needed. He finished the work required for us to be reconciled and sealed for salvation. For eternity. Forever living in fellowship with God.

Now the picture of sacrifices and offerings are those of worshipping God. Living in harmony and unity while serving the One who atoned and satisfied the debt we owed. Forever in His presence.

Let's Pray

Holy Father, I worship You. You paid my debt. You forgave my sin. Your sacrifice of Jesus was the final perfecting work to restore our relationship. Thank You. In Jesus' name. Amen.

Call to Action

You don't have to strive and work for your salvation. He did it. Accept it. Write it out.

August 21

Grace and peace be multiplied to you in the knowledge of God and of Jesus our Lord;
2 Peter 1:2

The more you know the more you have. Open His Word. Study it. Talk with Him. This is the most important relationship you will ever have. This is the only relationship you will find pure grace and increasing peace. He is the giver of good gifts. Nothing else can compare.

He enters the space of your soul and speaks blessings that cannot be uttered. There are no words that can accurately describe the fellowship He brings. But you know it when you have it. You have that peace that passes all understanding. Unspeakable joy. Anointed with His Spirit.

The more you know Him the more joy and peace you experience. It doesn't pale. It doesn't fade into nothingness. Instead, it becomes richer and more profound. The more you have the more you want. And He faithfully provides when you ask with no doubting.

Let's Pray

Holy Father, thank You for grace and peace. The joy You fill me with makes me want more of You. Increase my knowledge of Your Word so that I can know You more. Multiply the joy so that I can pour out for You. Help me spread Your good news. In Jesus' name. Amen.

Call to Action

Do you have God's multiplication factor going on inside you? Write it out.

August 22

And this I pray, that your love may abound still more and more in real knowledge and all discernment,
Philippians 1:9

The multiplication factor God places in you is the catalyst for you to multiply the love you give. You open your heart to Him so that He can do the work in you and then you take what He gives you and you do the work for Him. It is the best working relationship you will ever have.

He is the best coworker. He shows up at the perfect time. He won't steal your favorite pen. He always answers your questions. The answers may not be exactly what you are wanting but His answers are always correct. You never have to doubt the quality of His work.

His motives are genuine. His sincerity is unmatched. He is the definition of dependable. He will never abandon His job. His productivity makes your productivity even better. You are the best working team. You will not find anyone better to stand beside you through everything.

Let's Pray

Holy Father, without You all the work I attempt is shallow and meaningless. But when I have You with me and I am depending on You, everything is rich. Thank You. In Jesus' name. Amen.

Call to Action

How can you become a better coworker? Ask God to show you. Write it out.

August 23

Also it is not good for a person to be without knowledge,
And he who hurries his footsteps errs.
Proverbs 19:2

There is no shortcut in obtaining knowledge. I look back to my days in school and remember thinking I could wait until the night before a test to study. I sat in classes and listened and took notes so surely that would be enough. Sometimes it was but sometimes it wasn't.

When it came down to regurgitating what I had learned, it required time and attention sitting with the subject matter to truly know the material. Gaining more than I had when I started. Then being able to explain it either on a test or on a written paper or even in speech.

When I was able to teach it to someone else was the point where the knowledge had been sealed in my brain. Explaining in a way someone else then learns and obtains what I have worked for so long. Taking the gift of knowledge and sharing it over time.

Let's Pray

Holy Father, You created our brain to continually learn. It is a life-long process. You fill us and then desire for us to share what You have given. Lead us in this sharing. Thank You for filling us to overflowing. I love You, Lord. In Jesus' name. Amen.

Call to Action

Do you have knowledge to share with someone else? What is it? Write it out.

August 24

"For the earth will be filled
With the knowledge of the glory of the LORD,
As the waters cover the sea."
Habakkuk 2:14

There is an inherent knowledge of God that even those who claim to have no belief in Him hold. The Creator is always known by the created whether or not the created recognizes Him. If He isn't recognized there will remain an inexplicable longing for knowledge of Him.

Knowing Him is to know His glory. Replacing the longing with actual knowledge fills a void that exists without knowledge. The absence of knowledge is ignorance. Willful ignorance causes separation from God. Willful ignorance of God is betrayal.

God calls us to relationship with Him. Relationships take time and knowledge. They require intentionally learning each other. God knows all there is to know about you. What do you know about God? Do you want to know Him better? What do you need to do to make that happen?

Let's Pray

Holy Father, thank You for continually teaching me about You. You make Yourself available to me constantly. I love realizing Your presence with me. In Jesus' name. Amen.

Call to Action

Don't wait! Dive into His Word. Ask Him to reveal Himself to you. Write it out.

August 25

O LORD, what is man, that You take knowledge of him?
Or the son of man, that You think of him?
Psalm 144:3

God thought so much of you that He gave His only Son to die on the cross so that you could have eternal life with Him. He wants you that much. He desires a relationship with you. He patiently waits but He won't wait forever.

Ignoring Him is rejecting Him. Saying that you will read His Word later is saying you don't want to know Him now. Giving attention to other stuff instead of giving attention to Him is refusing His love. Idolatry is making your stuff more important than Him.

But how He loves you! He is calling you into a relationship with Him. He wants to reveal His love to you if you just accept it. It isn't hard to meet Him because He is right here. Right now. He wants your attention. He wants your acceptance. He wants you to know Him.

Let's Pray

Holy Father, You hold Your children in a loving embrace. God, I feel Your hug. It is gentle but firm. There is peace and joy. There is comfort. There is calm. In Jesus' name. Amen.

Call to Action

If you have rejected Him before, will you renew your relationship with Him now? Write it out.

August 26

"How long, O naive ones, will you love being simple-minded?
And scoffers delight themselves in scoffing
And fools hate knowledge?"
Proverbs 1:22

You know the old saying, "You can't teach an old dog new tricks." There is truth in that sometimes. And sometimes it is stubborn determination and a refusal to learn. Stuck in the rut of life and mindset that keeps you from learning anything other than what you have always known.

Going so far to ridicule those who want to learn more and sitting in that stubborn determination to think you already know everything you need to know. Insulting others' efforts in obtaining knowledge. Considering your knowledge superior to others in prideful arrogance.

Ask God on which side you sit. Are you always on a quest to learn more? Or are you stubbornly ridiculing others for their quest for more knowledge? Are you open to knowing where you sit? Are you open to learning more about God as He reveals more about you?

Let's Pray

Holy Father, open our eyes and ears to truth and knowledge. God, in all areas of our lives. Give us discernment. God, when things get hard, You help. You are faithful. In Jesus' name. Amen.

Call to Action

Answer the questions. Does it change in different circumstances and situations? Write it out.

August 27

For if we go on sinning willfully after receiving the knowledge of the truth, there no longer
remains a sacrifice for sins,
Hebrews 10:26

This verse has impacted me greatly recently. Stopping to consider the impact of this verse convicts me into awareness of sin in my life. Is there willful sin in my life that needs to be confessed and removed? Constantly asking God to reveal my sin so I can repent.

The sacrifice of Jesus was sufficient for all my sin. But if I refuse that gift of forgiveness, then I am refusing to confess. I am refusing to repent. I am refusing to call myself a sinner in need of a Savior. Instead of standing on the Rock, I am trampling His blood under my feet in defiance.

Jesus was perfect. I am not. He knows I am not perfect. He knows I need Him. He knows my sin sneaks up on me and the enemy wants me to remain in it. But He made the way for me to escape it. He provides the path for me to take which leads away from the death-hold of sin.

Let's Pray

Holy Father, show me my sin so that I can turn away and live in salvation. God, You are victorious over the grave of sin. Resurrect me so I can live with You. In Jesus' name. Amen.

Call to Action

Is there anything that you are holding onto that you need to give to Him? Write it out.

August 28

and to know the love of Christ which surpasses knowledge, that you may be filled up to all the fullness of God.
Ephesians 3:19

If you know you know. If you have been on rock bottom and felt the hand of God lifting you from the pit, you know the love of God which is incomprehensible. His gentle hand reaches down to offer you assistance to get out of the mud of your circumstances.

When you know His hand is on you, those circumstances look different. They may be the exact same but your perspective shifts to know the peace of God in the middle of it. That is what surpasses knowledge. He changes your view and transforms your heart and mind.

He fills you with His abundant peace. And you know that He will work all things out for your good. That is a peace that no one and nothing can steal from you. It is yours. He will faithfully pull you from any pit you fall into. He will never leave you.

Let's Pray

Holy Father, Your love goes beyond everything. It cannot be measured by human standards. Thank You for your unending love. I love You, Lord. In Jesus' name. Amen.

Call to Action

Can you recall a time you felt the hand of God in the midst of difficulty? Write it out.

August 29

a corrector of the foolish, a teacher of the immature, having in the Law the embodiment of knowledge and of the truth,
Romans 2:20

Knowing the truth and giving it to others requires humility and patience. Sometimes our audience doesn't want the truth. Sometimes they want it, but they can't reach it because they need something else before arriving where you are teaching. It is your job to give what is needed first. Trying to teach a lesson on advanced mathematics to a toddler just doesn't work.

As growth in knowledge increases, the lessons become more advanced. The teacher acknowledges the level of the students and changes the lessons accordingly. Then there comes a point where the teacher can no longer be effective because the student has attained maturity.

We are all on a life-long mission to know God. We are constantly learning and growing in our knowledge of Him. He is the best teacher, and His lessons are always enriching.

Let's Pray

Holy Father, thank You for teaching me. Thank You for allowing me to learn more about You. Help me to grow in the fullness of You. I love You, Lord. In Jesus' name. Amen.

Call to Action

Ask God to help you with a specific lesson you are dealing with right now. Write it out.

August 30

Now for this very reason also, applying all diligence, in your faith supply moral excellence, and in your moral excellence, knowledge,
2 Peter 1:5

He bought it knowing the brakes didn't work. He had taken some classes in high school and believed he could get them working again. Every evening after work he came home and worked on that four-wheeler. He was determined. He purchased parts and today the brakes work.

Is there something worthy of your time and energy? Diligently seeking answers to questions until you discover the truth brings satisfaction. Desiring excellence for your outcomes. Having pure motives in the work you are doing. Believing God can do abundantly beyond for you.

Faith is the catalyst for excellence. Knowing you have God on your side makes your work succeed. Trusting His plan for your life, for your every moment, adds peace to each step. So, there you are, working, moving, in faith, in excellence, in peace, for God.

Let's Pray

Holy Father, thank You for giving us work to do. Give us the strength we need to do that work. God, let the work show Your excellence. Let us be living testimonies. In Jesus' name. Amen.

Call to Action

Can you boast in the excellent work God is doing in your life? Write it out.

August 31

And He will be the stability of your times,
A wealth of salvation, wisdom and knowledge;
The fear of the LORD is his treasure.
Isaiah 33:6

The value of your portfolio cannot compare to the wealth of treasure God provides to you through salvation. There are no adequate financial resources on this earth to replace the exorbitant richness of a relationship with Him. There are no caps on His treasury.

When markets decline and seemingly fail, our Father's wealth is stable. In your life, you may even experience strong increases in your wealth of relationship with Him. He supplies all your needs and then some. That revelation alone has value untold.

Do you know how great His treasury is? His love poured out for you never ends. Are you holding out your hands and catching what He is pouring? Are you gaining wisdom and knowledge of His goodness poured out for you? Hold out your hands and catch it all.

Let's Pray

Holy Father, the vastness of Your wealth cannot be counted. There is no number that can be placed on its value. Because of Your love, we have great wealth in You. In Jesus' name. Amen.

Call to Action

Are you adding to your wealth of relationship with God? What has He given you? Write it out.

*"THE BEGINNING OF WISDOM IS:
ACQUIRE WISDOM;
AND WITH ALL YOUR
ACQUIRING, GET
UNDERSTANDING."*
PROVERBS 4:7

September

"The beginning of wisdom is: Acquire wisdom;
And with all your acquiring, get understanding."
Proverbs 4:7

I watched all three of my children go through school. The youngest just graduated from high school this year. He started kindergarten the same year my oldest started college. They all grew up too fast. And even though their formal education may be over (not sure if another college student is in our future) their learning experiences are not.

My oldest is a teacher. My second is an attorney. My third is a manager at a flooring store. And even though they may think they have learned a lot, there is a lot more to learn. I am convinced that our learning never ends. New experiences bring new learning opportunities.

Learning comes sprinkled with understanding and wisdom. Knowledge alone doesn't solidify understanding. You can be told something and may learn all about it but until you go through it yourself, you don't understand it. Combine knowledge and understanding with a heavy dose of God's grace and then you find wisdom.

There is no shortcut to wisdom. You can't get it from a textbook. It isn't inherited from your parents. Watching a YouTube video will not teach it to you. There is only one source.

God provides wisdom. He gives you opportunities to learn and understand and as you do, He imparts wisdom. Wisdom is the marriage of God's grace with experiential knowledge and understanding.

September 1

Solomon's wisdom surpassed the wisdom of all the sons of the east and all the wisdom of Egypt.
1 Kings 4:30

Solomon asked God for wisdom. God gave Him wisdom and so much more. Solomon had no reason to doubt God. Just read Proverbs and Ecclesiastes and you will find that his gift of wisdom was recorded for us to consider. God gave him words to provide guidance for us.

His words echo with truth and grace. Wisdom on the pages of God's Word. Wisdom recorded for all to see. Study it. Take what you study and put it into practice. Apply the words to your life.

But don't be mistaken. Wisdom is God-given. The wisdom of the world will lead to destruction, but the wisdom of God leads to eternal life. The wisdom of the world leads to heart ache, but the wisdom of God leads to peace. Which path of wisdom will you follow?

Let's Pray

Holy Father, You give good gifts. You have given us minds and hearts that connect to be used for Your glory. Life experiences teach us to lean hard into Your Word. Without Your Word we would be lost. Without Jesus we would have eternal death. Thank You for life. Thank You for giving us Jesus. Thank You for giving us Your Word so that we can know You. In Jesus' name. Amen.

Call to Action

Have you read those two books of the Bible? Will you commit to doing so? Write it out.

September 2

For wisdom is protection just as money is protection,
But the advantage of knowledge is that wisdom preserves the lives of its possessors.
Ecclesiastes 7:12

All the money in the world cannot buy you salvation. It can buy you stuff but, in the end, you won't be taking any money on your final journey into eternity. It may be helpful in this journey you are on right now, this journey within this world, but this journey is just temporary.

How could you use your money to make an eternal difference? The resources you have belong to God. Are you using them for His glory or are you using them for your glory? Your glory is just a dim shadow of God's glory. You can't buy glory, but you can use your money for His glory.

Making wise money decisions requires talking with God. I have made some mistakes in my life because I didn't talk with Him first. Hard lessons learned tend to keep you from making more mistakes. He is the best financial advisor. Give Him your portfolio and watch it grow.

Let's Pray

Holy Father, all glory belongs to You. Sometimes we forget that all we have is because of You. Forgive us. Give us wisdom in stewarding Your resources. In Jesus' name. Amen.

Call to Action

The first line in your budget should be GOD. How will you use what He gave you? Write it out.

September 3

Make your ear attentive to wisdom,
Incline your heart to understanding;
Proverbs 2:2

Pride steps in and grips your neck. You have heard the same lecture a million times and you refuse to listen to it one more time. At eighteen, you are an adult and know everything you need to know about life. That was me. Many years ago. Young and naïve. I didn't want to listen.

It took some years to learn I was wrong. Many mistakes later, I make the same lecture. I try to be the voice of reason. It is hard to teach a lesson to someone that hasn't had the experience. Once the experience is had, the teaching becomes more urgent. The lesson is more important.

And you finally get it. You finally understand the words spoken over you all those years ago. Words spoken from hard experiences. Words spoken attempting to keep you from getting hurt. But they must learn the lesson themselves, so they understand.

Let's Pray

Holy Father, thank You for protecting me through stupid mistakes. Thank You for working out stubbornness and pride in me. Continue to remove it from me because there is still quite a bit left in me. Protect my young people from hard lessons. I trust You with them. In Jesus' name. Amen.

Call to Action

Is your heart burdened by the choices of others? Ask God to help you and them. Write it out.

September 4

Conduct yourselves with wisdom toward outsiders, making the most of the opportunity.
Colossians 4:5

From the outside looking in you may not know the turmoil inside the house. From all appearances everything looks perfect. The dirty laundry is hidden, out of view. The conduct of the occupants may not reveal the truth of the condition of relationships. You may not see it all.

From the inside it might be a train-wreck. Hearts are broken. Words are harsh or nonexistent. Loneliness in a house full of people. Dust covers the one Book that could heal the condition of the household. But silence and sadness reign and stifle the searching hearts.

But God sees it all. He sees the hearts and knows the longing. One kind word turns into two. Words soften. Silence is broken. Loneliness is defeated. The dust is brushed off and the spine of that Book cracks open. Occupants begin living again. From the outside looking in, God is home.

Let's Pray

Holy Father, come and have Your way in my home. It belongs to You anyway. Bathe us in Your righteousness. Let this place be a beacon of light in a dark and dying world. Take our messes and make messages of hope for others to witness. I love You, Lord. In Jesus' name. Amen.

Call to Action

Do you have messes turned to messages of hope? Would you share with others? Write it out.

September 5

For the LORD gives wisdom;
From His mouth come knowledge and understanding.
Proverbs 2:6

Can you hear Him? He is calling you. He wants you to hear His voice. The best place to start is in the pages of the Letter He wrote to you. He gave you a lot of history to show His redemption. He wants you to understand what it took to bring You back to Himself from the grave of sin.

His perfect reconciliation awaits you in those pages. He would love to reveal His love and wisdom to you. He will take it from those blessed pages and place it delicately in your chest. Gently nestling it in the crevices of your heart. Expanding it so that there is no empty space left.

And when it starts seeping out of you, He will add more. He will take what you spill out and spread it on someone else. Then the filling of that one will begin to look like yours. Then they will spill out and spread onto others. Be filled! Overflow for Him!

Let's Pray

Holy Father, You are pouring out of me. You have filled me, and I am overflowing with joy for the work You have done in my life. I am eternally thankful for the redemption of my wicked, sinful soul. You saved me from my sin. I love You, Lord. In Jesus' name. Amen.

Call to Action

Leave your Bible open. Read it every day. Ask Him for understanding. Write it out.

September 6

When pride comes, then comes dishonor,
But with the humble is wisdom.
Proverbs 11:2

We have nothing to boast about except for the wondrous love of our Savior. No success of ours is attributable to anything in us but in the miraculous work of our Creator. When we attempt to gain glory for ourselves, falling from that pedestal will certainly be painful. Because it isn't ours.

Giving Him the rightful place of honor takes us low before Him in reverence. Us, taking a posture of praise. Him, taking a posture of worthiness and love, hovering over His beloved. Isn't that just like Him? Coming down meeting us at our lowest point. Leaning in close. Breathing on us and rejoicing over us. Singing His song over His beautiful creation.

Knowing He holds all the honor and living in that truth keeps us in our posture of praise. Keeping Him in His place of honor denies pride from taking hold. Letting Him hold us so that we are protected and can boast in His grip. Tell of His love for you!

Let's Pray

Holy Father, forgive me when I try to take any honor. It isn't mine but it is Yours. I worship and adore You. You alone are worthy of my praise. I love You, Lord. In Jesus' name. Amen.

Call to Action

Do you need to step down off a pedestal? Better to do it willingly than to fall. Write it out.

September 7

The mouth of the righteous utters wisdom,
And his tongue speaks justice.
Psalm 37:30

Growing up in Southern Baptist churches, we would attend Sunday School. It was always held an hour before the worship service. Sometimes there would be literature used that guided us through a topical study or specific books of the Bible. It was a time to learn and grow in understanding God's Word. Sunday School has turned into Connect Groups. Same practice.

As young adults, my husband and I had a teacher in Sunday School that always held our attention, as he did with everyone. His daily walk matched the lessons he taught. He was a humble teacher with a heart to share God's love with everyone he encountered. He passed away many years ago. His passing left a void in that classroom for a little while.

There is no specific lesson I can recall. No passage of scripture that stands out from the many lessons he taught. His constant testimony is the memory I hold of him.

Let's Pray

Holy Father, oh, that we may leave such a legacy of being living testimonies of Your goodness. Build that up in us so that others can know You. We praise You. In Jesus' name. Amen.

Call to Action

Do you have memories of someone that made an impression on you? Write it out.

September 8

Wisdom is better than weapons of war, but one sinner destroys much good.
Ecclesiastes 9:18

I am a sinner saved by grace. My sin destroyed too many good things. Jesus nailed my sin to the cross and covered it with His blood and washed me white as snow. He redeemed the wickedness in me and replaced it with His righteousness. Now I am a child of the King of Kings.

There is no weapon that can form against me that will prosper. He surrounds me to protect against any fiery arrows coming my way. I am sealed and set apart for His purposes. He has a plan for me, and nothing can separate me from His love. He has the victory.

He causes me to step on level ground. His Word is sweeter than honey. He will never leave me. He will never forsake me. He has good plans for me. I will sing His praises forever. I am His and He is mine. He is Master. He is Creator. He is Savior. Will you praise Him now?

Let's Pray

Holy Father, I am hidden in the cleft of the Rock. You protect me. You are my shelter and refuge. I can rest in peace knowing Your security for me. The power of Your salvation is given to me through the blood of Jesus. I love You, Lord. In Jesus' name. Amen.

Call to Action

How has God worked in your life to provide protection and security? Write it out.

September 9

And I saw that wisdom excels folly as light excels darkness.
Ecclesiastes 2:13

Stepping carefully through the house in the early morning hours while it is still dark, I make my way to fill the water kettle. I flip on the light above the stove to give just enough light to see my way around the kitchen. The light of my screen adds a little more light to the dark morning.

Hours later, the sky begins to show signs of light. The color shifts from black to gray to pink to brilliant blue. Too many hues in between to even list. God spills out the light of day in excellent array. His light reveals everything that was hidden. Even the shadows give in to the light.

Will you allow Him to shine light on your dark places? Invite Him into those spaces so nothing remains hidden. Ask Him to remove the folly and replace it with wisdom. Trust Him with your secrets. Trust Him to reveal and replace darkness with the Light of His love.

Let's Pray

Holy Father, Your Light shines brightly for all to see. Thank You for removing the darkness from in us. We bask in the glory of Your beautiful colors. Your brilliance is too great for us to fully see. Keep us in Your Light. You alone are worthy of all praise. In Jesus' name. Amen.

Call to Action

Give Him access to your dark spaces. He will Light it up. Give Him your praise. Write it out.

September 10

The LORD by wisdom founded the earth,
By understanding He established the heavens.
Proverbs 3:19

He molded the earth, already knowing its dimensions and shape. Placing it in just the right spot for the life it would hold. He considered the cost before the first ray of light exploded onto the earth and heavens. Before you do anything, you turn the light on. To navigate a dark space, illumination is necessary. The light shows the way. The light exposes the work in front of you.

His plan was well thought out. Already anticipating what you and I are doing at this very moment. Even what we will do tomorrow. He knew the choice Eve would make but His love was greater than any choice any of us makes. He desired us anyway. He loves us anyway.

His creation was designed to support life. His creation was designed to provide everything needed for us to dwell with Him. He knew what we needed. Now we just need to seek Him and trust His provision for our lives. He has already prepared everything for us.

Let's Pray

Holy Father, thank You for thoughtful consideration when creating everything we need for life. Most of all for Jesus. Without Him, we could not dwell with You. In Jesus' name. Amen.

Call to Action

Consider God's creation. What is your favorite part? Write it out.

September 11

My son, give attention to my wisdom,
Incline your ear to my understanding;
Proverbs 5:1

You know what to do. Just do it. The consequences will be there waiting for you if you don't do it. So why put yourself through the hurt when you know what will happen. You have been warned. You get to decide the best choice of action. Listen to reason or don't. It is up to you.

We wrestle with decisions instead of taking them to God. He allows us space to fall. He is always waiting to pick us up but when we don't look at Him in our choices, we are prone to stumble. Be still and know Him. Be still and ask Him for help with that hard decision. Trust His direction.

He will not lead you wrong. He may have some lessons to teach you along the way, but He will not leave you in the middle of struggles. But you must keep your gaze fixed on Him. That is your choice as well. Know that if you keep your eyes on Him, His way is much easier to follow.

Let's Pray

Holy Father, bind my wandering heart to You. I am prone to veer off the path You have set before me. Easily distracted. God, I want my eyes focused on You and nothing else. The world leaves me battered and bruised, but You heal my wounds and call me loved. In Jesus' name. Amen.

Call to Action

Clear the film off your eyes so you can clearly see God. What is He showing you? Write it out.

September 12

There is no wisdom and no understanding
And no counsel against the LORD.
Proverbs 21:30

We are bombarded with fake news and false promises. Sometimes it is hard to distinguish the good from the bad. The bad has become so good at convincing you to accept it so it keeps trying to win you over. Perilous times require powerful prayer. Pray without ceasing.

Praying without ceasing is finding Him in your thoughts as you go through life. Living every day aware of His presence and talking with Him as you do the people around you. Since He never leaves you, it is easy to have a continual conversation with Him. He can follow your random thoughts. He doesn't mind your tangents. He cares about everything you care about.

He will give you discernment to know the difference between lies and truth. The more you know Him the easier it becomes to follow Him. Seek Him and know Him. You will be glad you did.

Let's Pray

Holy Father, I know You are constantly with me. Guiding me. Holy Spirit interceding on my behalf when I don't know what to pray. Thank You for Your presence. Thank You for making a way for fellowship with You. I rest in Your presence. I love You, Lord. In Jesus' name. Amen.

Call to Action

Do you need Him with you all the time? I know the answer but tell Him. Write it out.

September 13

*"Who has put wisdom in the innermost being
Or given understanding to the mind?"*
Job 38:36

God's sovereignty is revealed in Job 38 and 39. He sets the record straight after Job's friends lectured him. God lays it all out. From the whirlwind, He spoke to Job. He didn't speak to those friends. Job was the intended audience of this reminder. And maybe you and I are too!

The best counsel on earth is not the best if it is given without the consultation of God. Surround yourself with others that seek His counsel. Remove yourself from any place that is dishonoring to God. Ask Him to show you those places and people that don't deserve your attention.

Well intentioned friends can even provide you with bad advice. We all have moments with lack of discernment. That is where grace comes in and offers reconciliation back into the sovereign arms of God. God restored Job and He will restore you too.

Let's Pray

Holy Father, thank You for restoration and reconciliation. Thank You for setting us straight. Show us where we stray from Your counsel and bring us back. We want to stay right here with You. You are where our hearts belong. I love You, Lord. In Jesus' name. Amen.

Call to Action

Where do you seek counsel? Has God given you a friend that gives Godly counsel? Write it out.

September 14

Wisdom strengthens a wise man more than ten rulers who are in a city.
Ecclesiastes 7:19

Those in authority are not always seekers of Godly wisdom. Nor do they want to heed wisdom when shared. Their lofty opinions blind them to the power available through the wisdom from God. Positions of influence can be wasted by those holding them in ignorance.

A wise person will gain more wisdom. It is directly attributable to the relationship with the Wisdom-Giver. Wisdom will not turn away from Him. His strength is offered to those who diligently seek Him. Wisdom will make effective use of the available strength.

Use discretion when listening to earthly rulers. Stay in God's Word so you are prepared for enemy attacks. There is no better wisdom to be found. There is no better war book. Search the pages for every ounce of treasure you can find. God will faithfully reveal Himself to you.

Let's Pray

Holy Father, we need Your wisdom. We live in a sin-infested world. We need Your salvation. We need Your strength to stand firm. Forgive our sins, there are many. Allow us to walk in a manner worthy of Your calling. Thank You for grace and mercy. In Jesus' name. Amen.

Call to Action

Make a list of people in authority and commit to praying for them. Write it out.

September 15

For wisdom will enter your heart
And knowledge will be pleasant to your soul;
Proverbs 2:10

My New American Standard Bible is The New Inductive Study Bible compiled by Precept Ministries International. If you know anything about Precept or Kay Arthur, you know that diving into scripture is encouraged. Through the years that I have studied in this version, I have colored and written and marked passages throughout the text. Following cross references and digging into the who, what, when, where, why, and how opens a perspective on the scripture that you may not have from reading alone. Taking notes and highlighting key words and phrases unlocks truth. I may not have many passages memorized but digging into my Bible has allowed me to recall passages when talking with others. God faithfully gives me recall when needed.

I love studying my Bible. There are torn pages, and the cover is getting worn but I love holding it. I love flipping through the pages. May I encourage you to have a physical Bible for studying.

Let's Pray

Holy Father, I love Your Word. I love digging in and learning more about You. Thank You for the best teacher ever! Holy Spirit speaks to me through the text. I love You. In Jesus' name. Amen.

Call to Action

Do you know how to study your Bible? Not just a Bible study but God's Word. Write it out.

September 16

My son, let them not vanish from your sight;
Keep sound wisdom and discretion,
Proverbs 3:21

From the youngest to the oldest, staying in God's Word is not only beneficial it is necessary. It is never too early and never too late to open His love letter to you. Be assured you will always learn something. Your time will not be wasted inside His Word. Open it with your family.

Teach your children how to love God's Word. Read it to them from the day they are born. When they ask questions, look them up together. See what God's Word has to say about issues they face. Lay the foundation for the rest of their lives and you will be giving them the best future.

Stay involved in a congregation of like-minded believers. Show hospitality and kindness. Make a family practice of worship, Bible study and prayer. God will bless your efforts. Walk in a manner worthy of His calling on your life. Set an example for your family.

Let's Pray

Holy Father, please forgive me for being so busy when my children were younger. God, they all believe in You and for that I am thankful. God, let them fall in love with Your Word. Grow them in their knowledge of You. Give them wisdom and discernment. In Jesus' name. Amen.

Call to Action

Commit to studying God's Word. Involve your family. Plan and keep it. Write it out.

September 17

Through insolence comes nothing but strife,
But wisdom is with those who receive counsel.
Proverbs 13:10

Here is my mouth getting me in trouble again! Unwelcomed advice falls on deaf ears. I know this. I have lived this. Let someone tell me something I don't want to hear, and it normally gets buried with the useless ideas in my brain. So why would I offer unsolicited advice?

Depending on who it is and what it is, your unsolicited advice may be the counsel needed. But the delivery matters. The voice of experience can be important for the inexperienced. Wise counsel gingerly offers helpfulness coated in compassion and respect. Not, I told you so.

Thinking before speaking is a learned talent for me. Not that I have mastered it, because I haven't. But I am learning. Let me encourage you to do the same. Hopefully, that is not unsolicited advice! I prayerfully encourage you to think before sharing your wisdom.

Let's Pray

Holy Father, sometimes I need a muzzle. God, instead of that, will You fill my heart with words that only represent You. Allow any encouragement or admonishment to be delivered in love. God, allow me to help others. I love You, Lord. In Jesus' name. Amen.

Call to Action

Do you hear yourself giving out unsolicited advice? Is it always welcomed? Write it out.

September 18

This wisdom is not that which comes down from above, but is earthly, natural, demonic. For where jealousy and selfish ambition exist, there is disorder and every evil thing.
James 3:15-16

Have you ever considered jealousy as being evil or demonic? The spirit of jealousy takes your mind and heart captive. In that prison, it is impossible to have compassion. Breaking the bonds can only be done through repentance and forgiveness. Pray for God to release you.

Holding onto it only strengthens its power over you. Jealousy hoards bitterness. It hardens your heart. It gives space to the enemy that doesn't belong to him. Give it to God and take your space back from the enemy. Send him on his way away from you. You belong to God.

Ask God to continually show you any forces of evil that attack you. Ask Him to expose it and to let you know truth. He will unlock chains and loose binds that hold you hostage. Don't give the enemy a foothold in your heart and mind. You are a child of God.

Let's Pray

Holy Father, I need Your protection from the enemy. He wants my mind and heart. He has no authority over me because I am Yours. You reign in my heart and mind. In Jesus' name. Amen.

Call to Action

Do you face attacks from the enemy? How will you enter battle? Write it out.

September 19

But the wisdom from above is first pure, then peaceable, gentle, reasonable, full of mercy and good fruits, unwavering, without hypocrisy.
James 3:17

Purity in its finest. Untainted. Followed by generous peace. It comes softly with no boisterous movement. No nonsense. Filled with mercy. Exhibiting exquisite fruit. Not tossed back and forth. Genuine and sincere. Characteristics of wisdom. Characteristics of those with wisdom.

It isn't boastful or bragging. It is full of confidence in the One who gives it. There is no confusion but clarity. Indecisiveness will not be found in wisdom, but certainty will. Respect and reverence accompany it.

The beholder knows it is there but doesn't discuss it. They hold it as a secret treasure. They protect and guard it. They use it with great discretion. It will not be misused. It does good for all its days. Its time is well spent. Purposefully intentional.

Let's Pray

Holy Father, You give good gifts. Accept our worship as a pleasing aroma. We taste and see that You are sweeter than honey to our lips. We drink Your living water. In Jesus' name. Amen.

Call to Action

Ask Him to grow your relationship with Him in wisdom and understanding. Write it out.

September 20

And Jesus kept increasing in wisdom and stature, and in favor with God and men.
Luke 2:52

Imagine God wrapped in the flesh of a child. His brain and body develop just as yours and mine did. When did He know? Did He know all along? Was He born knowing He is God? He increased in wisdom and stature. He gained attention. He is still gaining attention.

The Author of all wisdom born as a baby into the world He created lowered Himself for us to be closer to Him. He experienced all the hurt that we experience. He faced all the temptations we face. He endured persecution and our sin-death so we wouldn't have to. He rose victoriously so we could too. And He thinks enough of us to reconcile us to Himself.

We have His favor. We undeservedly receive His grace and mercy. When our faith fails, His stands firm. We are held by the Creator of the universe. He loves us.

Let's Pray

Holy Father, You gave me Your only Son to be sacrificed for my sins. He willingly took my place on the cross. I should have hung and been buried in an eternal grave, but Jesus stepped in and took what I deserve. My thanksgiving is meager, but please accept it. In Jesus' name. Amen.

Call to Action

We undeservedly receive His mercy. He deserves all our praise and worship. Write it out.

September 21

Neither have I learned wisdom,
Nor do I have the knowledge of the Holy One.
Proverbs 30:3

God imparts wisdom. For the one to whom wisdom is given, it is a precious gift. By nature of its existence, it multiplies. It is sown by God and He tends its garden. He is the keeper of wisdom.

He is careful with giving it as gifts. He knows who will properly steward this precious gift with integrity and honor. He measures out the right portion accordingly. He supplies more at just the right time. He is generous with some because He knows it will be put to good use.

If you receive this precious gift, in whatever portion given, guard it. Protect it as you would precious jewels. Although, it is not to be hidden. Along with it comes confidence in the Giver. Boldly trust Him. Realize the power He has placed in you that accompanies wisdom. He will faithfully execute His reason for placing it in you. Your responsibility is obedience.

Let's Pray

Holy Father, it is a posture of obedience You desire from us. Forgive us for our disobedience. Turn us around so that we are enjoying Your fellowship with the gifts You have given us. You lavish us with more than we deserve. Thank You, Holy Father. In Jesus' name. Amen.

Call to Action

If you could measure wisdom, how would you do it? Do you have an example? Write it out.

September 22

She opens her mouth in wisdom,
And the teaching of kindness is on her tongue.
Proverbs 31:26

Her laugh is unmistakable. When I hear it, I laugh. It is contagious. I have known her since I was one year old, and she was born. She has always been there. Even though we do not live in the same town, we can always pick back up where we left off. We are connected not only by blood, but by God. We are soul sisters. We are cousins. We are friends.

I share with you about her because today is her birthday. You can tell her happy birthday without knowing her. Go ahead. She will giggle when she reads this and thinks of so many people telling her happy birthday. Her face will explode with joy.

Kindness drips from her tongue. She is welcoming with her listening ear. She leans in with keen interest. Always making mental notes of a person she has just met and will surely remember them the next time she sees them. Her love of others is a result of her love of God.

Let's Pray

Holy Father, thank You for my cousin, my friend, my sister in You. You knit us together not just by kinship but by the blood of Jesus. Bless her today and always. In Jesus' name. Amen.

Call to Action

Is there someone you want to bless today? Send them a note of encouragement. Write it out.

September 23

The mouth of the righteous flows with wisdom,
But the perverted tongue will be cut out.
Proverbs 10:31

I want justice as much as you. I really do. But I can get angry by some of the junk I hear and see happening in this world today. It makes my blood boil. I imagine just reading this may cause you to think of something that has caused you to spout off in anger. Listen, I am right there with you.

When I get to that boiling point, I must remind myself to stop. Exploding in a fit of rage will not do anyone any good. My explosion will only cause more anger to rise in me. It would only add fuel to the combustion. I would be a ticking time bomb waiting for an unsuspecting bystander.

Then I would look just like the stuff that made me angry in the first place. Go ahead and laugh. You know I am right. You know you are guilty of the same thing. Check your anger. If your meter is running high, you may need to take a little break and get some God perspective.

Let's Pray

Holy Father, thank You for Your Holy Spirit interceding on my behalf. When I get close to being out of control, You contain me. You temper my outrage and remind me that You are the Giver of justice and that all will be made right with You. You are worthy of praise. In Jesus' name. Amen.

Call to Action

Did this hit you hard? Maybe not but maybe it did. If so, talk with God about it. Write it out.

September 24

A scoffer seeks wisdom and finds none,
But knowledge is easy to one who has understanding.
Proverbs 14:6

It always causes me to wince. Maybe not an outward motion of disgust but an inward sense of anguish. It feels like my heart has been wounded. And it has been increasingly common recently. Expletives pouring from mouths revealing the contents of hearts. Uttering God's name in vain.

I know there will be plenty of people calling me names and thinking all kinds of thoughts about me for even bringing this up but let's be honest here. That is the very problem. What is in our hearts that need to flow out of them? What is pouring out of your heart?

Your words reflect what you believe and hold in your heart. Word vomit full of vulgarity and cursing only reflects those same things about you. If you are a child of God, examine your speech. Ask God to rid your heart and mind of anything that is not pleasing to Him.

Let's Pray

Holy Father, remove word impurities in me. Let the language coming from my mouth be sweet, pleasant, and true. We know that bitterness flows out when it is present in us. Replace it with honey. Let our speech reflect You in our lives. We praise and honor You. In Jesus' name. Amen.

Call to Action

Ask God to give you a good mouth washing as you pray the same for others. Write it out.

September 25

So teach us to number our days,
That we may present to You a heart of wisdom.
Psalm 90:12

Our time on this earth is so short. It is just a vapor that appears for a moment and then disappears. The vapor has no intention, but we do. We intentionally do nothing, or we purposefully do something. We either make good use of our time, or we waste it.

I will admit to wasting much of my time. I have confessed that to God and asked Him to help me be intentional with the time He has given me. Old habits are hard to break, but with His help I know He will redeem what I have wasted. He is redeeming it even as I write.

Being intentional requires discipline. Purposefully making use of each moment. Rising in the morning knowing God has a purpose for you and you must rise to the occasion and be ready for whatever it is He has in front of you. He has created you and me for His good pleasure.

Let's Pray

Holy Father, thank You for knowing the length of our days. Will You fill them with the knowledge of Your salvation? Give us wisdom to use our time to honor You. Not just to stay busy, but to be intentional servants for Your kingdom. I love You, Lord. In Jesus' name. Amen.

Call to Action

What is your intentional purpose today? Someone needs you to fulfill it. Write it out.

September 26

Dead flies make a perfumer's oil stink, so a little foolishness is weightier than wisdom and honor.
Ecclesiastes 10:1

Our trash bins sit in front of our parking area. Easy access to drop bags in as we come and go. But the accumulation of trash can accumulate an unpleasant odor. We could relocate the trash bins, or we could lessen the amount of trash we collect. Either way, elimination is key. Remove what stinks and the odor goes away. Remove the offensive perpetrator and the problem is eradicated. Sounds easy. Making changes can be more difficult than it seems though.

Practicing a new path can be daunting. It is an unknown. This isn't about trash bins. This is about removing what produces an unpleasant aroma in your worship, in your life praise. Foolishness has no place in the life of a believer. Harbored bitterness mounds like stinky trash.

Take out your trash. Get rid of it. Ask God to reveal the unpleasant odors coming from you. Then ask Him to replace them with fragrant incense that is pleasing to Him.

Let's Pray

Holy Father, reveal and remove from me what is unpleasant to You. Create in me fragrant notes of worship and praise that is pleasing to You. Let all be for Your glory. In Jesus' name. Amen.

Call to Action

You already have a mental list of your stinky trash. Confess it to God. Write it out.

September 27

Do not speak in the hearing of a fool,
For he will despise the wisdom of your words.
Proverbs 23:9

Foolishness will not listen to wisdom. You may be able to clearly see a path free of struggle for your loved one and attempt to guide them down that path but if folly is their focus, your attempts to guide will be rejected. Your prompting and prodding may place a wedge between you.

May I suggest praying? Seems like a logical thing to do, right? And you may already be doing it. Do some more. Pray without ceasing. Ask God to intervene. Ask Him to clear the blinders off the eyes of the one that seems to be determined to hit a brick wall. Ask Him to keep your loved one from stumbling and crumbling. Ask Him to redeem your loved one.

We all have those people in our lives. The ones we want so desperately to live for God but seem to be going in the wrong direction. It may seem that all your efforts on their behalf are wasted. No prayer is wasted with God. He hears your cry and will be faithful. Trust Him.

Let's Pray

Holy Father, I trust You with all my loved ones. In Your perfect timing, You will and have created in them a heart that desires You above anything else. I love You. In Jesus' name. Amen.

Call to Action

Who are your loved ones? Who is it that you are bringing before God's throne? Write it out.

September 28

Daniel said, "Let the name of God be blessed forever and ever,
For wisdom and power belong to Him."
Daniel 2:20

I shared with my husband recently how I long for heaven. Not wanting to die but wanting the eternal presence of God in a tangible sense that this life seems to keep dim. We have known many who have passed away recently. Only God knows their real eternal home but from the life we witnessed in them, we believe they are experiencing God's presence like never before.

We believe they are worshipping with unadulterated, unfiltered praise. There is no holding back. No hesitation. Unwavering expressions of praise to our Holy God. The blessings they are pouring out would explode windows. It is too great for these temporary human forms to know.

But while we are here, in this human form, we will offer the best praise we can. We bless His Holy name. We give Him all honor. We lift open hands to Him. We bow before His throne.

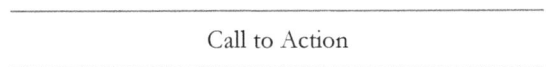

Let's Pray

Holy Father, we have nothing to bring but hearts that need You. We give what we have and ask that You accept it. You are holy. There is none greater than You. In Jesus' name. Amen.

Call to Action

Spend time praising God. Tell Him how you long for Him. Write it out.

September 29

The rod and reproof give wisdom,
But a child who gets his own way brings shame to his mother.
Proverbs 29:15

As a child, I knew my limits. I knew when I passed those limits there would be consequences. Being the middle of five children, I had the two older ones I would watch and learn from and the younger two didn't seem to get the same lessons I did from observing the older ones. Quite a dynamic situation! Somebody was always getting in trouble. And sometimes others would get in trouble just by association. I remember one such time. Indulge my reminiscing.

I have no idea what happened. The circumstances completely escape me. But the fall-out is just as fresh now as it was then. My dad was the disciplinarian in our family. He would administer that discipline on our rear ends. I was summoned for my reckoning. The wall received it instead.

He told me to cry. And I did! He extended mercy to me. I knew what mercy was on that day. He withheld my punishment that I probably deserved. And that is what Jesus did for you and me.

Let's Pray

Holy Father, thank You for the gift of mercy that I don't deserve. Please forgive me for continuing to need it. Please help me to walk in righteousness. In Jesus' name. Amen.

Call to Action

Have you met mercy? When were you first introduced? Write it out.

September 30

for I will give you utterance and wisdom which none of your opponents will be able to resist or refute.
Luke 21:15

The words God gives you to speak on His behalf will never be returned to you without gain. If they are truly from Him, you can be assured He will use them for His gain. His plans always prosper. They always succeed. There is nothing that can stop them from flourishing.

Many may try to ridicule what God is doing in you, but they have no power over you. The enemy may attempt to block you from moving forward in the direction God is sending you, but he will fail. With God all your efforts with Him will be incomprehensibly good.

Keep moving forward with Him. Seek Him with all your heart and mind and soul and strength. He is faithful to meet you when you humbly approach His throne. He is true to His promises. He will never leave you or forsake you. You are sealed by the power of His salvation.

Let's Pray

Holy Father, so great a gift is Your salvation. We can only fall prostrate at Your feet in gratitude and worship. We give you all praise and honor and glory. I love You. In Jesus' name. Amen.

Call to Action

What assignment does He have for you? What are you waiting for? Go! Get busy. Write it out.

*AND HE WAS SAYING TO THEM,
"THE HARVEST IS PLENTIFUL,
BUT THE LABORERS ARE FEW;
THEREFORE BESEECH THE LORD
OF THE HARVEST TO SEND OUT
LABORERS INTO HIS HARVEST."
LUKE 10:2*

October

And He was saying to them, "The harvest is plentiful, but the laborers are few; therefore beseech the Lord of the harvest to send out laborers into His harvest."
Luke 10:2

You can't carry the load alone. I can't carry the load alone. Spread the work around and the burden lessens. There is plenty of work to go around, but there aren't plenty of willing workers. Before you and I begin our work, we need to recruit more workers. Finding workers is work.

I hired someone this week. I placed a job advertisement and had over fifty applicants. I narrowed the field down to eight and arranged interviews. The first applicant did not come. I feared this was the beginning of the end of my search. Concerned others may not show up, I started making calls to confirm appointments. I had six interviews that day with three strong candidates.

I asked for references and found I still had three strong candidates after hearing positive stories on all three. I had a difficult decision to make. All three seemed to be a good fit for the role. One took another position before I could move further, leaving me with two qualified candidates.

One more phone call to each candidate. Reviewing resumes one more time. Praying for a firm decision. Sleeping on it to wake for confirmation. The choice was obvious. I made my choice, and the chosen candidate accepted the offer.

I have recruited a worker to come alongside me in the work I have to do. God lined it all up. Without His blessing, I would not be anticipating her start date. I trust God to provide. I am thankful He produces workers when they are needed the most.

October 1

"Now when you reap the harvest of your land, you shall not reap to the very corners of your field, nor shall you gather the gleanings of your harvest.'"
Leviticus 19:9

God abundantly provides. In His abundance, He provides enough to share. His Word instructs us to give out of the abundance He provides. But it is to be shared with the needy. What does that look like? How do you discern who is truly needy? It isn't always the person at the traffic light holding a sign asking for help. They may need help but not necessarily for what they are asking.

Credible organizations abound for you to join. Their missions are clearly stated, and accountability is important to them. It isn't hard to find one that you can support. It could be as easy as asking your pastor to direct you to one that fulfills your heart's desire to help.

Many accept volunteers and financial donations. You may have more time on your hands than financial resources and using your abundance is honoring to God, no matter the format. Blessing others brings blessings to you. We all have something to give.

Let's Pray

Holy Father, thank You for Your abundant provision. Direct us in sharing. In Jesus' name. Amen.

Call to Action

Do you already have a special mission? Will you recruit others to join? Write it out.

October 2

"Do you not say, 'There are yet four months, and then comes the harvest'? Behold, I say to you, lift up your eyes and look on the fields, that they are white for harvest."
John 4:35

There is always a harvest waiting to be brought in from the fields. It may be next door or around the corner. Maybe it is in the coffee shop behind the counter. It could be that co-worker that has been asking questions about your church. It could be that little one sitting in the highchair.

Someone else may have planted the seeds. Someone else may have watered the soil. Someone else may have fertilized the field. Someone else may have pruned dead branches. Someone else may have added support to a drooping stalk. It could be you that comes along for the harvest.

Ask God to give you discernment to know what you need to do in your harvesting opportunities. You may need to sow a seed. You may need to water the soil. You may need to add fertilizer. You may need to pull out your pruning shears. You may need to add support. You may see ripe fruit.

Let's Pray

Holy Father, bless the work of our hands and hearts as we minister to others. God, help us to discern ripe fruit ready for harvest. Thank You for preparing the harvest. In Jesus' name. Amen.

Call to Action

Where are you? Waiting to be harvested or out there gathering the harvest? Write it out.

October 3

"Speak to the sons of Israel and say to them, 'When you enter the land which I am going to give to you and reap its harvest, then you shall bring in the sheaf of the first fruits of your harvest to the priest.'"
Leviticus 23:10

Your first efforts were made possible by God. He gave you the ability to do the work. You can't accomplish anything without Him. Why would you think you get the first results of your efforts? And why would you think the first fruits belong to the government? Give to God first.

As a young believer, I heard stories of people's faithful, radical giving. Out of the little they had; they were faithful to give a tithe to God. If you don't know, the word tithe means tenth. Out of everything they would give the first ten percent back to God. Their stories always encouraged me because they shared how when they came to a desperate situation with no resources, God always provided for their needs. In their faithfulness, they found God to be faithful.

It's our turn. It all belongs to Him anyway. We get to use it.

Let's Pray

Holy Father, thank You for Your faithfulness to us. We enjoy the provision You give. Help us to be faithful in giving back to You. It is all Yours. In Jesus' name. Amen.

Call to Action

Do you tithe? Will you commit to stewarding resources so you can? Write it out.

October 4

And sow fields and plant vineyards,
And gather a fruitful harvest.
Psalm 107:37

Apple harvest in North Georgia brings thousands of visitors. Many of those visitors are fascinated by the idea of farming but live in cities with asphalt, concrete, and buildings galore. The farming life is foreign and therefore the attraction for a weekend getaway. The tasty harvest is just a bonus for a fall retreat. The slower pace is really the draw but only for a quick moment.

These wannabe farmers are so frenzied in their routines, slowing down to appreciate the cycle of life for these crops is too boring for them. Appreciating the time and effort it took to get the fruit ready for harvest is missed by the many visitors. They appreciate the results though.

And, so, it is with the harvest of souls for the kingdom of God. The process provides rich experiences not to be missed in preparation for the harvest. Then enjoy a cornucopia.

Let's Pray

Holy Father, thank You for the abundance of flavors and textures You give. You make this world a colorful masterpiece in each season. We take pleasure in Your bountiful harvest. Please find pleasure in the harvest we bring for Your kingdom. In Jesus' name. Amen.

Call to Action

What is your farming experience? Thank God for your favorite harvest. Write it out.

October 5

Prepares her food in the summer
And gathers her provision in the harvest.
Proverbs 6:8

Remember those plans you made in January? Do you see the results? Did you stick with it and make progress toward your goal? Have you reached your goal? Are you enjoying the product of your efforts? You are holding mine in your hand right now.

Preparing for the work ahead is worth the return. God gave you the work to do and you are doing it. Keep going and don't stop. He will use your current work for your next task. He is always teaching and preparing us for what is to come.

The labor pains you have endured are giving birth to something wonderful. You have devoted time and effort, blood and sweat, tears and laughter, to this labor of love. Your attention has been focused on obtaining the completion of this work. Praise God as you enjoy the fruits.

Let's Pray

Holy Father, our work never ceases. Thank You for giving us work to do. Let us continually be working to further Your kingdom in all we do. Bring fruit from our work. It is all for You. Find it as a pleasant fragrance of offering. Yours is the glory forever. In Jesus' name. Amen.

Call to Action

Go back and see how you have done with your plans. Do you see results? Write it out.

October 6

"But when the crop permits, he immediately puts in the sickle, because the harvest has come."
Mark 4:29

Watching. Waiting. Testing. Observing conditions for the right moment to gather. Not waiting a moment longer for fear of spoilage and loss. Taking it too early could produce the same results. Perfect timing requires careful attention and experience and discernment.

Equipment is in place. Storage bins are sitting ready to be filled. Workers are gathered. Clouds on the horizon cause panic. No time to waste. The harvest must happen now.

The wind blows. Rain threatens. Dark clouds swirl overhead. But then when it seems work will stop the sky splits into a brilliant blue, a stark contrast to the waving grains of gold. And gold is gathered. Precious gold loved by the Farmer.

Let's Pray

Holy Father, You sow, water, grow and bring to full maturity. We are Your harvest, God. Collect us into Your heavenly storehouses. Preserve us. Multiply us. We eagerly await Jesus' return for His bride. We are waiting with excited anticipation. All praise and honor are Yours. We worship at Your feet. We love You, Lord. In Jesus' name. Amen.

Call to Action

Are you excited about the eventual return of Jesus? If not, prepare for it. Write it out.

October 7

"According to what I have seen, those who plow iniquity
And those who sow trouble harvest it."
Job 4:8

Job's friends are notorious for their bad advice and harsh accusations. Occasionally they made accurate statements. They had good intentions but didn't always have their facts straight.

Were their admonishments reflective of their own actions? They were stirring the pot. Throwing untruths in Job's face when they knew his character. With friends like this, who needs enemies?

The most well-meaning people among us, even ourselves, are prone to stir up contention and strife. It seems to always come back on us. This isn't karma! This is God's correction of one that has strayed away from good intentions. Good intentions require good actions for good results.

The soil and seeds must be in good condition for the harvest to be prosperous. If the soil doesn't have the proper nutrients, seedlings will fail to thrive. If the seeds are hollow shells, nothing will sprout. Good soil and good seeds together with water and sunshine create good harvests.

Let's Pray

Holy Father, help our actions and intentions be pleasing to You. In Jesus' name. Amen.

Call to Action

Do a check on your intentions and actions. Ask God to reveal discrepancies. Write it out.

October 8

The sluggard does not plow after the autumn,
So he begs during the harvest and has nothing.
Proverbs 20:4

The planning and preparation are continual. Purposefully expecting the next season and doing what needs to be done to be ready assures adequate provisions. Like looking at the sky and anticipating rain and picking up your umbrella to be prepared for the eventual.

Part of planning involves saving money. Wasteful spending leaves you broke. Budget so you can save for vacation or a big purchase instead of piling up debt that you will spend the rest of your life paying. Debt makes you a slave. Live frugally. Give generously. Debt is not your friend.

Retirement is a goal for many. I fear for many it becomes a time to wait for death. Losing sight of your purpose for living can be dangerous to your health. Plan and prepare to serve differently. Continue in the work God has for you to do. Prepare spiritually, physically, and financially.

Let's Pray

Holy Father, thank You for work. Thank you for giving us purpose and mission. We want to serve You well. Guide us in our work. Help us to stay engaged in the mission of building Your kingdom. Direct our stewardship of Your resources. In Jesus' name. Amen.

Call to Action

Do you have a budget? May I encourage you to seek God's will in using money. Write it out.

October 9

Like snow in summer and like rain in harvest,
So honor is not fitting for a fool.
Proverbs 26:1

Some things just don't belong together. Flip flops and socks. Fill a cracked container with water. Using salt instead of sugar. Using sugar instead of salt. Riding a bicycle backwards. It just doesn't work well. It is awkward. It may even be frustrating or disgusting.

Turn on the news and you will hear and see story after story of people being honored for both good and evil. Depending on who you listen to you will hear different opinions. Honor does not belong to evil. Honor is to be reserved for righteousness. Righteousness and evil cannot coexist.

Do you give honor where it doesn't belong? Think about that. Treating someone with respect and honor for your own personal gain is not honoring them but insulting yourself. It certainly isn't honoring to God. Place honor only where it belongs. Use it wisely.

Let's Pray

Holy Father, You are worthy of all honor. God, help us to see others through Your eyes. Help us to love them and to bestow honor in a manner that is just and right. Keep us from being people pleasers but let us be pleasing to You. All honor is Yours. In Jesus' name. Amen.

Call to Action

Ask God to help you treat others the way you would want to be treated. Write it out.

October 10

"While the earth remains,
Seedtime and harvest,
And cold and heat,
And summer and winter,
And day and night
Shall not cease."
Genesis 8:22

God's incredible creation of earth is rotating around the sun bringing all the seasons in consistent order. His orchestration of this pattern is masterful. The Master of the universe put it all into motion with the words of His mouth. He will keep it moving at His good pleasure.

He fashioned winter cold for dormant rest to prepare for spring blooms of color and life. Cool spring blooms usher vivid life into summer sun and warmth. The summer sun draws life up and ripens fruit in preparation for autumn harvest. The abundance of autumn harvest gathers provisions for the winter cold of dormant rest. And so, it begins again. Consistent rotation.

The same with our lives. We come into the world fresh and new. Kisses from our Creator are still in our view. We grow and mature. Many seasons experienced in this journey of life. And before we know it our winter season is upon us beckoning us back to our Creator. Enjoy the journey.

Let's Pray

Holy Father, Your creation groans for You. We need You in every season. In Jesus' name. Amen.

Call to Action

What season are you in right now? Yes, I know autumn, but in life. Praise God for it. Write it out.

October 11

"You shall work six days, but on the seventh day you shall rest; even during plowing time and harvest you shall rest."
Exodus 34:21

I am nearing the end of drafting this book and have scheduled out how much I need to write each day. I have a self-imposed deadline. I have been working on this for eight months. I am ready to see its birth. The pages are full and pregnant. The labor pains have been long and tiring.

I am writing this page on Monday morning. I rise early before I go to work to type out words on my screen. Some days are easier than others. Some days I just stare at the brightly lit screen in a dark room with nothing to show when I finally get ready for work. It has been quite the journey.

Yesterday, Sunday, I rose early as usual. I sat at my desk and opened my laptop. Before I touched the pages of this book, I journaled a prayer. I opened my Bible and read a passage. I closed my laptop and thanked God for Sabbath rest. He was faithful to honor it. I am blessed by Him.

Let's Pray

Holy Father, thank You for providing rest for me. God, You know how tired I get. You know all my struggles. You have been faithful to me, and I am thankful. In Jesus' name. Amen.

Call to Action

How have you received God's blessing when you listen to Him? Write it out.

October 12

He who gathers in summer is a son who acts wisely,
But he who sleeps in harvest is a son who acts shamefully.
Proverbs 10:5

My husband's backyard garden produced corn, okra, squash, green peppers, tomatoes, and watermelon this year. He just recently mowed it down with his tractor. He harvested enough corn and okra to add to our freezer. We enjoyed garden to table meals while it lasted.

We don't rely on this food, but we are thankful to have it. We are also thankful for farmers who work to provide food year-round. The work of farmers feeds the world. If you know a farmer, thank them. Go buy some local produce and enjoy the fruits of their labor.

What a blessing it is to have access to food! Pray for nations that may not have the abundance we have here in America. Seek ways to help people in your community that may not have the abundance you have in your household. May God bless the sharing!

Let's Pray

Holy Father, thank You for the people that grow our food. Bless their efforts and multiply the goodness of their bounty. God, protect our food supply. In Jesus' name. I love You, Lord. Amen.

Call to Action

Make a list of local ministries that provide food for those in need. Commit to help. Write it out.

October 13

Now He who supplies seed to the sower and bread for food will supply and multiply your seed for sowing and increase the harvest of your righteousness;
2 Corinthians 9:10

Last year, I planted zinnia seeds. I had freshly cut flowers all summer. As I cut, more would come. Blooms multiplied each time I took one for a vase. Finally, as growing slowed, I left blooms to dry. I collected many dry blooms to save as seeds but others that looked small, I left them on the stems and pulled them all up when I cleaned out the bed.

This year I didn't plant seeds. My attention has been on other matters. Early in spring I saw evidence of life peeking through the bottom of that bed. God took some of those seeds and planted them for me. I have enjoyed zinnias this year without planting a single seed.

I am looking forward to the harvest of those other matters from this year. I am praying God multiplies the harvest. I still have seeds saved. I still have the promise of future harvests.

Let's Pray

Holy Father, You are the Master Gardener. Your fields are always abundantly producing prolific harvests. Thank You for producing a harvest in our hearts. In Jesus' name. Amen.

Call to Action

Ask Him to sow more seeds in your heart and allow yours to multiply. Write it out.

October 14

"So every good tree bears good fruit, but the bad tree bears bad fruit."
Matthew 7:17

Only silent tears fell. Pain expressed not in sadness for her but in sadness for those who remain to miss her. Pain for self in missing her. A life well-lived remembered by many. Stories of memories. Memories made during that life well-lived. Her fruit evident in those tears.

The reflection you saw when you looked at her was not of herself or her parents or siblings or husband but of God. Kindness from her constant smile. Generosity from her kitchen. Love from the time she spent with her people. Years of loyalty to her people. Years of faithfulness to God.

Her casket was covered in a beautiful blanket of every kind of light pink flower imaginable, just the shade of her gentle cheeks. A beautiful tribute to a beautiful soul. Hers was a soul that set an example for others who come behind her. A soul that left a mark for God.

Let's Pray

Holy Father, thank You for the example of good fruit that we get to witness in others. Traits that are indicative of a relationship with You. Help us to bear good fruit. Create in us hearts and minds that are quick to offer compassion and kindness. In Jesus' name. Amen.

Call to Action

Who has sown a seed in you that causes you to want to live differently? Write it out.

October 15

Then God said, "Let the earth sprout vegetation: plants yielding seed, and fruit trees on the earth bearing fruit after their kind with seed in them"; and it was so.
Genesis 1:11

Two pear trees were planted on the hill. Their first year, they received regular watering. There was one pear on one tree that first year. No fruit on the other. The second growing season, only rain watered the trees. The leaves were eaten by pests and no fruit appeared on either tree.

Maybe it is time for pruning and giving a little attention to the trees. Perhaps the third growing season will see improvements in both trees. Or perhaps the trees will need to come down. Maybe the location doesn't give optimal conditions for survival.

God planted each of us in a specific location. He has given us the tools we need to thrive. Unlike the pear trees, we can take action to change conditions so we can accomplish the work God has given us to do. He has given us fruit to bear and seeds to sow.

Let's Pray

Holy Father, You give attention to our every need. You provide for every detail. Thank You for Your care and precision over us. Help us to sow and reap good fruit. In Jesus' name. Amen.

Call to Action

What details has God worked out for you? Will you thank Him? Write it out.

October 16

"You did not choose Me but I chose you, and appointed you that you would go and bear fruit, and that your fruit would remain, so that whatever you ask of the Father in My name He may give to you."
John 15:16

Chosen. Appointed. Sent. Fruitful. Eternal. Receiver.

Have you ever considered owning any of these descriptions? Well let me inform you of something. If you are a child of God, these descriptions belong to you. Upon your realization of your need for a Savior, you became all these things and more. You came into your true existence.

He chose you before the world existed. He has had His eye on you forever. Fully known by Him. Appointed for excellent work. It is your assignment from God. He has given you something to do. Sent to do that work and to be fruitful as you do it. You are a missionary right there. You are promised eternal life with Him. You are an heir. Your inheritance is straight from God.

Claim your rightful place in His kingdom. He has given it to you.

Let's Pray

Holy Father, You have equipped us for Your purposes. Help us live in it. In Jesus' name. Amen.

Call to Action

Do any of these descriptors intimidate you? Talk with God about it. Write it out.

October 17

(for the fruit of the Light consists in all goodness and righteousness and truth),
Ephesians 5:9

It lives in the good that you do. It dwells in righteousness. It abides in truth. The fruit that comes from God is seen when it dwells within you. You can't help but let it be seen. It peeks out like little rays of sunshine peeking through your windows in early morning hours.

The light explodes through cracks and crevices. Dispersing into a million vibrant colors. Piercing the eye of the beholder. Light bouncing off goodness, off righteousness, off truth. Penetrating dark spaces exposing anything that needs to be buried at the foot of the cross.

When you have been in the Light, you are ruined for good. The dark vanishes. What the light gave, the dark cannot take back. All revealed and cleansed by the Light.

Let's Pray

Holy Father, Your Light shines in and through us. Thank You for illuminating the path in front of us and guiding us in Your goodness, righteousness, and truth. God, allow us to carry Your Light in this broken world so that we can be beacons of hope for others. In Jesus' name. Amen.

Call to Action

Are you hiding your light? The Light that is within you? Ask God to help you let it shine for all to see. In Him is all goodness, righteousness, and truth. Write it out.

October 18

Then he prayed again, and the sky poured rain and the earth produced its fruit.
James 5:18

The grass was crunchy. It wasn't supposed to be. It had been weeks since any rain had watered the earth. My heart matched the grass. I was crunchy. The grass wasn't the only thing that needed a good rain shower. My heart needed a downpour. The drought was sucking the life out of me.

He met me in my petitions. He heard my cries. He reached down into my pit of dry dusty bones and stretched them over with sinew and flesh. He breathed fresh wind into my lungs. He set my heart ablaze for Him. He opened my eyes and revealed truth. He rescued me.

Now I must not stay silent. His favor over me demands praise. I cannot allow the rocks to cry out in my place. What once were dry bones rattling have been lifted to life, prepared for battle. The battle cry is going out. The trumpet is sounding the alarm for war. Armed by God.

Let's Pray

Holy Father, dust off dry bones and reconnect them with tissue. Will You strengthen us for the battle we face is grim? We know we have victory in You and have nothing to fear. You prepare us to bear much fruit. We are willing and ready for Your assignment. In Jesus' name. Amen.

Call to Action

Do you have your assignment? Are you preparing for harvest? Write it out.

October 19

And the seed whose fruit is righteousness is sown in peace by those who make peace.
James 3:18

Through the blood of Jesus, righteousness is imparted on those who are covered in it. Only by the blood. Only by the perfect sacrifice of our perfect Savior. In our sinful state, He thought us important enough to die for us. He gave His life so we could be called righteous.

Jesus gave us His righteousness. One by-product of righteousness is peace. The calming of your soul in the middle of chaos is peace. When everything seems wrong and upset, the presence of Jesus in your life ushers in the presence of peace. Peace does not exist outside of Jesus.

His gift of peace multiplies. He takes the turmoil of our lives and inserts peace. Incomprehensible peace. He wraps it around your shoulders and nestles it in your heart. He gives you plenty so that you can share. He shares with you so that you can share with others.

Let's Pray

Holy Father, the peace that You give me keeps me going. When up ahead seems scary and dark, You reassure me with Your peace. You calm my anxious thoughts. You hold my racing heart in Your grasp so gently and breathe life into my weak lungs. In Jesus' name. Amen.

Call to Action

What does God's peace feel like to you? Describe it in your own words. Write it out.

October 20

Behold, children are a gift of the LORD,
The fruit of the womb is a reward.
Psalm 127:3

I have a bad habit of isolating myself. Pulling away to be alone. Then when I get there, I feel lonely. Ha! Crazy, huh? Understand, I am never completely alone because there is no where I can go to get away from God. For that I am thankful! But He doesn't want me to isolate myself.

So, He gave me three children. He blessed me with three healthy pregnancies. He blessed me with three easy deliveries. He blessed me with three people that were a product of the love He had for me and my husband. We don't deserve them, but God blessed us richly with them.

This is my story. Yours may be quite different. I will not attempt to imagine your story because it is yours, not mine. I would love to hear your story. Someone may need to hear your story. Someone may need to hear your heart. I pray you find blessings in the story God gave you.

Let's Pray

Holy Father, thank You for the blessings of Ashley, Andrew, and Adam. You allowed me to birth three incredible individuals. I ask Your blessings on them. For their relationships with You. For them to walk in a manner worthy of Your calling for them. In Jesus' name. Amen.

Call to Action

Share your story with someone. Someone needs to hear it. Before you do, write it out.

October 21

"My fruit is better than gold, even pure gold,
And my yield better than choicest silver."
Proverbs 8:19

There is no manufactured price tag sufficient to carry the value of the gifts God bestows on His children. The cross could not hold it for long. The grave could not keep it contained. The value of life given to relieve the debt of my sin has no limit. There are not enough digits to count it.

But you and I hold the gift. How can that be? A love so great that the cross couldn't keep it and the grave couldn't contain it is held in these temporary vessels within the confines of our souls. Consider that your soul holds the power of the One who created you. He knows no boundaries!

With Him there is limitless power. Our human attempts to define weight or force or any measure of anything only scratches the smallest of etchings into the vastness of who He is. No amount of gold or silver or precious stones can define His value. He is worthy of all praise.

Let's Pray

Holy Father, I don't know what I would do without You. I would be lost and searching for something I couldn't find. There is nothing I can do that is worthy of Your grace and mercy, but You give them anyway. I am in awe of You. I love You, Lord. In Jesus' name. Amen.

Call to Action

The world's net worth is not greater than the love of God. Thank Him for His love. Write it out.

October 22

They will still yield fruit in old age;
They shall be full of sap and very green,
Psalm 92:14

Have you sat down to talk with someone beyond your years? They know stuff that you don't. I promise you could learn a thing or two from someone who is your senior. You could say the same about yourself. You have experiences that may benefit someone else.

I have known many people throughout my life who have wisdom far beyond mine. I love hearing them talk. The stories and lessons they have learned are rich indications of the hand of God. Provision and protection in perils. Examples of faith in action. Most are willing to talk with you.

Go and listen to someone. Ask them to share their salvation story. They may ask you to share yours. Be prepared to hear some amazing stuff! Take a snack to share too. It is always a blessing to break bread together. It doesn't matter if you are older or younger. Go listen. Go share.

Let's Pray

Holy Father, thank You for the fellowship You give us with others. God, keep me from isolating myself so that I can listen to others and share in return with them. Place people in my life that will enrich it and perhaps allow me to do the same for them. In Jesus' name. Amen.

Call to Action

Make a list of people, older and younger, that you want to visit. Then do it. Write it out.

October 23

The fruit of the righteous is a tree of life,
And he who is wise wins souls.
Proverbs 11:30

My family tree is loaded! My dad had twelve siblings. My mom had four siblings. I have four siblings. And we have not even included spouses and children and grandchildren. And we are not going back beyond my grandparents. It is full. There are at least three preachers in the tree, an uncle, my dad, and my grandfather. Others have testified of God's goodness outside of the pulpit.

There have been plenty that are not loud with their sharing like the preachers in the family but each one that has called on the name of Jesus as Savior has been a witness of His goodness to the people around them. Many are quick to tell you how He has worked in their lives.

It all started with one person believing. One person surrendering to the Lordship of Jesus started multi-generational belief. If you are the first one in your family to believe, consider the impact your life may have on the kingdom of God. Be fruitful and multiply.

Let's Pray

Holy Father, thank You for those who came before me and help me to lead the generations after me. Use my life to further Your kingdom. I am here and willing. In Jesus' name. Amen.

Call to Action

Can you trace your spiritual legacy through your family tree? Are you growing it? Write it out.

October 24

"My Father is glorified by this, that you bear much fruit, and so prove to be My disciples."
John 15:8

A pastor mentioned recently that if everyone in that service were involved in the church as the Bible describes the early church that there would never be the need to ask for volunteers. The work would be spread around, and everyone would be working within their calling.

Imagine if we got up out of our seats and became involved in teaching and praying. Going to work in the children's ministry holding babies while parents lead in other ways. Picking up trash from the grounds. Cleaning toilets. Visiting home-bound brothers and sisters. Sharing a meal with a family. Reaching out to help in a time of crisis. Giving resources to keep the doors open.

All of this while joining together to study God's Word to know Him. Everyone has a different gift. Even if you know someone fulfilling what you are led to do, you become involved. You never know what need exists until you are actively participating in the body of Christ.

Let's Pray

Holy Father, You know our hearts when it comes to working in Your kingdom. You have equipped us to be involved. Let us move in confidence within your will. In Jesus' name. Amen.

Call to Action

Do you know what your spiritual gift is? Ask a pastor to help you with it. Write it out.

October 25

Death and life are in the power of the tongue,
And those who love it will eat its fruit.
Proverbs 18:21

The words stung quickly. I didn't even have to think much about the impact because they punched me in the gut. Immediately the downward spiral began. From the mountain top all the way to the bottom of the valley in one question. It left me feeling nauseous.

The words were meant to be encouraging. Words to cause you to examine yourself and ask God to reveal truth. They did that and I didn't like the implication. I didn't like the reflection I saw when considering such a short question. "If all have a problem with you, are you the problem?"

Does my tongue get me in trouble? Or am I edifying others through the words I speak? Am I ripping anyone apart without fully realizing the power of the words I speak? Do I turn others away because of my words? Considering this quietly today.

Let's Pray

Holy Father, hold my tongue so that only life is spoken. Allow my words to provide encouragement and edification. Guard my mouth as You guard my heart so that the flow is only from Your goodness. Let me remember the power I hold. In Jesus' name. Amen.

Call to Action

Listen to your words before you speak. Do you need to sit a while with this too? Write it out.

October 26

When you shall eat of the fruit of your hands,
You will be happy and it will be well with you.
Psalm 128:2

After baking a loaf of sourdough bread, I slice it and freeze it. I love toasted slices. So many possibilities with a slice of sourdough bread. French toast. Sandwich. Cream cheese and just about any topping you want. Olive oil and spices. Butter. Jelly. Peanut butter. You get the picture.

For a non-cook, my bread makes my heart sing. Watching it come together from a few simple ingredients to being this slice of heaven that I get to enjoy is a personal pleasure. It is an indulgence. It is a gift from God. From the work of my hands, God allows me to make bread.

What work are you doing that makes you happy? It doesn't have to be tangible. Whatever work you do, do it as if you are doing it for God. Because you are. He takes delight in the efforts you make to honor Him. Go ahead! You can smile!

Let's Pray

Holy Father, accept the work of our hands as an offering of praise to You. You have given us the ability to do certain things, and we want it to honor You. Allow others to see evidence of You through our work. We praise You for what You do for us. In Jesus' name. Amen.

Call to Action

If you haven't figured out the work that makes you happy, think about it and write it out.

October 27

"I will abundantly bless her provision;
I will satisfy her needy with bread."
Psalm 132:15

Did you have enough to eat today? If your kitchen is anything like mine, there is always an abundance. My husband is the cook in our household, and he always prepares more than enough. He doesn't want anyone to get up from our table hungry. We keep disposable trays for guests to take leftovers. It is what he does. God blesses us abundantly.

There are those that have an abundance. There are those that don't have an abundance, though. There are those that may go to bed hungry tonight. I pray that it is not you. I pray you have sufficient resources to provide sustenance for your family. Even abundance.

Will you prayerfully consider giving to a local food bank? There are organizations that provide groceries for those that need a little extra help. God knows the intent of your heart when you give. He also knows the intent of any recipients from these organizations. Ask Him to bless it.

Let's Pray

Holy Father, will you show us who and how to help? Give us discernment in our giving so that it is useful and not harmful. Use our overflow to benefit others. In Jesus' name. Amen.

Call to Action

Look up local food banks. Make a list and call to see how you can help. Write it out.

October 28

He rained down manna upon them to eat
And gave them food from heaven.
Psalm 78:24

The Israelites wandered in a desert forty years. There were no crops to provide for the multitude. Food was scarce. But their complaints weren't. They cried out to Moses wanting to go back into slavery because their bellies were grumbling. They were willing to trade freedom for food.

When God heard their cries for help, He provided. He gave just the right amount. Just for the day and enough for the Sabbath on the day before. He rained down provision. He placed the food at their feet. They did nothing to deserve it, but He gave it. Bread to keep them alive.

He did it again for me and for you. He gave us the Bread of Life. He places Him before us, and we get to choose to take and eat and live. We didn't do anything to deserve Jesus, but He gave Him anyway. Are we willing to trade the freedom He gives us for any temporary satisfaction?

Let's Pray

Holy Father, You not only care about our spiritual condition, but You also care about our physical condition. You rained life down in the form of our Savior. You continue to sustain us with His bread of life and living water. I praise You for Your abundant provision. In Jesus' name. Amen.

Call to Action

Take time today to praise Him for His goodness over you. Write it out.

October 29

She looks well to the ways of her household,
And does not eat the bread of idleness.
Proverbs 31:27

This woman of Proverbs 31 set the standard for all women. She knew what was needed to provide for her family and community. She didn't sit around waiting to be told what to do, she got up and did it. I am sure she didn't waste her precious time scrolling through social media.

She was one busy woman. Her value is far greater than precious stones. She gives her husband no reason to distrust her. She looks for work to do and enjoys it. She is a deliberate shopper. She wakes up while it is still dark so she can prepare food for her family and those who work for her. She operates many profitable businesses. She finds ways for them to profit more. She keeps a light on for security. Her hands stay busy. She helps others. Her family is well clothed. Her husband is well-known. She is a teacher and a blessing to her children. She doesn't ask for praise, but it finds her anyway. Study this woman. Ask God to help you follow her example.

Let's Pray

Holy Father, help me to walk in a manner worthy of Your calling. Allow my life to bring you honor and glory. Thank You for Your Word to guide me. In Jesus' name. Amen.

Call to Action

Consider your life and ways you can become more like this woman. Write it out.

October 30

"Do not worry then, saying, 'What will we eat?' or 'What will we drink?' or 'What will we wear for clothing?'"
Matthew 6:31

God is all about the details. He is the Master Artist and Master Administrator and Master Physician. He cares about your feet as much as He does your head. He cares about the words you think as much as He does the ones you speak. There is not one thing that is hidden from Him.

His care extends from the furthest reaches of space to the core of the earth. His care defines your DNA. Blood pumping through your veins was designed to keep you alive. The blood of Jesus was designed to keep you alive. He cares about your eternity. He cares about your choices.

If you are covered by the blood of Jesus, there is nothing to worry about. The best decision you will ever make is to know Him and accept His care for you. The next moment is His. Hold out your hands and give it to Him. Trust Him with it. He really does know best.

Let's Pray

Holy Father, in Your infinite love and mercy You surround us with Yourself. You never leave us or forsake us. We are held securely in Your tender care. Thank You. In Jesus' name. Amen.

Call to Action

When I am fully aware of His presence, He gives me assurance. Can you relate? Write it out.

October 31

For even when we were with you, we used to give you this order: if anyone is not willing to work, then he is not to eat, either.
2 Thessalonians 3:10

Have you eaten today? Does your morning routine include skipping breakfast, or do you have a meal first thing when you wake up? I normally eat within two or three hours of waking up. I will have a warm cup of decaf coffee or hot tea soon after rising. Something I have noticed though, the warm beverage or the food does not prepare itself. I must get up and work to make it happen.

I know! If you know your Bible and look at today's verse, you will tell me this is Paul's exhortation to lead a disciplined life of productivity. He was speaking of people that had developed habits of laziness. Laziness brings starvation. You don't work; you don't eat.

So, what about the needy? There is help that helps and help that hurts. Teach someone to garden and they will have food. Hand someone a cheeseburger and they will expect you to hand them another one. You decide which one you want to give.

Let's Pray

Holy Father, keep us mindful of the help we offer. Let it be beneficial. In Jesus' name. Amen.

Call to Action

How can you sow seeds of helpfulness? There is work to be done. Write it out.

I WILL PRAISE THE NAME OF
GOD WITH SONG
AND MAGNIFY HIM WITH
THANKSGIVING.
PSALM 69:30

November

*I will praise the name of God with song
And magnify Him with thanksgiving.
Psalm 69:30*

Pumpkins are ripe. Leaves are falling. The harvest is finished. The weather has shifted to cool, crisp mornings. The earth is beginning its cycle of rest from the busy growing season. The abundance is realized in pantries and hearts. Autumn is here.

Along with this shift, comes a natural desire for thankfulness. Looking back over the year and seeing God's hand weaving all things together for your good. Both challenging times and good times have proven His faithfulness. He has been your constant companion.

So, prepare a celebration. Make this one a celebration to remember. Pull out the best of the best that you have. With the setting of each place at the table, record another blessing. This table will be full of the richness He has added to your life.

Share your table with others. Bring guests in to see the bounty He has given you. Ask others to see theirs. Always remembering that God is the source of your blessings. Without Him, your table is empty. Boast in Him and of His goodness.

From the harvest, serve food full of His flavor. Seasoned with love. Aromas enticing all who gather. Mouths watering in anticipation of the feast.

Drink in His goodness. Be drunk only in His Spirit. Enjoy the fruit of His Vine.

Let's fill this Thanksgiving table with offerings of praise to God.

November 1

Let the word of Christ richly dwell within you, with all wisdom teaching and admonishing one another with psalms and hymns and spiritual songs, singing with thankfulness in your hearts to God.
Colossians 3:16-17

Will you join me in giving thanks? You have seen it and maybe done it before. Perhaps you do it every day. Is it a daily practice you have been doing for years? Not just in November, but throughout the year? Writing out your gratitude. Counting your blessings.

November seems like a suitable time to refocus gratitude. Returning to the One who gave everything to you. Expressing your offering of thanks in all things.

Are you willing to join me? Are you willing to share it with others so they may be encouraged to do the same? The thanks are to God always. But by sharing you will bring others to the Thanksgiving table. What is one thing for which you are thankful? Allow others the blessing of knowing what God does for you?

Let's Pray

Holy Father, all thanks be to You. You shower us with blessings. Give us the ability to see blessings each day. God, allow us to live in gratitude. In Jesus' name. Amen.

Call to Action

After writing your gratitude, read it aloud to yourself. Write it out.

November 2

That I may proclaim with the voice of thanksgiving
And declare all Your wonders.
Psalm 26:7

Consider His wonders. Those you can see and those you can't. They are too numerous to count but you can begin anytime. Today even. Begin counting the wonders of God today. Begin with one a day or more. Three is a great number. Or five.

In a clear night sky, stars abound. Get away from city lights and stare up at the sky. Or go to the ocean and watch the sky turn from dusk to velvet covered in diamonds. Can you count them? Probably not. Now imagine that is the number of wonders for you to behold.

They shimmer and twinkle. All doing their own thing. Shining their reflective stardust just for you to see. It may be unimaginable to know their distance. But God made all of them. And He takes delight in you sitting there admiring His work.

Let's Pray

Holy Father, thank You for the stars. Seeing them reminds me Your work is always shining to behold. You took great care in creating them. And you allow me to enjoy seeing them. Your wonders always amaze me. I love You, Lord. In Jesus' name. Amen.

Call to Action

Have you enjoyed the night sky recently? How did it make you feel? Thank Him. Write it out.

November 3

They were all struck with astonishment and began glorifying God; and they were filled with fear, saying, "We have seen remarkable things today."
Luke 5:26

Witnessing the wonderful healing power of God leaves you awestruck. No words can express how remarkable it makes you feel. His power so overwhelming, you stand in amazement. But for God it is His ordinary existence displayed as extraordinary miracles, beyond comprehension.

Experiencing His power emits fear in the beholder. Not the scared out of your mind fear but the reverential awe kind of fear that leaves you breathless. Amazed in wonder, leaving you full of laughter and tears all at the same time. Like falling on your knees in worship kind of fear.

He has that same power every day. It never fades. It never will. We miss it when we take our eyes off Him. We miss it when we forget to pay attention to Him. Don't miss His power. Stay alert for all the remarkable things He is doing in and around you.

Let's Pray

Holy Father, I become speechless amid displays of Your power. My throat may tighten but I want to shout. Laughter bursts forth with tears. You are amazing. Thank You. In Jesus' name. Amen.

Call to Action

Immediately something came to mind. Did you thank Him? Write it out.

November 4

"and My people who are called by My name humble themselves and pray and seek My face and turn from their wicked ways, then I will hear from heaven, will forgive their sin and will heal their land."
2 Chronicles 7:14

The humbling comes first. You can't move on without it. The rest will do no good without that first step. Recognizing your need for humility brings you into a posture ready to seek Him. Brings you bowed low so that you are at His feet in submission to Him.

Then you pray and seek His face and turn from all wickedness. In praying, you glorify Him, admit His sovereignty. You seek to know Him. To fully know Him. You repent, confessing your sin and moving away from it entirely. Now you are ready for what He has for you.

He hears. He forgives. He heals. His ears never fail to hear a prayer prayed through the right posture. Jesus finished the work of forgiveness on the cross, so you just needed to admit that you needed it. He is the Great Physician who performs, not practices, all healing.

Let's Pray

Holy Father, we are wicked people in need of Your forgiveness. We turn away from the sin that separates us from You. Heal our land, the soil of our hearts. Thank You. In Jesus' name. Amen.

Call to Action

Thank Him for the healing you have witnessed, whether someone else or yours. Write it out.

November 5

to the only God our Savior, through Jesus Christ our Lord, be glory, majesty, dominion and authority, before all time and now and forever. Amen.
Jude 1:25

God of all time. He is the beginning and the end. No limit. Infinite. Forever.

My brain struggles with that thought. Maybe because I get tired and want to quit. Perhaps because from where I sit, people die. What I know and have seen is birth and death with truly little time between. We just see a vapor of a moment in the timeline of God.

He is everlasting. His glory never dims. His majesty never fades. His dominion never ceases. His authority is complete and perfect. And it all was long before we existed and will continue forever. What a privilege to know Him!

Let's Pray

Holy Father, You are our Savior and Lord. Your kingdom has no limits or constraints. Your measure of time is so different than what we know and understand. Our miniscule minds are amazed by Your grand design. All honor and glory belong to You. We are thankful to get to be part of Your design. We love You and thank You, Lord. In Jesus' name. Amen.

Call to Action

Our time is limited on earth, but we can spend eternity with Him. Are you thankful? Write it out.

November 6

The LORD'S lovingkindnesses indeed never cease,
For His compassions never fail.
They are new every morning;
Great is Your faithfulness.
Lamentations 3:22-23

As each day ends, I excitedly go to bed. After a full day, my body and mind need renewal. I love early morning, but coming to the place of rest, where I know I can relax and rest as I close my eyes for one last chat with God brings great contentment.

Matter of fact, I get grouchy if I don't get to bed on time. My brain starts shutting down and I don't think clearly. At times I get silly. I tell my family I am turning into a pumpkin. They already know. It is like I become a different person. I need my rest.

The next morning, there they are. God's compassions, waiting for me. He has regenerated my brain so I can think again. He has refreshed my energy for a new day. His faithfulness continues with me as I enter new opportunities to witness for Him.

Let's Pray

Holy Father, great is Your faithfulness and I want to share it with others. Give me courage and boldness in speaking about Your compassions. Thank You for rest. In Jesus' name. Amen.

Call to Action

Ask God to give you His rest and then thank Him for His faithfulness. Write it out.

November 7

And do not be conformed to this world, but be transformed by the renewing of your mind, so that you may prove what the will of God is, that which is good and acceptable and perfect.
Romans 12:2

There is a battle going on for your mind. The enemy wants you to believe all kinds of lies. As long as you do, you are susceptible to his influence. He has a slight hold on you even though you are sealed by the blood of Christ. He doesn't deserve to have any influence over you.

What are the lies you believe? For me, they are that I am not good enough, no one wants to be around me, I am not smart like some people. And don't even get me started on the way I look. I have carried many lies with me for as long as I can remember. They are lies. I am tired of them.

When the lies try to convince me to do anything contrary to the Holy Spirit's voice in my head, I must listen carefully to Him. The more I do this, the less I believe those lies. God gave me the ability to think rationally. He created my mind to follow Him.

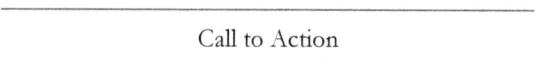

Let's Pray

Holy Father, thank You for my mind. Thank You for Your Holy Spirit guiding me. Thank You that You made me just right. You are the one I want to please. In Jesus' name. Amen.

Call to Action

Do you believe lies? Ask God to show you and then thank Him for truth. Write it out.

November 8

"THE SPIRIT OF THE LORD IS UPON ME,
BECAUSE HE ANOINTED ME TO PREACH THE GOSPEL TO THE
POOR.
HE HAS SENT ME TO PROCLAIM RELEASE TO THE CAPTIVES,
AND RECOVERY OF SIGHT TO THE BLIND,
TO SET FREE THOSE WHO ARE OPPRESSED,"
Luke 4:18

The good news of Jesus is the best news you will hear today. It is the best news you can share. There is nothing that is better. Getting a raise is not better. Getting engaged is not better. Getting a good report from the doctor is not better. Nothing compares to the good news of salvation.

Jesus paved the way to salvation. He is the avenue we take to reach the fullness of the knowledge of the power of salvation. His strength carries us to the foot of the cross and gently sets us down in His presence where He proceeds to transform us into His bride. His love pours over us.

Such a great love should be shared. He gave it to you. He wanted you to have it, so He freely gave it to you. He wants you to share it with others. He wants you to be a vessel of His Word so that the message of the good news spreads. There is someone in your life that needs to hear it.

Let's Pray

Holy Father, thank You for the good news of salvation. Will You anoint us to take this message and handle it appropriately so that others will come to know You? In Jesus' name. Amen.

Call to Action

Who do you need to share with? Thank God for the sharing before you do. Write it out.

November 9

Every person is to be in subjection to the governing authorities. For there is no authority except from God, and those which exist are established by God.
Romans 13:1

Do you vote? As an American citizen, it is your choice to participate in the electoral system. If you don't vote, why? In a democratic nation, all citizens are given the right to have a say in the authorities elected to office. It is our responsibility to take part in this process.

Prayerfully considering candidates is an important part of our citizenship. Researching candidates should be done before casting your vote. Knowing where they stand on issues helps you to make your choice. Don't rely on what others tell you unless you trust them completely.

Ask God to help you in your decision. Understand that He is the One that will place people into authoritative positions. Once done, trust God to guide leadership in making wise decisions. Always seek God in knowing the truth about governing authorities. And then pray for them.

Let's Pray

Holy Father, I trust You to protect our nation. You have blessed us with freedom and for that I am thankful. Guide our leaders to follow You. In Jesus' name. Amen.

Call to Action

Are you thankful for the opportunity to vote? Ask God to guide you. Write it out.

November 10

Be anxious for nothing, but in everything by prayer and supplication with thanksgiving let your requests be made known to God. And the peace of God, which surpasses all comprehension, will guard your hearts and your minds in Christ Jesus.
Philippians 4:6-7

I had part of this passage taped on my bathroom mirror for months. I needed the reminder. Anxiety plagues me sometimes. My pulse quickens. I sweat. My stomach tightens and cramps. I blame it on caring. Having enough passion about something to get worked up about it.

But is it? Or is it a lack of faith on my part? Is it just part of who I am? I am not qualified to answer those questions, but I do know God knows. I know that He will listen to my prayers even when I am anxious. He tells me not to be anxious, and I must listen to Him.

So, I take deep breaths. I stop and talk with Him when anxiety strikes. No matter the situation, my thoughts immediately turn to Him and this passage. I ask Him to speak truth into the situation over me. He gives me His peace. He pours it over my head like a soothing balm.

Let's Pray

Holy Father, thank You for your faithfulness in calming my anxiety. Thank You for caring and for the peace that passes all understanding. I love You, Lord. In Jesus' name. Amen.

Call to Action

Do you need to ask God to help you with anxiety? Thank Him as you ask Him. Write it out.

November 11

Consider it all joy, my brethren, when you encounter various trials, knowing that the testing of your faith produces endurance. And let endurance have its perfect result, so that you may be perfect and complete, lacking in nothing.
James 1:2-4

It is a hard pill to swallow. Trials seem like burdens, not somewhere to find joy. I don't go about seeking a trial just so I can find joy. Trials find me without me seeking them.

Clouds that have silver linings and rainbows remind us of hope. Clouds that pound us with rain and lightning do not always produce the same reaction. God doesn't change in different situations. He will be with you through them all.

On the other side of those tough times, you may not always realize the results He has worked out in you. But then again, you may realize it when the next trial comes along. Your perspective will be completely different and the joy you find in the faithfulness of God will be full.

Let's Pray

Holy Father, sometimes trials hit in rapid succession. Sometimes I just can't seem to catch a break between them to breathe and realize Your joy. Help me to trust You. Give me joy in full measure. Allow my trials to bring You honor and glory. In Jesus' name. Amen.

Call to Action

Can you give God thanks for your trials? Write it out.

November 12

"Cease striving and know that I am God;
I will be exalted among the nations, I will be exalted in the earth."
Psalm 46:10

Up against deadlines, man-made deadlines. Setting priorities. Looking at the clock and knowing you have five minutes to be on time with ten minutes of driving time remaining. In hour two of waiting to be seen by the doctor. Laundry is piled high. Dinner needs to be prepared.

All the things that need your attention can wait. Breathe. Give God your attention. Pushed against a deadline? Ask God to help. Deciding what is next? Ask God to help. Uncertain if grace will be offered when late? Ask God to help. Impatiently waiting for a doctor? Ask God to help. Household chores piling up with kids running wild? Ask God to help.

God is on His throne. Unhurried. Patiently waiting. Always on time, even if I am late. Not concerned with the condition of your house but of yours and your family's hearts and minds.

Let's Pray

Holy Father, I exalt You. Stop me in my tracks when I get so crazy with the concerns of this world. Remind me You are in control and have it all worked out. In Jesus' name. Amen.

Call to Action

Thank God for His patience. Ask Him to help you be still and know that He is God. Write it out.

November 13

Set a guard, O LORD, over my mouth;
Keep watch over the door of my lips.
Psalm 141:3

My mouth gets me in so much trouble. It can be quicker than my reasoning skills. I am working on it, but I haven't mastered holding my tongue. And let's not talk about facial expressions. The two together can really cause me problems. Listening to Holy Spirit softens my words and face.

God knows I need Holy Spirit. Without Him, I am like a two-year old loaded up on sugar needing to know all the answers to all the questions in rapid sequence, with no breath in between. Some of my questions don't even make sense.

He watches and knows my actions and words before I do. He wants to be so much a part of me that what flows out of me is nothing but good. He is faithful to provide His goodness so that I am careful with my actions and words; encouraging and edifying words dripping with love.

Let's Pray

Holy Father, turn my messes into messages of Your grace. Teach me to hold my tongue. Guard my heart and mind so that my mouth is also guarded. Thank You for Your faithfulness. Thank You for Your Holy Spirit helping me. I love You, Lord. In Jesus' name. Amen.

Call to Action

Do you have a mouth that runs wild? Thank God for guarding it. Then let Him. Write it out.

November 14

"For My thoughts are not your thoughts,
Nor are your ways My ways," declares the LORD.
"For as the heavens are higher than the earth,
So are My ways higher than your ways
And My thoughts than your thoughts."
Isaiah 55:8-9

I expected to stop by her house before going to work. Gathering all my stuff, getting into the car to face another work week. I had plans to go out of town for work. I left my breakfast in the car thinking I would be right back. My dad, sister and aunt were there. She was well cared for.

On the side porch, my aunt warned me before entering the house. I didn't know what to expect even with her warning. It was a noise I will never forget. And if you have been there, you know what I mean. That rattle. Nearing the end. I stood by her bed as my mom slipped into eternity.

She didn't need her physical body any longer. It was no good for her. God had something new for her. His plans for her were to remove her from the prison of cancer and restore her health. Why He didn't on this side of heaven, I don't know. I am thankful He knows better than me.

Let's Pray

Holy Father, thank You for perfect healing. Thank You for knowing all things. Thank You that we can rest in Your higher thoughts and ways. Thank You for peace. In Jesus' name. Amen.

Call to Action

Thank Him for the peace He gives when you don't understand. Write it out.

November 15

"If it be so, our God whom we serve is able to deliver us from the furnace of blazing fire; and He will deliver us out of your hand, O king. But even if He does not, let it be known to you, O king, that we are not going to serve your gods or worship the golden image that you have set up."
Daniel 3:17-18

Even if the prayer is not answered the way I expect, I will worship God. Even if the healing doesn't happen the way I expect, I will worship God. Even if the persecution presses in on all sides and attempts to take my life, I will worship God. "Even if" can be scary but worth it.

When faced with the option to worship some worldly idol or God, what will you choose? Most of us would say, God. We won't freely admit to worshipping idols. But let's examine reality. Is there anything that you put before God? Anything that takes priority over God?

Standing in pressure from the world and being able to say, God comes first, is faith in action. Even if God doesn't deliver me from this pressure, this pressure is not my master. The world doesn't own me. God is my Lord. Jesus is my Savior. Holy Spirit is my constant helper.

Let's Pray

Holy Father, thank You for being the God of deliverance. You rescue us from fiery furnaces of our own making. You alone are worthy of all praise. I love You, Lord. In Jesus' name. Amen.

Call to Action

What has been your "even if" position? Thank God for blessing you in it. Write it out.

November 16

Now to Him who is able to do far more abundantly beyond all that we ask or think, according to the power that works within us, to Him be the glory in the church and in Christ Jesus to all generations forever and ever. Amen.
Ephesians 3:20-21

God's power works within us. Sit with that thought for a minute. He can do far more abundantly beyond what we can ask or think. Far more abundantly. You are not able to imagine what the power of God can do within you. All glory is His in all generations.

Witnessing His power and realizing the magnitude of His love working in us draws us closer to Him. You want more but you are only human and sometimes you limit what you receive because of rebellion and ignorance. Lay aside anything that hinders the power of God in your life.

He is forever faithful to do what you need when you need it. Your stubbornness may place an obstacle in the way of receiving. He will still be faithful, but will you be faithful? Will you accept His abundantly beyond that He wants to do for you through His power that is in you?

Let's Pray

Holy Father, I have witnessed Your power. I have received Your abundantly beyond. I have seen generations of blessings. God, thank You. I am in awe of You. In Jesus' name. Amen.

Call to Action

Are you thanking Him for the abundantly beyond in your life? Write it out.

November 17

Then Mordecai told them to reply to Esther, "Do not imagine that you in the king's palace can escape any more than all the Jews. For if you remain silent at this time, relief and deliverance will arise for the Jews from another place and you and your father's house will perish. And who knows whether you have not attained royalty for such a time as this?"
Esther 4:13-14

I have not attained royalty status by world standards, but I am a child of the King of Kings so I could be considered royalty. You too. We can claim it. It is okay. And not only royalty but we are where we are in all of history for a purpose that God ordained just for us. So put on your crown.

With crown on your head, find your purpose. It may change as years go by. It will shift and get rearranged by the situations you experience. Changing baby diapers may shift to changing parent diapers. Sitting under someone else's teachings may shift to you being the teacher.

Whatever you find to do, God will use it for His glory. Give it to Him. Give Him access to your heart and mind and hands and feet so that you are living fully inside the purpose He has for you right now. Don't overthink it. Go and do. Wear your crown and then place it at the feet of Jesus.

Let's Pray

Holy Father, I bow before Your throne. Use me for such a time as this. In Jesus' name. Amen.

Call to Action

What do you get to do for Him? Thank Him for working it out in you. Write it out.

November 18

Therefore there is now no condemnation for those who are in Christ Jesus.
Romans 8:1

Jesus took all our sin and abolished it when He finished the work on the cross and in the grave. He gave us a fresh start. He removed all condemnation and gave us His righteousness. We no longer wear filthy rags, but we are clothed in His pure white robes.

No shame belongs to us. He removed it. He lifted all guilt and forgave us. He gave us a seat at His table. He even held the chair. He prepared the feast.

If we are clothed in His righteousness, seated at His table, what do we owe back to Him? Everything! He laid down His life so we could be redeemed from the bond of sin. We are no longer condemned to hell and the grave because of His perfectly pure sacrifice.

Let's Pray

Holy Father, You know our hearts and minds can cause us to live condemned when we really aren't. You removed that death sentence from us when You gave us Jesus. You gave us Your Son so that we can live in Your holiness. Your favor toward us is undeserved but You give it anyway and give us so much more than we could ask. Thank You, Holy Father. In Jesus' name. Amen.

Call to Action

Will you accept His gift of redemption? Will you thank Him for your salvation? Write it out.

November 19

So there remains a Sabbath rest for the people of God. For the one who has entered His rest has himself also rested from his works, as God did from His.
Hebrews 4:9-10

My body knows when rest is needed. There is a natural tendency for me to hit a brick wall. This is God's way of telling me to stop working. It isn't just my body that needs rest, it is my mind and heart. My soul needs rest just as much as my body. This is the rest God prescribed.

There is a difference between God given rest and me just randomly taking a break from work. When it is up to me, my brain is still engaged which causes my body to hold onto tension. This is not the rest I need to feel rested. Letting my work wait, refocusing my brain away from it, is rest.

Seeking Him instead of anything else and laying aside busyness lets me breathe. That time prepares me for the work that is to come. The to do lists can wait. Organize your time so that your Sabbath rest is intentional. God is faithful to provide.

Let's Pray

Holy Father, we desperately need the rest that You give us. We work so hard and become exhausted without it. We want to be effective in our work. Help us. In Jesus' name. Amen.

Call to Action

Will you thank God for Sabbath rest? And for the work He has for you. Write it out.

November 20

Jesus said to him, "I am the way, and the truth, and the life; no one comes to the Father but through Me."
John 14:6

I am not capable of doing anything without Jesus. I cannot breathe or sleep or eat without Him. He is my source of life. He is the only way to the Father. He defines truth. Take Him away and what am I left with? Nothing. I am left with nothing in His absence.

He is my Provider. He is my Sustainer. He is my Healer. He is my Savior. He is my love. He is my Comforter. He gives me peace. He gives me joy. He is my Rock. He is my Defender. He holds victory over death. He is my Creator. He is my Protector. He is my Shepherd.

Will you recognize Him as all those things and more? Will you give Him praise for being your source of life? Will you thank Him for providing the way, the truth, and the life you have in the Father? You are not capable of doing anything without Jesus.

Let's Pray

Holy Father, all praise to You for Jesus. For the sacrifice of Your Son. We are nothing without You. Thank You for life. Thank You for Your love. I love You, Lord. In Jesus' name. Amen.

Call to Action

Who is Jesus to you? Is He your Savior? Thank God for Jesus. Write it out.

November 21

What is man that You take thought of him,
And the son of man that You care for him?
Yet You have made him a little lower than God,
And You crown him with glory and majesty!
Psalms 8:4-5

God thinks of you. The Most High God takes thought of you. You are on His mind. He has plans for you. He has a purpose for you. He thought of every detail needed to make you. Every hair on your head is numbered by Him. The beating of your heart is in rhythm with His.

He cares for you. Every hurt you have ever experienced has been felt by Him. The worries and concerns you carry around; He is willing to carry for you. Excitement and joy come from Him. He loves to see you smile. He loves to hear you laugh. He wants you to call Him.

He crowns you with glory and majesty! He shares His glory with you. He wraps you in His majesty. You get to wear a crown that is placed on your head by God Himself. The King of Kings crowned you. You belong to Him. He cherishes you with an everlasting love.

Let's Pray

Holy Father, Your love surpasses anything we can imagine. Oh, that You take thought of us and crown us with glory and majesty! We worship and adore You. In Jesus' name. Amen.

Call to Action

As you polish your crown, thank God for it. He loves to hear your voice. Write it out.

November 22

Therefore He is able also to save forever those who draw near to God through Him, since He always lives to make intercession for them.
Hebrews 7:25

Jesus has God's ear. He mentions you to Him. They may have full conversations about you. What have you given them to talk about? Maybe you wish you hadn't given them that to talk about. Here's your chance to change the topic of conversation. Give them something good!

He welcomes your change because when you turn away from what keeps you from Him, you are drawing closer to Him in the process. His saving grace is yours. He thwarts the attacks of the enemy without you even knowing it when you are covered by His grace.

There you are being talked about in heaven because you are sitting at the foot of the cross. Not because of some scandalous mess you have gotten yourself into but because the grace of God covered you and gave you a seat right there. Enjoy being in that seat!

Let's Pray

Holy Father may my life be worthy of the breath You breathe into me. Keep me from creating messes of my life so that You are pleased. I love You, Lord. In Jesus' name. Amen.

Call to Action

What do you think they are saying about you? Can you give thanks for it? Write it out.

November 23

For the LORD will not abandon His people,
Nor will He forsake His inheritance.
Psalm 94:14

No matter how many times you trip and fall, God is always there to catch you. He knows your weaknesses. In those weaknesses, His strength is revealed. He picks up the pieces of broken you and molds them back into the right places. Your messes become His masterpieces.

He wants your surrender. He wants your open hand to receive what He offers. He wants your attention. He wants your recognition of who He is in your life. He wants you to live with Him. He is always with you. He will never leave you. But He doesn't want you to leave Him.

What do you need to surrender to Him? Are you prone to wander? Do you lose sight of Him because of the busyness around you? Will you allow Him to captivate you? He is always right there waiting for your attention. Will you give it to Him?

Let's Pray

Holy Father, You are so quick to forgive when I wander away from You. You pull me back into Your loving arms and remind me that You love me. Please forgive my wayward wanderings. Keep me securely in Your grasp. Thank You for never leaving me. In Jesus' name. Amen.

Call to Action

Express your gratitude to Him for His steadfast love. Write it out.

November 24

I will sing of the lovingkindness of the LORD forever;
To all generations I will make known Your faithfulness with my mouth.
Psalm 89:1

Looking back for just a moment. Remembering some struggles. Lots of struggles. But also remembering blessings poured out on us. So many blessings. When we didn't know, God did. When we were just along for the ride, God drove. And He is still driving.

It is amazing to trace God's hand back through so many years. I was nineteen. He was twenty-four. The odds were not in our favor, but we found God's favor. When you have His favor, He works all things together for your good. It has truly been miraculous to see His hand at work.

We have endured, survived, flourished, multiplied, prospered, committed, recommitted, and leaned heavily on God. Marriage is not always easy. But God has been with us and kept us together for three and a half decades. His lovingkindness endures forever.

Let's Pray

Holy Father, thank You for my marriage. Thank You for bringing us together and keeping us there. We could not do this life without You. We praise You. In Jesus' name. Amen.

Call to Action

Your relationship with God is the most important one. Thank Him. Write it out.

November 25

"but whoever drinks of the water that I will give him shall never thirst; but the water that I will give him will become in him a well of water springing up to eternal life."
John 4:14

That first sip sets your heart on fire and makes you want to explode out of your skin. When you realize His mercy and grace are for you and that Jesus died on the cross for your sins so that you can live in fellowship with God, you become a new person. You have tasted the living water.

You turn on the tap and it flows in and through you. Situations may attempt to slow the flow but in relationship with Jesus, nothing can stop the flow. It is alive. It makes you alive. His flow of life never runs dry. When it comes to a slow drip, open the faucet. Let Him refill your reservoir.

How do you do that, you ask? Open His Word and read. Ask Him, without doubt, to fill you with His fresh supply. He will faithfully provide you with streams of mercy that flow deep and wide. Look nowhere else but to Him for your rehydration. His water is the best.

Let's Pray

Holy Father, thank You for the water filling me so that I can become a well springing up pouring out on others so they will do the same. God, Your supply never ends. In Jesus' name. Amen.

Call to Action

Join me in thanking God for His living water. Give Him praise. Write it out.

November 26

Let them also offer sacrifices of thanksgiving,
And tell of His works with joyful singing.
Psalm 107:22

Are you feeling the sacrifice of thanksgiving? Maybe it is hard to be thankful today because life has bruised you up and left you a little sore. I know thanksgiving can be hard to get out because of situations. That is where the sacrifice comes in. When it is hard, do it anyway.

Offering your sacrifice of thanksgiving in the face of hard times may lighten your burden. Giving God praise for who He is and the wonderful work He has done on your behalf, shifts the focus away from the situation and onto the One in control of all situations. Sing praise to Him.

Joyfully raise your voice in song. He loves to hear you sing to Him, even if it is off-key. He made that voice and loves to hear it directed at Him. So, sing until thanksgiving becomes easy and light. Sing praise to the One who loves you. Sing with joy in your thanksgiving.

Let's Pray

Holy Father, thank You for speaking to me through music. I love to sing praise to You. Please find this offering of thanksgiving acceptable and pleasing. You fill me with joy unspeakable in the presence of praising You. Thank You for music. In Jesus' name. Amen.

Call to Action

You know what to do. Sing. Worship. Then thank Him for the opportunity. Write it out.

November 27

Jesus said to them, "I am the bread of life; he who comes to Me will not hunger, and he who believes in Me will never thirst."
John 6:35

I took my sourdough starter out of the refrigerator yesterday morning. If you know anything about sourdough starters, you know that they must be fed. Basically, you just add flour and water and leave it to grow. The fermentation in the starter bubbles and expands the mixture. Once it has expanded, it is ready to be used as a rising agent in bread.

Last night I mixed the dough. Using more flour and water with a little salt, I added the starter. I mixed it until it was all incorporated. The starter was well distributed throughout the dough. Folding it together a few times builds its strength. It had to sit overnight to rise again.

This morning bubbles were visible in the dough. It had risen. One final rest in the refrigerator before it goes in the oven later today. The heat applied to the dough will bring it to its completion. Ready to take a bite? You don't have to wait. Taste and see that the Lord is good.

Let's Pray

Holy Father, thank You for causing us to rise up to eternal life. In Jesus' name. Amen.

Call to Action

How has God seasoned your life? Have you thanked Him for it? Write it out.

November 28

Therefore, having been justified by faith, we have peace with God through our Lord Jesus Christ,
Romans 5:1

Believe. Trust. Have faith in the One who is faithful. Your faith justifies your presence before His throne. Because of the blood of Jesus, you have faith. He gave you His Holy Spirit to dwell in you. Unseen but fully present. A personal presence of peace just for you.

Closer than any family. Closer than any friend. He knows you more intimately than you know yourself. He sees what you can't. He knows what you don't. He is constantly aware of your needs. He is constantly providing for your needs. He takes care of what you can't.

Close your eyes and look at Him. Your vision will never be clearer than when you fully realize His presence in you. He does not leave you. He is always there. Even when you try to move, He is still there. You can't go anywhere that is outside of His presence. So, praise Him now.

Let's Pray

Holy Father, Your everlasting presence washes over me and holds me securely. I love being wrapped in Your arms. Thank You for constant peace. I know that You are my Savior. I trust You with everything. I am Yours. I love You, Lord. In Jesus' name. Amen.

Call to Action

Have you received the gift of peace from God? How will you thank Him? Write it out.

November 29

Your faithfulness continues throughout all generations;
You established the earth, and it stands.
Psalm 119:90

The sun came up over the horizon this morning. Proof that the earth is still spinning. Rotating around that giant orb of light that keeps us in a certain pattern of movement. God established the gravitational pull and keeps everything in the universe perfectly aligned. He holds it all.

The enormity of His work and level of infinitesimal detail shouts to His divinity. Organized but creative. Known but mysterious. Amazing and wonderful. Quiet but loud. Gentle and strong. Loving but chastising when needed. Compassionate but exacting. Beginning and the end.

Go outside and look. Stand in one place long enough and you will see the proof of movement. Mark it. See how God moves the earth. Then let Him move you. His faithfulness will move you in perfect alignment with Him. Follow His lead as He navigates you around Himself.

Let's Pray

Holy Father, Your works are too wonderful for me to comprehend. Thank You for allowing me to witness Your greatness. Your majesty brings me to my knees in awe of You. My mind and heart cannot contain or begin to understand all of You. You are wonderful. In Jesus' name. Amen.

Call to Action

Go outside. Behold His creation. Drink it in. Thank Him for the pleasure of it. Write it out.

November 30

But we should always give thanks to God for you, brethren beloved by the Lord, because God has chosen you from the beginning for salvation through sanctification by the Spirit and faith in the truth.
2 Thessalonians 2:13

I am thankful for you. Thankful that God gave me this book so that you and I could journey through this year together. I am thankful for the salvation He provided for us. I am thankful that His sanctification continues as we continue our growth in Him.

You are loved. You are chosen. You are favored by God. He rejoices over you. You are blessed by Him. He speaks truth over you. You are held by Him. He is your protection. He is your shelter. He is your refuge. He is your anchor. He is your constant help and provider.

As you finish this month and move into the final month of the year, be blessed. I pray you enter the Christmas season full of hope and wonder. I pray you experience the love and grace of our Savior as you celebrate His birth. Rejoice in peace as you give thanks for all He has done.

Let's Pray

Holy Father, thank You for the gift of friends. Thank You for our sweet fellowship through these pages. It is for Your glory and honor. We praise Your Holy Name. In Jesus' name. Amen.

Call to Action

Tell Him of your thankfulness for all He has done for you. Write it out.

For a child will be born to us, a son will be given to us; and the government will rest on His shoulders; and His name will be called Wonderful Counselor, Mighty God, Eternal Father, Prince of Peace.
Isaiah 9:6

December

For a child will be born to us, a son will be given to us;
And the government will rest on His shoulders;
And His name will be called Wonderful Counselor, Mighty God,
Eternal Father, Prince of Peace.
Isaiah 9:6

Wonderful Counselor.

Mighty God.

Eternal Father.

Prince of Peace.

The eternal hope of a Savior wrapped up in clean linen. The innocence of a baby drawing shepherds to the place of His birth. Light led the way to the place He lived. Alive. Breathing. Wiggling. Small fingers. Small toes. Chubby cheeks. Eyes seeing His world from a new perspective. Ears hearing noises He created. His creation holding Him. Him entering His creation as a baby. Magnificent innocence. All powerful God in helpless babe. For you. For me.

December 1

And Mary said: "My soul exalts the Lord,"
Luke 1:46

Simple devotion to the Almighty God. Mary praised God for the assignment. She exalted Him with her voice. Abandonment to any other thought but intentionality to the assignment presented to her. The hardest, most wonderful assignment for a young woman.

She was made for this assignment. Her body prepared to carry God's Son. Innocence bears innocence. Nestled into a pure womb. A sacred space for God to lay His Son. Gently. Quietly.

Let's Pray

Holy Father, may I find such devotion to You as I see in Mary. You have asked me to carry Your Son in my heart and mind, not so different than the assignment You gave Mary. Prepare me for the assignment You give me. I exalt You. In Jesus' name. Amen.

Call to Action

God has given you an assignment. Write it out. Whatever He calls you to He will prepare you.

December 2

"And my spirit has rejoiced in God my Savior."
Luke 1:47

Look deep within. Setting aside all distractions. Allowing, even commanding, everything inside to settle and get still and quiet. Silence. Listen. Now rejoice. Rejoice in the Savior of the world.

Mary was in awe of God. Deep in her core she knew Him as Savior, even as she carried her Savior. Within her core resided the Savior of the world. She bore Him. He physically grew within her body.

He grows within a willing vessel. Will you be a willing vessel that rejoices?

Let's Pray

Holy Father, I rejoice in You. You alone are worthy to be praised. I am a willing vessel to be used for Your honor and glory. Fill me with Your Holy Spirit. In Jesus' name. Amen.

Call to Action

Your life is given by God to worship Him. Rejoice, for the Savior of the world has come and will return. Write out your praise to Him.

December 3

"For He has had regard for the humble state of His bondslave;
For behold, from this time on all generations will count me blessed."
Luke 1:48

Mary not only had a front row seat in the life on earth of Jesus, but she had an integral part. Her body held the Savior of the world. The Creator using the woman of His creation to create in her the physical body of the Creator Savior. Did you get that? Think about it. Let your brain wrap around it and consider Mary's role.

A young woman, a teenager, innocence to hold the most precious gift ever given. Her warm womb nurturing, growing the Messiah. Her blood pumping life into the Life-Giver. Her lungs filtering the air from the Breath-Giver. He created her so she could help create Him.

Let's Pray

Holy Father, Creator, You take what the world considers meager and turn it into magnificence. Wonderful is Your name in all the earth. There is no greater. You are worthy of all praise. In Jesus' name. Amen.

Call to Action

Consider Mary. Now consider your role in the kingdom of God. His creation of Mary was no different than the creation of you. What is your role in His kingdom? Write it out.

December 4

"For the Mighty One has done great things for me;
And holy is His name."
Luke 1:49

Mary, in awe of the personal, magnificent, wonderful gift of life. Both the preparation of her few years and for what would be. She may not have all the details nailed down, but she knew the provision of God would be more than sufficient to meet her needs. He had already proven it. And she testified of what He had done.

He is still doing wonderful things. He gave the greatest gift ever. He is still giving Him. Still offering Him to anyone. Anyone willing to look to Him for eternal life-giving provision. Willingness to accept the gift of the Savior.

Let's Pray

Holy Father, You are in the gift giving business. No greater gift has been given than that of Your Son. Thank You for the sacrifice You made on my behalf. In Jesus' name. Amen.

Call to Action

What has He done for You? Will you take time now to praise Him for His provision in your life? Write it out.

December 5

"AND HIS MERCY IS UPON GENERATION AFTER GENERATION TOWARD THOSE WHO FEAR HIM."
Luke 1:50

Mary knew the writings of David. She had heard them spoken her whole life. Passed down from generation to generation, she was well acquainted with scripture. Her mind and heart were knit together from hearing and believing and living with the scriptures. That's how we know Him. To live with Him. Not just Sunday morning messages, but daily dwelling so that generations will know Him.

Holding reverential fear of the Most High only places Him in the proper place in a life. He is God. He is Creator. He is Master. He is Life-Giver. He is Healer. He is Savior.

Let's Pray

Holy Father, You are Most High. Great is Your mercy toward me. Thank You for allowing me to know You. Thank You for generations before me pouring into me so that I can pour into those coming after me. In Jesus' name. Amen.

Call to Action

No matter what your history holds, God holds your future. What action can you take to provide the Presence of God for generations after you? Record it here and somewhere you will see it over and over. Write it out.

December 6

"He has done mighty deeds with His arm;
He has scattered those who were proud in the thoughts of their heart."
Luke 1:51

Humility draped around Mary's shoulders. Holding her in a quiet embrace. Clothed in strength. Not her strength. The strength of the One she carried. The same One who carried her. The same One who has been and will be doing mighty deeds for eternity past, present and future.

In awe and reverence, her willing submission could contain no pride. She was raw and vulnerable to the mighty hand of God. She was set apart to be the mother of the Savior of the world, the Savior of all humanity.

Let's Pray

Holy Father, the gift of Your Son only brings me low into a place of submission to You. There is nothing in me apart from You that is worth boasting. All praise is Yours. You are Almighty. In Jesus' name. Amen.

Call to Action

Lay aside pride and approach the throne of grace. What will you give Him praise for today? Write it out.

December 7

"He has brought down rulers from their thrones,
And has exalted those who were humble."
Luke 1:52

Mary continued praising God. She knew that the economy of God could be upside down from the world's perspective. And here she was, a young virgin, esteemed for having the position of mother to Messiah.

Imagine her with head bowing low. Possibly on her knees. Hands raised in full submission to her Almighty God. Everything she had laid out for Him. Her very life as an offering for service to the King.

She was given an honorable role. The unlikely given the most prestigious position. She accepted in humility.

Let's Pray

Holy Father, thank You for the example You have given me in Mary. Hers was the most unique position and mine is no different. Guide me, as you did Mary, in living a life of service to You. In Jesus' name. Amen.

Call to Action

Your turn. Claim the service God has given you. What will you do with it? Write it out.

December 8

"HE HAS FILLED THE HUNGRY WITH GOOD THINGS;
And sent away the rich empty."
Luke 1:53

Mary found the provision from God to be astounding. Good things filling barren places. Abundance replacing lack. Could she have been referring to the womb now filled with the one that would pave the way for the very One in her own womb? Emptiness replaced by life.

The longing of every soul waiting to be filled with His richness. Life in her womb ready to offer life to all. Anyone waiting and wanting to be filled. His fullness poured into the hungry.

Let's Pray

Holy Father, thank You for the offering of abundant life. Thank you for the provision You continually offer. Your gift is exceedingly beyond anything I could ever imagine. In Jesus' name. Amen.

Call to Action

Have you found yourself drenched in the goodness of God? Mary did. Overwhelmed by the fullness, she poured out praise to God for the goodness He gave. How has He provided for you? Write it out.

December 9

"He has given help to Israel His servant,
In remembrance of His mercy,"
Luke 1:54

Mary recalled the promises she had heard. Scripture replaying in her mind. She knew His mercy triumphed. And here she was, in the middle of the story unfolding of His ultimate display of mercy. He was extending it beyond the confines of her womb and giving it to Israel and to you and to me.

Israel repeatedly turned their backs on Him. We do too. But there is always a longing to go back. To return to Him. And there He is. Waiting for us to lay aside all that weighs us down and attempts to keep us from Him. He offers mercy. The weight lifted off for us. He took it. Removed it. And He doesn't want us picking it back up.

Let's Pray

Holy Father, thank You for mercy. In all my messes, You are patiently waiting for me to turn away from those traps and run back to You. Thank You for accepting me back time and time again. In Jesus' name. Amen.

Call to Action

Do you need to return to Him? Let Him know. Write it out.

December 10

"As He spoke to our fathers,
To Abraham and his descendants forever."
Luke 1:55

He is still speaking. The pages of His word. The promptings of His Holy Spirit. He is still speaking.

It can be hard to listen in the madness of our everyday lives. Get still and quiet long enough to hear. Silence can be deafening for ears accustomed to constant noise. Even in quiet the thoughts race to take first place. The noise in my brain can be louder than the noise surrounding me.

He is still speaking. Listen.

Let's Pray

Holy Father, please forgive me for rushing and running outside of earshot. Pull me back into reach of Your voice. In Jesus' name. Amen.

Call to Action

Do you find yourself becoming so overwhelmed with life that you miss Him in it? What can you do to get alone with Him to truly listen to what He has for you? Are you willing to be still and know Him? Will you make a dedicated effort to make it happen? Write it out.

December 11

Therefore, beloved, since you look for these things, be diligent to be found by Him in peace, spotless and blameless,
2 Peter 3:14

Walking in peace. Walking spotless and blameless. Only by His redemption. His righteousness spilling out onto and into us. Ushering us into His presence. Where we are welcomed. Where we are wanted. Where we are called. Him, making us righteous.

I am looking for the new things He has promised. His salvation brings these promises into the lives of those who believe in Him. Beyond what we can comprehend is the goodness of eternity with Him. Only because He came as a baby to provide the perfect, sinless, offering that we could not provide on our own.

Let's Pray

Holy Father, thank You for the promises You give for me to have eternity with You. Your Son was given so that I could be in Your presence. I love you, Lord. In Jesus' name. Amen.

Call to Action

Will you give Him praise for His promises? Tell Him what His love for you means to you. Express your gratitude for the baby that changed the world. Write it out.

December 12

"I am the Alpha and the Omega," says the Lord God, "who is and who was and who is to come, the Almighty."
Revelation 1:8

He is here. He was here before us. He has been here all along. Emmanuel. God is with us. God in human form.

He never leaves. He is constant. Never failing. Never faltering. Steady. Not shifting. Not being thrown about by any random wave wanting to knock Him off His throne.

He is Master. He is the beginning and the end. He doesn't revolve around our desires. We were created to revolve around Him. We were created to dwell in Him and for Him to dwell in us.

Expect His constant presence. Anticipate His all-consuming love.

Let's Pray

Holy Father, You are the beginning and the end. Apart from You there is nothing. You are worthy of all praise. I desire Your continual presence. In Jesus' name. Amen.

Call to Action

What offering of praise do you have for the Almighty? Write it out.

December 13

"For He has had regard for the humble state of His bondslave;
For behold, from this time on all generations will count me blessed."
Luke 1:48

Generation upon generation passed down the anticipation of the long-expected Messiah. Generations after will be filled with wonder of the coming of the Messiah to His young mother, Mary. He knew her long before she was born. He would choose her to mother Him.

She knew the One she held in her womb was more than her Child, He was her Master. The strength given to her through the power of God held her heart together. She welcomed the position of being His mother. She welcomed the trials in rejoicing for the Savior of the world.

She didn't shy away from the task at hand. She embraced the moments fully aware of her position of lowliness and honor. Oh, to be chosen to be the mother of Jesus!

Let's Pray

Holy Father, You chose Mary, in her humble state, to hold in her womb the very lifeblood the entire world needs for salvation. She is blessed among women. Thank You for giving us the example of her obedience. In Jesus' name. Amen.

Call to Action

Consider Mary as she learned of her condition. Would you be so courageous? Write it out.

December 14

For my eyes have seen Your salvation,
Luke 2:30

Simeon had waited for this moment his whole life. The salvation of the world. The promise fulfilled in flesh. The baby Messiah in his arms. Simeon felt the reverence and moved gently and quietly, feeling fully the magnificence in his midst.

His life and death depended on the arrival of the Child. And here He was. The weight of the Babe in his arms. The weight too great to bear. Did the Babe hold Simeon more than Simeon held the Babe?

Word became flesh. Simeon could depart in peace having held Salvation in his arms.

Let's Pray

Holy Father, the weight of Your love, mercy and grace presented to us in the flesh of Your Son is incomprehensible. Thank You for the Preeminent Gift. In Jesus' name. Amen.

Call to Action

Simeon's eyes beheld the Word made flesh. His arms held Emmanuel. Have you held a newborn baby and wondered at the creation? Imagine holding your Savior. What thoughts go through your mind? Write it out.

December 15

Nicodemus, who had first come to Him by night, also came, bringing a mixture of myrrh and aloes, about a hundred pounds weight.
John 19:39

Nicodemus met Jesus under cover of darkness after witnessing tables being overturned in the temple. Jesus presented Nicodemus with the love story of God and the path to salvation for all who believe. Nicodemus continued to follow Jesus from a distance.

John records the help Nicodemus gave to Joseph at the burial of Jesus. His continued interest in Jesus brought him to offer an exorbitant weight of spices. Was this an offering of belief?

We aren't told if Nicodemus believed in the message of salvation. But the actions he took and the record of his participation in the burial points to his continued interest in Christ. Do your actions point to your continued interest in Jesus?

Let's Pray

Holy Father, our curiosity leads us to wonder. We seek Your face in this dark world as Nicodemus sought Jesus in dark streets and tombs. God, draw us to seek You in the light of life. In Jesus' name. Amen.

Call to Action

Declare your belief in Jesus. Write it out.

December 16

At that very moment she came up and began giving thanks to God, and continued to speak of Him to all those who were looking for the redemption of Jerusalem.
Luke 2:38

She had been walking these passages for decades. The fasting and prayer left her mind and body aware and able. But this visitor stirred her to excitement, and she couldn't keep quiet, thanksgiving on her tongue.

The air was electrified by the very presence of this Little One. Did she hold Him? Did He offer soft grunts of stretching because that body was a tight fight for One so great?

This little body held the redemption of Jerusalem. She knew this. Like Mary, Simeon and Nicodemus, she had been listening and studying and knew the scriptures. She knew the world had been waiting on Him. She knew the world needed Him. And here He was. In the flesh. Within her reach. Behold the Lamb.

Let's Pray

Holy Father, Your redemption was in the presence of Anna. We rejoice with her in the perfect redemption given to all mankind. In Jesus' name. Amen.

Call to Action

Can you sense the presence of Jesus? Will you rejoice as Anna did at His arrival? Write it out.

December 17

But when he had considered this, behold, an angel of the Lord appeared to him in a dream, saying, "Joseph, son of David, do not be afraid to take Mary as your wife; for the Child who has been conceived in her is of the Holy Spirit."
Matthew 1:20

Thrust into this story, he served as a quiet, strong, willing participant. No different than Mary, given a position in history only he could play out. He received reassurance, but it came in dreams. On the outside, opinions, judgments, and dangers, all followed him.

The earthly role of father to the Messiah was gifted to Joseph. To raise, teach and nurture into adulthood prepared for a cross made from wood, the material of his earthly profession. The Holy Father selected the wood that provided the tool for the completion of His work on earth.

Joseph did what was needed of him and was taken out of the picture. He didn't linger, wringing his hands. He didn't worry that the job he performed wasn't good enough. He did what he knew to do and trusted the Master.

Let's Pray

Holy Father, You complete what we can't. Your strength is sufficient in all tasks that You give to us. We trust You with all things. In Jesus' name. Amen.

Call to Action

Are you a willing participant in the story of Jesus? What is your role? Write it out.

December 18

Now when they had gone, behold, an angel of the Lord appeared to Joseph in a dream and said, "Get up! Take the Child and His mother and flee to Egypt, and remain there until I tell you; for Herod is going to search for the Child to destroy Him."
Matthew 2:13

He felt threatened. Word of His birth had him scrambling to secure his throne. He would not sit back and allow a foretold Child to overtake his position as king. So he decimated a generation.

His agenda was to maintain control. He wasn't the first one to want what didn't belong to him. And he certainly wasn't the last. Doing whatever it takes to secure our position, we all will lie and cheat and steal and destroy to hold on to what destroys us in the end. He lied to locate the Messiah. Deception was no match for Truth. His royal position ended in his own demise.

The Child, protected from the murderous king, escaped the enemy's plot. His position was more secure than any earthly king. His Royal Heritage was unmatched. Herod couldn't destroy the gift of Christmas.

Let's Pray

Holy Father, we invite You into the celebration of the season and know the gift of Your Son is the reason for the celebration. Remind us, Holy Father. In Jesus' name. Amen.

Call to Action

Consider what may be stealing your Christmas and take action to change it. Write it out.

December 19

And suddenly there appeared with the angel a multitude of the heavenly host praising God and saying,
"Glory to God in the highest, And on earth peace among men with whom He is pleased."
Luke 2:13-14

Shepherds hanging out in a field. Sheep settling in for the night. Counting sheep. Making sure none have gone astray. Heavy eyes. Wanting sleep. Fiercely protective over their flock.

A light unlike anything they have ever seen blinds them. There's a gift a few hills over. Good news. Extraordinary joy. The Savior. Messiah. The Lord. A baby. In a feeding trough.

Shepherds get around. They went to see the child. Amazed by everything they had witnessed, they couldn't keep quiet. After seeing the baby in the manger, they had the privilege of sharing the good news. Raised eyebrows. Wondering minds. From that field in the middle of the night, ripples went out of the good news. Stories shared from town to town.

Let's Pray

Holy Father, like the shepherds we want to be the bearers of good news for a lost world. Give us knowledge and wisdom to share the message of salvation. In Jesus' name. Amen.

Call to Action

Place yourself in the shoes of the shepherds. What would you do? Write it out.

December 20

After coming into the house they saw the Child with Mary His mother; and they fell to the ground and worshiped Him. Then, opening their treasures, they presented to Him gifts of gold, frankincense, and myrrh.
Matthew 2:11

The very presence of the Holy Child was the greatest gift ever. His gift brought eternal hope. His gift was the only sacrifice that could save our souls. But the gift of the Messiah wasn't the only gift brought to Bethlehem over 2,000 years ago. Magi from the east came bearing gifts for King Jesus.

Upon arriving they fell to their faces in worship. The visitors brought worldly grandeur with fine spices and precious metal. Costly gifts. The travelers bowing low and timid, desperately wanting to stare into His deep eyes to behold all of Him.

They traveled far to worship. They traveled far to bring gifts. They traveled far to bring their gift of worship.

Let's Pray

Holy Father, our worship pales in consideration of the grand display offered by these wise men. May our gifts and worship be found acceptable in Your eyes. In Jesus' name. Amen.

Call to Action

Gifts come in different packages. What gift do you have to offer King Jesus? Write it out.

December 21

For a child will be born to us, a son will be given to us; And the government will rest on His shoulders;
And His name will be called Wonderful Counselor, Mighty God, Eternal Father, Prince of Peace.
Isaiah 9:6

Wrapped up in layers of cloth, He was placed in an animal feeding trough, sitting in a dark, cold barn with animals and their mess. He was placed amid us, in our mess. He left the comfort of His home to join us in ours. In all our mess, He shows up. Because we need Him.

He came. As Wonderful Counselor. As Mighty God. As Eternal Father. As Prince of Peace. Perfect protection. Everlasting provision. Rely on Him.

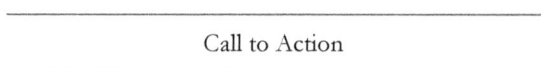

Let's Pray

Holy Father, You provide everything we need through Jesus. Let us seek Your counsel in all things. Remind us that You are Mighty God. We need You, Eternal Father. Grant us the peace that only You can so we can know the protection and provision that is abundantly beyond our comprehension. In Jesus' name. Amen.

Call to Action

Spend extra time today to recognize the wonderful gift you have in Jesus. Praise Him for the abundance of peace He offers. Accept that offering of peace and acknowledge your need for Him. Write it out.

December 22

When Elizabeth heard Mary's greeting, the baby leaped in her womb; and Elizabeth was filled with the Holy Spirit.
Luke 1:41

A holy moment for Elizabeth to realize the presence of her Savior. Deep in her womb she knew the movement stirred by His presence. Her baby connecting with Mary's baby. A holy moment filling Elizabeth with the Holy Spirit.

Peace flooding Elizabeth. Joy leaping in her womb and soul. The presence of Emmanuel was encapsulated in the womb of Mary. Exuding joy spread out and landed in Elizabeth and the baby in her womb.

Maybe your joy is an inner peace that rises in your chest and fills your senses with silent anticipation that all is well. Or maybe your joy is a smile across your face even when times are tough. Knowing His presence is joy.

Let's Pray

Holy Father, Your presence continues to fill us with joy and peace. God, allow us to live fully aware in awesome anticipation of the goodness You pour into us. In Jesus' name. Amen.

Call to Action

Do you need to sense His presence? Get quiet. Get still. Seek Him. Praise Him. Write it out.

December 23

Therefore let us draw near with confidence to the throne of grace, so that we may receive mercy and find grace to help in time of need.
Hebrews 4:16

Flesh draped Jesus. Perfect Son of God. Full of mercy. Giver of grace. Creator. Savior. Helper. Friend.

In the wretched condition of our hearts and minds, He stepped in. Desiring us to turn to Him. Coming close to us so we could be close to Him. Him, desiring relationship with us.

He reached out to us. He rescued us. He restored us to Himself. He redeemed.

Keeping our eyes fixed on Him, He made the way for us. Stripping all tightly wrapped temptation away. He stripped Himself down to a Child and offered us what no one else could. The perfect, blameless sacrifice to take our sins. His perfect Christmas gift.

Let's Pray

Holy Father, Your redemption is perfect. Thank You for redemption. In Jesus' name. Amen.

Call to Action

His perfect gift was complete. He accomplished the total retribution of our sins. He took what we deserved and in place of wrath we have redemption. Will you give Him praise? Write it out.

December 24

"Cease striving and know that I am God;
I will be exalted among the nations, I will be exalted in the earth."
Psalm 46:10

Furiously shopping until the very last minute to fulfill all the lists. Nestle the packages under, around, on branches of the tree. Presents that will be unwrapped like the unwrapping of the Savior before He hung on a tree.

Gifts, food, table settings, and stockings, all ready for the big day. Can pure joy be wrapped in snowman wrapping paper? Red ribbons curled atop boxes stacked around the decorated tree, like the blood dripping from our Savior on a tree. Anticipation of the coming celebration.

But if that is all there is to Christmas, the boxes will be empty reminders of unfulfilled wishes. Joy is not wrapped in paper packages. Joy is wrapped in Christ. Exalt Him so that He is the focus of the season.

Let's Pray

Holy Father, we want Christ to be the focus of our Christmas celebrations. Forgive us when He is not and turn us around so that He is again. In Jesus' name. Amen.

Call to Action

What have you celebrated this season? The gifts or the Gift? Write it out.

December 25

But the fruit of the Spirit is love, joy, peace, patience, kindness, goodness, faithfulness,
gentleness, self-control; against such things there is no law.
Galatians 5:22-23

The real Christmas list. The one that exists outside of the packages littered all over the floor. Not contained in a cardboard box that becomes the favorite toy. It didn't require any financial resources from you. The only effort it required from you is accepting the Gift.

Once the Gift is accepted, evidence of His existence in your life drips with the list instead of shiny new toys sitting under the branches of your Christmas tree. You sit under the branches of His tree. His lineage includes you.

Faith becomes evidence in a life living the list of Christ's presence.

Let's Pray

Holy Father may the evidence of Jesus in me be prominent in my life. Let love, joy, peace, patience, kindness, goodness, faithfulness, gentleness, and self-control pour out of me because of You. In Jesus' name. Amen.

Call to Action

How will you accept His gift today? Express your acceptance. Write it out.

December 26

In the beginning was the Word, and the Word was with God, and the Word was God. He was in the beginning with God. All things came into being through Him, and apart from Him nothing came into being that has come into being. In Him was life, and the life was the Light of men. The Light shines in the darkness, and the darkness did not comprehend it.
John 1:1-5

It all starts in the beginning. Nothing starts without a beginning. Jesus is the beginning of life. He ushered the world into being as He ushers us into life from death. Our sin keeps us separated from Him, but He reconciles us to Himself by making a sacrifice for us. So that we begin fresh with Him.

Each day we are given a fresh start. The beginning of the day is the perfect time to seek Him and accept His gift of reconciliation, leaving the past and moving forward in the newness of Him. His mercies are new each morning.

As you come to the end of the year, consider what you need to do to start fresh with Jesus. Finish this year by cleaning out the junk to make room for a new beginning focused on Him. You have a few days to clean out. Get busy!

Let's Pray

Holy Father, prepare us for a new focus. Prepare us for intentional devotion to You. We commit each day to You. Grow us in the New Year. In Jesus' name. Amen.

Call to Action

What are you getting rid of that keeps you from devotion to Christ? Write it out.

December 27

And let endurance have its perfect result, so that you may be perfect and complete, lacking in nothing.
James 1:4

Finish strong. Rest and contemplation seem to be common themes for the last few days of the year. Many are considering the past year with dreams of the next. We celebrate successes and mourn struggles.

God has been with you through it all. Holding you up in the struggles and cheering you on in the successes. He is with you as you finish one year and prepare to enter another.

Through it all your strength has come from Him. He is working in you to bring completion to this year. What do you need to do to recognize Him in all things?

Let's Pray

Holy Father, Your hand in my life has been evident over the past year. I praise You for the blessings You have poured out on me. Continue working in my life so that it may be honoring to You. In Jesus' name. Amen.

Call to Action

Make a list of your blessings. Make a list of your struggles. How has God worked throughout both? Write it out.

December 28

This hope we have as an anchor of the soul, a hope both sure and steadfast and one which enters within the veil,
Hebrews 6:19

Sinking your anchor into the hope of Jesus is the only way to end or begin a year. Keeping that anchor firmly secured to that hope and holding on with everything in you. He is steadfast and sure and there is nothing else that will hold you as securely.

Check the ropes. Are the knots tight? Make sure the ropes are not fraying. Devotion to time with Him in His word. Talking with Him. Praising Him. Showing hospitality. Intentionally focusing on Him.

Creating new habits and laying aside anything that keeps you from living fully in God's will is the best place to start dwelling in the security of His hope. Starting fresh. New mercies.

Let's Pray

Holy Father, You set my anchor. Tie the ropes off so that I will not be shaken and battered by the storms that are sure to come. Thank You for being my shelter of hope. In Jesus' name. Amen.

Call to Action

Have you started your list of goals for the new year? Do those goals include intentionality with God? Write it out.

December 29

Whatever you do in word or deed, do all in the name of the Lord Jesus, giving thanks through Him to God the Father.
Colossians 3:17

The work of your hands gives evidence to your faith. Raising children. Caring for patients. Cleaning houses. Cooking meals. Managing an office. Maintaining your household. Whatever the work is it points to your faith. Your attitude and behavior while doing that work is a testimony to where your heart and mind reside.

Evaluate yourself. Consider your daily routine and determine how others may perceive you based on the work you do every day. What is the testimony you are giving them? Is it honoring to God?

Spend time today seeking God's evaluation of you. Lay His beside yours and compare the two. Consider areas of your life that may need an adjustment. Seek His help with the adjustment.

Let's Pray

Holy Father, allow the work of our hands to honor you. In Jesus' name. Amen.

Call to Action

Will you commit to intentionally working for God? You are His vessel. How will you work for Him in the coming year? Write it out.

December 30

"Every branch in Me that does not bear fruit, He takes away; and every branch that bears fruit, He prunes it so that it may bear more fruit."
John 15:2

Are you still pruning from yesterday? That evaluation brought to light areas of your life that may need to be changed. Do you need to continue your time with God today toward repairing areas so you will produce an abundance of fruit next year? This is the perfect time to do it.

Open your Bible and spend time focusing on Him. Go to Psalms and Proverbs. Go to Matthew 5-7. Ask the Holy Spirit to teach you. Praise God through reading His word.

Do you know Him as Lord and Savior? Do you know the salvation that only comes through the blood of Jesus? Do you know He died as the perfect sacrifice for our sins? He rose on the third day to prepare a place for us. He rose to give us new life and provide the way to that new life.

Let's Pray

Holy Father, it is only by our confession that Jesus is Lord that we can come to You and lay our requests before Your throne. We praise You that You cared for us so much that you gave Your Son to die in our place. Thank You, God. In Jesus' name. Amen.

Call to Action

Continue planning your commitment to Him for the new year. Write it out.

December 31

The end of a matter is better than its beginning;
Patience of spirit is better than haughtiness of spirit.
Ecclesiastes 7:8

Here we are. The last day of the year. Looking forward to the journey into a new one with God. Leaving this one with the knowledge that He was with us through it whether we recognized Him. Determined to seek Him continually in the new year ahead.

Are you ready? Is there anything you need to do to finish strong? May I encourage you in your walk with Him. He will never fail you. He will never forsake you.

No matter what you faced this past year, His provision is always abundant. He will continue to provide in the new year. I pray you look back and recognize His hand in your life. I pray you look forward to what He has for you in the coming year.

Let's Pray

Holy Father, thank You for Your faithfulness. Keep me faithful. In Jesus' name. Amen.

Call to Action

Look back at your Call to Action from January. Did your plans change during the year? Did you establish plans this year that you will carry over into next year? What is it that you will leave behind this year? Write it out.

"FOR IF YOU REMAIN SILENT AT
THIS TIME, RELIEF AND
DELIVERANCE WILL ARISE FOR
THE JEWS FROM ANOTHER PLACE
AND YOU AND YOUR FATHER'S
HOUSE WILL PERISH. AND WHO
KNOWS WHETHER YOU HAVE
NOT ATTAINED ROYALTY
FOR SUCH A TIME AS THIS?"
ESTHER 4:14

Acknowledgements

There is always this fear of leaving someone out when it comes to recognizing those who have played critical roles in any endeavor. Please accept my apology now if I fail to mention you specifically.

Chuck Martin, the one who encouraged me the most. When I doubted, you believed. You have been by my side for thirty-five years. I would not have it any other way. Thank you for your patience. Thank you for listening.

Ashley, Andrew, and Adam, God blessed me with you three, and those you have brought into my life. You are my reward here on earth.

Behold, children are a gift of the LORD,
The fruit of the womb is a reward.
Psalm 127:3

Cindy Benefield, you were the first willing to read these pages. Your love and support have been constant in my life. Thank you.

Stacie Mote, thank you for laughing. Thank you for being my best friend and cousin. Thank you for trusting my navigation on trips. Thank you for reading these pages and the careful feedback you provided.

Sally Burkhalter, you are the iron that sharpens me. And then the balm that soothes. Thank you for your friendship. Thank you for drying and reading wet pages. Thank you for your encouragement.

Anita Howard, we need to go to lunch. Thank you for taking the time to read these pages. Your selfless dedication is unmatched.

MaryAnn Shea, you are my spiritual mother. Several decades of leadership, pouring into others, willing to speak hard words laced in mercy. Thank you.

Stacy Arquillo, that January walk on the beach brought us back together after many years apart. I pray you continue to seek God's plan for your service.

Heidi Cox, we also need to go to lunch. It was your suggestion that helped me finish this book. I was stuck and you gave me the exact thing I needed to get to the finish line. Thank you.

Max Carter, my fourth child. You listen to an old woman and treat her like a friend. Blessings to you on every endeavor.

Jessie Benefield, my heritage comes from you. You sowed seeds in all your children. Thank you for being my daddy.

Donna Benefield, my mama. I would not wish for you to be back with us because heaven is where you belong, but I know you would read this book. Your writing inspired me to write. I didn't know it until after you were gone. God gave it to me. Thank you for loving me unconditionally.

Nika Maples, thank you for your challenges and words of encouragement. Even though we have never met in person, I am eternally thankful for your friendship.

To my Creator, You know everything there is to know about me and yet You allowed me to write this book with hopes of bringing others closer to You. Please take it and do with it according to Your will. It is Yours.

About the Author

Bonnie J Martin is married to Chuck She is mama to Ashley, Andrew, and Adam; Nonnie to Grady and Maggie; and "extra mom" to Drew and Sarah, hoping to add Allie someday. She is a daughter, sister, aunt, niece, and cousin. Bonnie treasures her family.

By trade, Bonnie is a Certified Public Accountant. Her passion lies in serving God by spending early mornings writing. It is during this time that she takes what God gives her and clicks keys for His glory.

Bonnie enjoys composing pictures and turning them into inspirational images to share on social media. Many of her images can be found on her blog at www.bonniejmartin.com. She has nurtured several plants in her greenhouse for many years and clips blooms from seasonal flowers for vases.

Bonnie attends church at Crossroads Baptist Church in Valdosta, Georgia.